LIFE IN CHRIST

Register This New Book

Benefits of Registering*

- ✓ FREE **replacements** of lost or damaged books
- ✓ FREE **audiobook** – *Pilgrim's Progress*, audiobook edition
- ✓ FREE information about new titles and other **freebies**

www.anekopress.com/new-book-registration

*See our website for requirements and limitations.

Life in Christ

Lessons from Our Lord's
Miracles and Parables

The Miracles of Our Lord
Volume 6

Charles H. Spurgeon

We love hearing from our readers. Please contact us at www.anekopress.com/questions-comments with any questions, comments, or suggestions.

Life in Christ, Vol. 6
© *2022 by Aneko Press*
All rights reserved.
Revised edition 2022
Please do not reproduce, store in a retrieval system, or transmit in any form or by any means – electronic, mechanical, photocopying, recording, or otherwise, without written permission from the publisher. Please contact us via www.AnekoPress.com for reprint and translation permissions.

Unless otherwise indicated, scripture quotations are taken from the New American Standard Bible® (NASB), copyright © 1960, 1962, 1963, 1968, 1971, 1972, 1973, 1975, 1977, 1995 by The Lockman Foundation. Used by permission. www.Lockman.org. Scripture quotations marked "KJV" are from The Authorized (King James) Version. Rights in the Authorized Version in the United Kingdom are vested in the Crown. Reproduced by permission of the Crown's patentee, Cambridge University Press.

Cover Design: Natalia Hawthorne
Cover Painting: Matt Philleo
Editors: Ruth Clark and J. Martin

Aneko Press
www.anekopress.com
Aneko Press, Life Sentence Publishing, and our logos are trademarks of
Life Sentence Publishing, Inc.
203 E. Birch Street
P.O. Box 652
Abbotsford, WI 54405

RELIGION / Christian Life / Spiritual Growth
Paperback ISBN: 978-1-62245-820-2
eBook ISBN: 978-1-62245-821-9
10 9 8 7 6 5 4 3 2
Available where books are sold

Contents

Ch. 1: Plain Words with the Careless 1

Ch. 2: Christ's Curate in Decapolis 19

Ch. 3: Going Home 33

Ch. 4: The Physician Pardons His Paralyzed Patient 49

Ch. 5: The New Fashion 63

Ch. 6: Carried by Four 81

Ch. 7: The Gospel's Healing Power 99

Ch. 8: Sitting There 117

Ch. 9: First Forgiveness, Then Healing 133

Ch. 10: May I? 145

Ch. 11: The Great Physician Successful 163

Ch. 12: The Touch 179

Ch. 13: Sincere Faith 197

Ch. 14: Tell It All 215

Ch. 15: Cured at Last 233

Ch. 16: She Had Not Escaped Notice 249

Charles H. Spurgeon – A Brief Biography 267

Other Similar Titles 271

Chapter 1

Plain Words with the Careless

Seeing Jesus, he cried out and fell before Him, and said in a loud voice, "What business do we have with each other, Jesus, Son of the Most High God? I beg You, do not torment me." (Luke 8:28)

If we understand these words to be the exclamation of the evil spirit which tormented this poor demoniac, they are very natural words, and one can very readily understand them, for the presence of Christ is such a great torment to the prince of evil, that he might well cry out, *"Have You come here to torment us before the time?"* If we would force Satan to retreat, we have only to preach the Lord Jesus in the power of the Spirit, for this is the hell of devils. Hence it is that he roars so much against gospel preachers; he roars because the gospel makes him ache. But if these words be looked upon as the language of the man himself, they are most extraordinary. In fact, they are so singularly mad and foolish that we can only account for them by the fact that though it was a man who spoke, yet the devil was in him; for surely none but a man possessed with a devil would say to Jesus, who alone could bless him, "Depart from me!" or say, "Torment me not!"

And yet there are tens of thousands of men in this world who are saying just the same thing. Thousands of persons appear to be far more anxious to escape from salvation than to escape from eternal wrath.

They avoid heaven's love with scrupulous diligence, and the prayer of their life seems to be, "Keep me, Lord, from heaven! Prevent me from ever being saved! Give me the full swing of my sins, and let me live so as to ruin my soul!" Conduct most strange! From what source comes such folly? The desire and determination of some men to destroy themselves are fixed and resolute to the last degree. Their self-hate, and their suicidal avoidance of mercy's thousand exhortations and pleadings are so extraordinary that, I repeat, we can only account for men being so blind and maddened by the fact that Satan has the mastery over them, and leads them captive at his will.

Before I proceed to discuss the words themselves, there is, however, something to be learned from them. We may learn that *a man may know a great deal about true religion, and yet be a total stranger to it.* He may know that Jesus Christ is the Son of God Most High, and yet he may be possessed by a devil; no, as in this case, he may be a den for a whole legion of devils. Mere knowledge does nothing for us but puff us up. We may know, and know, and know, and so increase our responsibility, without bringing us at all into a state of hope. Beware of resting in head knowledge. Beware of relying upon orthodoxy, for without love, even with all your correctness of doctrine, you will be a sounding brass and a tinkling cymbal. It is well to be sound in the faith, but the soundness must be in the heart as well as in the head. There is as ready a way to destruction by the road of orthodoxy as by the paths of heterodoxy. Hell has thousands in it who were never heretics. Remember that the devils *believe, and shudder.* There are no sounder theoretical believers than devils, and yet their conduct is not affected by what they believe, and consequently they still remain at enmity with the Most High God. A mere head believer is on a par therefore with fallen angels, and he will have his portion with them forever unless grace shall change his heart.

> **Beware of resting in head knowledge.**

We learn also from the words of the text that there *are a great many bad prayers prayed in the world.* The man said, "*I beg You, do not torment me.*" He was earnest to get Christ to let him alone, very earnest. Many, many, many well-worded prayers, which have been excellent in themselves, have not had half so much earnestness in them as this. Both men and swine run hard when Satan drives them, but the best of us are slow indeed in going to heaven. A sinner's prayer for his own misery is often a grim and awful thing to look upon, from its horrible earnestness.

Alas, how often have we heard men offer prayers which it would be a very dreadful thing if God were to hear! What are oaths and blasphemies but prayers? – only they are prayers of the worst kind. A thousand mercies, indeed it is, that God has never granted the swearer's prayer, but has been pleased to spare him, though he has often invoked curses on his own head. Swearer, down on your knees this moment, and thank the Almighty that he has not taken you at your word! If you have ever made a league with death and a covenant with hell, and have asked that God would destroy you, be thankful that he has not done so. Take that as a sign of mercy, and pray that the longsuffering of God may lead you to repentance. I hope and pray that his having spared you is with the intent that he may save you eternally.

Now we shall come to the words themselves, though we shall not take them quite in the order in which they stand. The first thing to which I shall call your attention is *a mischievous misapprehension*. There are many foolish people in the world who imagine that Christ comes to torment them, and that his religion would make them miserable. The second thing is *a grumpy question: "What business do we have with each other?"* Many, many think that they have nothing to do with religion, nothing to do with Christ, and they ask, more or less contemptuously or earnestly, as their state of mind may be, "What business do *I* have with You, Jesus, Son of God Most High?"

First, we have to deal with a very mischievous misapprehension.

It is currently thought among mankind that to receive the gospel of Christ would be to cease to be happy, to give up all joyfulness and cheerfulness, and to doom one's self to a life of melancholy. I shall argue upon that point a little, and I shall begin by admitting some things which are frankly to be acknowledged. An honest man, when he has embraced a cause, must not go in for it blindly, but must be willing to make admissions where truth requires them, even if they should appear to be dead against him.

Now, I will admit that *if men will take joy in their sins, the gospel will, if it gets at their consciences, make them miserable*. It will act as salt to raw wounds, or as a whip to rebellious backs. There are some of you of this sort, whose pictures I could easily paint so that you would know yourselves at once. I have heard of and have personally known persons who have been in the habit of practicing glaring vices, say, for instance, drunkenness, and yet they have attended here with remarkable regularity. They have been pleased, either with the greatness of the congregation, or else with the particular manner of the minister, and they have come again and again, and there has been some kind of impression produced, so that they had a hankering after the best things. They have by and by reasoned with themselves, "I cannot go on as I have done and still continue there – the man makes his knife too sharp. I must give up my sins or leave him altogether." And so, after a while, feeling themselves rendered perfectly wretched by the sermons which they have listened to, they have given up even heeding the means of grace. Many and many a man has gone down those steps under the columns in front yonder, grinding his teeth, and stamping his feet, and vowing that he would never come again; and yet he is the very man who is sure to come again before long.

I am often very glad when that is the effect produced, for I have hope of men who have enough conscience left to be irritated by the truth. Better a wrathful hearer than a forgetful hearer. If the arrow irritates, let us hope that it has gone deep. I admit, then, I must admit it, that if men are resolved to keep their sins, it *will* be a very uncomfortable thing for them to hear about Christ Jesus, and holiness, and happiness, and sin, and the wrath to come. Jesus Christ's coming near them in the preaching of the gospel will torment impenitent sinners, and make them feel alarm and terror which they will try to drown by opposing the truth. Why, in the old Methodist times, when they took John Nelson, and pressured him to make him a soldier, they said, "Take the fellow away! Why, a man cannot nowadays get comfortably drunk, nor swear an oath, but what there is some Methodist sect or other who is sure to reprove him!"

> The Christian is a standing rebuke to the ungodly.

Just so; wherever true religion is in the world, it makes sinners sin uncomfortably. The Christian is a standing rebuke to the ungodly. A man who is honest, and sober, and decent, and pure, and who lives as a Christian should live, is such a rebuke to the wicked, that if they cannot burn him, and perhaps would hardly like to do so in these times, yet, if they can but ignore him, or insinuate that he is a hypocrite, and that he has some sinister motive behind him, they can then be a little comfortable at the service of evil, and warm their hands at Satan's fire. I trust this tabernacle will always be too hot a place for such of you who mean to indulge in secret sins and hold on to hidden wickedness. Never will I, so long as God spares this tongue, flinch from telling you of your sins, for if I did I should expect that your guilt would rest upon me, and that the blood of your souls would lie at my door.

O that I may have grace to be far more faithful, even though your praise should turn to animosity! Yes, I admit that if you mean to go to hell, you need not come to hear the gospel, because your doing so will only make you uncomfortable in this world, and will be of no service to you in the next.

Again, I must make another admission, namely, that *a great many people, at the time when they become serious for the first time, and give themselves to Christ, are rendered, for a time, very miserable.* There are some whose repentance is so exceedingly bitter that they make the very worst of company; they shun company themselves, and those who love merriment shun them. The terrors of the Lord are upon them, and they are feeling the burden of sin – it is no wonder that a cloud hangs over their brow. We read John Bunyan's life, and we cannot but admit that for years he was rendered, by religion, as wretched a man as he well could be; and many others have passed through just that same state of mind – some for days, some for months, and others even for years. But allow me to remind you that this is not at all the fault of our Lord Jesus Christ, for if these people had come at once to him, and obeyed the great gospel command, "Believe and live," they would have had instantaneous peace. Did you note that verse in the hymn which was given out just now? It told us that no preparations were needed before coming to Jesus. I will quote it again:

> This fountain, though rich, from charge is quite clear;
>   The poorer the wretch, the welcomer here:
> Come needy, and guilty, come loathsome and bare:
>   You can't come too filthy, come just as you are.

Now, if a soul will but cast itself at once upon the glorious work of the great Redeemer, it shall there and then be saved. If those who were so long in soul trouble had but come to Christ, and had trusted him, with all their sins around them, they would have had peace at once; and the reason why they were so long a time in misery was because they did not go to Jesus Christ, but kept on looking to themselves, looking for this feeling, and that good action, and that other experience, and dreaming that because they did not see these, they could not be saved. O that they had accepted at once the simple truth that the blood of Jesus Christ, God's dear Son, cleanses us from all sin. Now, if a man is under a physician, and he has a medicine sent to him, if he should be months in getting well, you cannot blame the physician if you find that the medicine stands untasted upon the shelf. Why, the man has been trying twenty other things, and he has only gotten worse and worse. It is a good thing that he wishes to be healed, but how much better would it be if he would but try the right medicine which alone can cure him! If he does not try the prescription, it is not the fault of the physician if he suffers a long time – it is his own fault. Even so, if a man will not believe in Jesus, do not blame the Master if he finds no salvation.

O poor troubled hearts, you need not go that roundabout way of sorrow, tempted, and tossed about, and tormented with a thousand doubts and fears; there is a far nearer and surer way to life eternal. If you come to Jesus Christ immediately, and fall down before the cross, and rest your soul simply there, you shall find joy and peace this very night – before you go to your rest, you shall know that you are *accepted in the beloved*. But even if this pain were necessary, notice this – is it not a very small cost to pay? – to be rendered wretched for a little time, if afterwards there shall come perfect peace, and if, especially, as the result of that there shall be eternal salvation in the world to come? Why, suppose a part of your foot has become diseased, and a bone has to be taken out, you do not say, "Oh! but the surgeon cuts so deep, and he has to use so many dreadful tools!" Of course he has to, but if he can save the limb, or preserve the life, nobody thinks of a little pinch so long as the life is preserved.

Ah! if you had to stand waiting for Jesus at mercy's gate in the cold, with the hailstorm of wrath pelting you, for ages upon ages, it would be a small thing to endure if you might afterwards enter into the rest which remains for the people of God. Even on that calculation, the thing is a good bargain, and he who is wise will reckon the cost to be all little enough.

But, now that I have admitted this, I want to ask those who say that Jesus Christ would make them miserable a question or two. I have admitted a great deal – now, be fair and open with me in return. You are afraid of being made miserable. *Are you so mightily happy, then, at the present moment?* You are afraid that if you became a Christian, you would be melancholy. Now tell me, are you so wonderfully full of joy at the present moment, so marvelously happy that you are afraid of damaging your little paradise? Excuse me if I say that I rather question whether those blissful fields of yours are so very delightful. I have my doubts about those charming pleasures of yours, and I suspect them to be more paint than reality.

Ah! my friends, we little know the miseries of the wicked. Take the drunkard, for instance – what a jolly, pleasant fellow he is! Yes, but what does Solomon say? *Who has woe?* Hear that word again, *Who has woe?* Why, this man whom the world calls "such a jolly fellow" has *woe* because he delays long at the wine, and mingles his strong drink. If men were rational, none of them would take the drunkard's woe for the drunkard's cheeriness. There is no comparison – he has a dear price, a heavy penalty to pay for all his apparent joy. Rare old liqueurs turn out to be depressing ruin, and fine sparkling wines end in darkness and death. It is so with all vices – they froth a little, and then turn to flat wormwood, the dregs by which all the wicked of the earth shall drink. Who does not know that the penalty of fleshly vices is too horrible for us to describe? A man cannot sin without bringing upon himself some sorrow even in this life. Wretchedness follows at the tail of transgression. Do not tell me that a working man who spends his money at the gin palace, or the beer shop, can have a happy home. The woman who gallivants about here and there, visiting this and that place of pleasure and amusement, and neglecting her own family, does not find it all happiness. I am sure she does not; her face is evidence to the contrary.

> A man cannot sin without bringing upon himself some sorrow even in this life.

Those who lie, and cheat, and swear, and forget God, I am quite sure, do not find so much joy as they profess to have.

So then, to make short work of the business, you who whine about religion as being melancholy are generally a set of hypocrites, so come here, sir, and let me tell you a little plain truth. Why, you pitiful creature, to tell me that religion would make you melancholy, when you are as melancholy now as you can pretty well live, and have to be looking after this excitement and that to try and forget yourself, for when you sit down in your sober senses, and calculate what you are, and where you are going to, you know very well that nothing could make you much more miserable than you are, and you are about as dull now as you could be! Do not make this mighty fuss about religion making you miserable, when you are miserable already; but, like a sensible man, find no fault with what you have not tried.

There is another question I would like to ask you, and that is, If you reply that you *are* happy now, I would be glad to know, *will the present happiness which you enjoy, or you say you enjoy, last you very long?* The leaves are now falling very rapidly from the trees, and they remind us that we too must die. Will your cheeriness and your reveling support you in the dying hour? Do you expect that these things will buoy you up amid the chill waves of the black sea of death? No; you admit that all your rare reveling must end then. Well, is not this a poor prospect for a dying pillow? Is this a wise choice to choose to die without a hope? And after death – what then? Will your present worldly delights minister comfort to you in another state? Do you expect that the gaieties and vanities of life, in which both rich and poor indulge, will be a comfort to you in looking back upon them, when your soul is separated from the body, and you stand before the bar of God? And if you die unsaved, and God condemns you, driving you from his presence, do you think that the merriment of the ballroom, the theater, and the drinking bar will, in their remembrance, yield drops of water to your burning tongue in eternity? Will these things be pillows for your aching heads in hell? Will the sinful joys of earth breathe the soft breath of consolation upon you, when Christ has said, *"Depart from Me, accursed ones"*? You know, very well, they will not.

Listen to me, then. These joys of yours which you are so afraid of losing, they are but bubbles, and they burst; they are mere child's toys, and you break them and are done with them; and you yourself will soon be where no more bubbles are blown, and no more toys made to sport with. Do not, therefore, make so much noise about your joy – there is nothing in it. Sirs, you might throw your joys to the dogs, and they would refuse them; for the joys that a man can know apart from Christ are unworthy of an immortal being – they are unsatisfactory, delusive, and destructive; and if the religion of Christ does take all such joys from you, it only removes from you mischief which you ought to be most glad to lose.

But now, we will go further in dealing with this mischievous misapprehension. You have a notion that if Jesus Christ should come into your heart, you would have to give up your pleasures. Now, *what pleasures?* The pleasures of the hearth and family fireside? The pleasures of seeing your children growing up around you to call you blessed? The pleasures of doing good? The pleasures of discharging your duties as in the sight of God? The pleasures of a quiet conscience? The pleasures of knowing that you can look both your fellow men and your God in the face? None of these pleasures will Christ take away from you. The pleasure of having a good hope as to the hereafter? The pleasure of having a good friend to whom to tell all your troubles? The pleasure of going to your heavenly Father with all your griefs and sorrows? None of these will Jesus take away, nor can I conceive of any pleasure that is worth calling a pleasure, which a man will lose by becoming a Christian.

Ah, yes! I know what you mean. You mean that *you will not be able to go after your sins.* Now I understand you. Why did you not say so before, and call a spade a spade? Call your sins *sins,* but do not call them pleasures; and learn that the pleasures of sin, which are but for a season, are but Satan's baits by which he takes souls upon his hook to their destruction. You shall lose no pleasure but that which is unhealthy, unfit for your soul, unsatisfactory in itself, and unworthy of your nature. If you come to the cross, you shall certainly find that

> Religion never was designed to make our pleasures less.

It multiplies our truest and purest pleasures a thousandfold.

"Oh," say you, "but I shall have to give up my liberty!" Your liberty? In what respect? Your liberty to be honest and to be upright? Your liberty to love your neighbor? Your liberty to be kind to the unthankful and the ungenerous? Your liberty to go about doing good? Your liberty to search, and judge, and know for yourselves? You will have to give up none of this in becoming a Christian. In fact, I dare to tell you, that you will have a liberty conferred upon you far more wonderful than any liberty which you as yet have known. "He is the freeman whom the truth makes free, and all are slaves besides." Jesus Christ gives a man such an independence of spirit that he fears no one, but does what is right, actuated by the spirit of right within him; and then he goes through the world fearless of oppressors, dauntless and courageous under all circumstances, the Lord's freeman. You will not, then, have to give up your liberty. Yes, I know what you mean – you mean *liberty to sin*, that is to say, *liberty to ruin yourselves*. Thank God, *that* liberty will be taken from you, for you never had any right to possess so terrible an engine of destruction; but it shall be so taken from you that you yourself will be glad to miss it.

Why, look at that swine yonder, wallowing in the mire. A miracle transforms it into an angel, but has not that angel liberty to go and wallow in the same filth as before? Certainly he has, but does he ever use it? No, it is contrary to his angelic nature to be found reveling in mire. So will it be with you. You will not care for those things which are now your delight, but, being made free from sin, you will count it foul scorn to serve it any longer. Oh! it will be no loss of liberty, but the unloosing of all your bonds.

Still you say, "If I were a Christian, it would make me melancholy!" What for? Why should it make you melancholy? Make you melancholy to think that, if you live, God will be your shepherd, and you shall not be in want? Make you melancholy to think that if you die, "Jesus can make your dying bed feel soft as downy pillows are"? Make you melancholy to believe that you are on the way to heaven, and that when the trials of this poor life are over, you shall be with Jesus forever? I cannot imagine it. Let not Satan's lie deceive you. It will drive your melancholiness most effectually away, if Jesus Christ comes into your soul.

Now, I will put a few things to you, with the deepest earnestness, for I long to see you turned from your evil ways, and saved by the sovereign grace of God. O that the Holy Spirit may press home upon you the arguments which I try to use. You have heard the story of the Savior who came from heaven to earth to die for his enemies. *Do you believe that he came on earth to make us miserable?* Can you look into the face of that Man who bled for sinners that they might live, and believe that he came here with the malevolent design of making men wretched? You know better; in your heart you know better. There must be joy in that which such a man works out; so gracious a Redeemer must intend our best happiness. Listen to his teachings, and I will ask you then whether *they tend to make anyone miserable.* Point me to a precept where the Savior bids us cease to rejoice.

I invite you to find in the Word a commandment against sober, solid, pure, and holy joy. I will find *you* words like these: *Rejoice in the Lord always; again I will say, Rejoice. Be glad in that day and leap for joy.* What day? A bright day? No. "*When people . . . falsely say all kinds of evil against you because of Me.*" He began his first sermon with the word *blessed,* and he repeated the word many times; and as he was at first, so he was at the last, for he was blessing his disciples when he ascended into heaven. He came into the world so that his teaching might make men blessed, both here and hereafter. I will ask you again *whether you notice in his followers any particular misery.* Some of them, through sickness, may be sad, and there may be some who profess to be Christians who do not have enough religion yet to make them happy, but most of us are a happy people. I will bear my witness, and speak for myself. I believe I have a spirit which delights in happiness, and that I am not naturally one of the dullest of mankind. I am not conscious now of being anything but simply honest in what I am about to say, and I can assure you that nothing has ever given me such joy as the knowledge that Jesus Christ is mine. I have had to suffer a great deal of pain lately, and nothing has assisted me to bear its sharpest twinges, and they have been sharp indeed, like the thought that "His way was much rougher and darker than mine."

I tell you, young men, you who want to see life, you must see Christ. You who want to have true happiness, a happiness to rise up and to sleep with, a happiness to live with and to die with – not the happiness of those silly butterflies that fly from flower to flower and are never content unless they are in the theater or the ballroom, but the happiness of a man that is worth calling a man – I tell you such solid happiness is to be found only in vital godliness. I am of the same mind as the poet Young, who said,

> A deity believed is joy begun; A deity beloved is joy matured:
> A deity adored is joy advanced; Each branch of piety delight affords.

God is my witness, I do not lie, there is a joy to be found in knowing Christ which all this round world besides cannot be found – search it through and through. *"If only you had paid attention to My commandments! Then your well-being would have been like a river, and your righteousness like the waves of the sea."*

One thing I will also say, and then be done with this point. You believe that religion is a happy thing, though you pretend you do not. You must confess, and you do confess, that *you desire to die like a Christian.* You like for the present, perhaps, to indulge in this folly and that iniquity, but you would like to die with Christ, would you not? Then if you would be like a Christian in death, you must be like a Christian in life. You have down deep in your heart, even though you may deny it, a consciousness that faith in Jesus is worth having, and that it would be worlds better for you if you were converted, and had the Holy Spirit dwelling in your heart. Now, do not restrain that thought. Do not, I pray you, quench that inward consciousness. Believe it, for it is true, and oh! may you today, by divine grace, be led to seek the Savior, and may you find him before you give sleep to your eyes or slumber to your eyelids. My longing for you is that you may be saved! My heart bleeds over the prospect of your eternal ruin. O that you may be led to Jesus! May you trust your soul into the hands of Jesus who was crucified, and you shall find that he does not torment you, but is comfort, fullness of comfort, to your spirit.

My time flies by me all too rapidly, and I shall want all there is left for the second point, which is a fretful question – *"What business do we have with each other, Jesus, Son of the Most High God?"*

"What have I to do with you?" This is a question which we have heard many times. Poor people often ask it. I heard a workman say, "Well, I have nothing to do with religion; I know it is all very well for my master, for ministers, and fine ladies, and aristocrats, and old women, but it is of no use to me. I have to work hard, and I have a family to bring up, and it has nothing to do with me." Now, give me your hand, my good fellow, and believe me, you are quite mistaken. Why, there is nobody in the world whom it has more to do with than it has with you, for *"the poor have the gospel preached to them."* Jesus Christ sends his gospel specially to those who labor and are heavy-laden. Moreover, I do not know anyone who could want it more than you do, for you have not very much in this life to cheer or comfort you. It is a hard fight to get through this world at all in times like these, but if you have a good hope for the next world to help you in the battles of this life, then you will bear your trials, and you will cheerfully endure the hardships which heavenly wisdom appoints for you.

> Jesus Christ sends his gospel specially to those who labor and are heavy-laden.

There are a great many working men and their wives here today who are members of this church, and I know if they were to stand up for the purpose – and hundreds of them could – each one of them would tell you that the best inheritance they have ever had has been an interest in Christ, and that they never found themselves so truly blessed as when they laid hold of eternal life and trusted in Jesus. It has everything to do with you working people; I love you, and I long that you may believe this great truth, and put it to the test.

But very often *the wealthy* say, *"What business do we have with each other, Jesus?"* Lavender kid gloves and the gospel are not always well agreed; the upper circles are none the nearer to heaven because of their imaginary elevation. There are also certain learned gentlemen who are instructed in metaphysics and philosophy who patronizingly inform us that the restraint of religion is a very proper thing to keep the working classes in some kind of order, but really they themselves are several degrees above it. Thus they say, as plainly as they can, *"What business do we have with each other, Jesus?"*

Ah! the greatest fools in the world are those who despise other people, and they certainly do this who say that a thing is good enough for others, but quite unworthy of such excellent people as themselves. Who are they that they should lift up their heads so high? God *made from one man every nation of mankind to live on all the face of the earth;* and I reckon that that which is good for the poorest garbage collector, with his bell, is also good for the richest nobleman with his stars and garters; and that which may be a blessing to the most ignorant, will also be a blessing to the most learned. O my brethren, educated, refined, wealthy as you may be, the gospel of Jesus has everything to do with you.

The giant minds of Milton and Newton found ample room in the gospel; they delighted to bathe, like leviathan, in the ocean of divine truth. Speak of philosophy? There is nothing so philosophic as the doctrine of the cross of Christ; and as to metaphysics, if a man shall delight himself in these, he shall find arm room and elbow room enough in the study of the doctrines of grace. Here the stoutest champions of logic may meet each other in the arena of debate. Here is room for the profoundest learning; and if you should study till you know all things, yet shall you find that the knowledge of Christ Jesus surpasses all knowledge, and that his cross is the most excellent of sciences. There is much to do with you, you great ones. May grace bow your necks to the yoke of Jesus.

"What business do we have with each other, Jesus?" says this and that individual in this vast assembly. There may be many here who are saying, "Religion has nothing to do with me." But, young woman, in your beauty religion will add a new charm to your attractions, an unfading luster, such as nothing else can yield. The knowledge of Christ Jesus shall give you a beauty of mind that shall last when the worm has furrowed that fair brow, and your well-fashioned form has dissolved into the old brown dust, which is the residue of all the living. Young man, with all your manhood about you, full of life and spirit, Jesus Christ has much to do with you. He can make you more manly than you otherwise would have been. He can bring out the noble points of your character, and educate you to be something more than school or university can make you. And you who are in business, this will help

you in your cares. You who have to toil, and plod, and bear the troubles of life, Jesus Christ will comfort and sustain you. And you gray heads, who can need Jesus Christ more than you? Here is your staff, your dying pillow, your immortal rest.

What has he to do with you? Why, I trust that you have much to do with him, and if you have not, yet at least he has something to do with you, which I will now show you. What have you to do with Christ? There are two or three matters in which all of you have to do with Christ, whether you will or not, and the first is this: *it is because of his intercession that you are alive today.* Your tree brought forth no fruit, and the Master said, *"Cut it down."* Why, then, does it stand? Why, because the Husbandman said, *"Let it alone, . . . for this year too."* Shall that tree ungratefully say, "What have I to do with the Husbandman" when it owes itself to him? Ah! friend, the Jesus whom you despised has interposed and lifted his pierced hand between you and the sword of justice, or your body would at this hour have been in the grave, and your soul would have been tormented in the pit! You have something to do with him, then. Do you feel no stirring of repentance at the thought? Does not the Spirit of God lead you to honor the author of your continued existence?

Again, you have this to do with Christ: that *it is entirely owing to him that you are now in a place where the gospel can be proclaimed to you.* O sinner, there could have been no hope, no gospel hope for you, if Jesus had not died. What balm would there have been in Gilead, what physician there, if Jesus had not come from heaven to save? The fact that you are able to hear me say, and that I am able to say it, *"Believe in the Lord Jesus, and you will be saved,"* that fact you owe to Christ. Otherwise, if we had met together, it would only have been to remind each other that we were under God's curse, and that when this life was over, we would go to a world of misery. Now we hear the silver trumpet sounding, with the love notes of the heavenly invitation, "Come to the banquet of mercy, you lame and blind!" The chief of sinners may come, and, if they trust in Jesus, they shall be saved; but were it not for the crucified Son of the highest, no note of hope could reach the ears of the guilty.

I remind you, further, that if you ask, "What have I to do with Christ?" the time is hastening when that question will receive a most conclusive answer. At the last great day, *if you have nothing to do with him as a Savior, you will have to appear before him as a judge.* The days of grace will then be over. The great white throne will be set in the heavens, and a congregation infinitely greater than any we have ever seen will be gathered around that dreadful tribunal. All men must put in a personal appearance at the last judicial inquest, and each one will hear his final sentence.

Ah, you cannot now escape! You cannot hide yourselves from the eye and hand of the judge! The mountains refuse to bow their heads to cover you, and the rocks will not open their flinty bowels to receive you! The eyes of fire find you out, and the voice of thunder says, *"I was hungry, and you gave Me nothing to eat; I was thirsty, and you gave Me nothing drink;" "Because I called and you refused, I stretched out my hand and no one paid attention"; "Depart from Me, accursed ones, into the eternal fire which has been prepared for the devil and his angels."* We *must* have something to do with Christ. You may get away today, or any other day, and go into the haunts of sin, and say, "I will not be followed by the arrows of the gospel," but the arrows of justice will surely overtake you. You may escape from the Savior, but you will rush into the arms of the judge. You may fly from your friend, but you will only make him your enemy. You may waste your life in neglecting him, but the next life will never end, and your neglect shall bring upon you a remorse which can never know an alleviation. *"What business do we have with each other, Jesus?"* The question is invested with great solemnity! Dear hearer, trifle no longer. Weigh well the question we have been considering, and never venture to ask it again.

> You may escape from the Savior, but you will rush into the arms of the judge.

Shall I tell you, before I close, what Jesus Christ may have to do with you, and what he has to do with many now present who have trusted him? It would be a thousand mercies, and a thing to sing of in heaven, if some who came here utterly careless today would go away impressed. I am so thankful to be able to preach to you again. I thank God I am able to be here. I thirst and pant to be at my solemn but beloved work again. I am so glad to be again employed by my Lord as the means of warning and pleading with poor sinners: I thought I could not better show my thankfulness than by seeking the conversion of some who are farthest away from seriousness. I do hope many of the people of God have been praying that a blessing may come. My own soul keeps praying as I speak. O that the Lord may hear me! I may have some here who have never heard the gospel before, and others who have only dropped in out of curiosity. May this be "a word in season" to such.

Some of us were once as careless, as godless, as hopeless, and as sinful as any of you can be, and Jesus Christ has had this to do with us: he showed us our lost estate; he broke our hearts, and then he bid us to look to him. Oh, happy day when we did so!

We saw him, by faith, hanging on the tree, and we believed that he had suffered there for us. We rested our souls upon what he had done, and ever since that day, instead of saying, *"What business do we have with each other, Jesus?"* we have felt that we have everything to do with him. He washed us from our sins; our sin could never have been taken away from us by any other means. He clothed us with his righteousness; we have no other righteousness to wear than that which he has worked out and brought in. Since we have been brought into fellowship with him, we have found it to be our pleasure to be obedient to his commands, our privilege to believe his promises, our joy to plead his name at the mercy seat, our elation at having conversation with him, and our delight to expect the time when we shall be like him, and shall see him as he is.

You are no judges of what the Christian knows of enjoyment, if you are not Christians yourselves. You can no more judge of spiritual delights than a horse in a field can judge of the pleasures of the mathematician or the astronomer. You have not the nature that qualifies you for it. There is another world inside this world, another life within this life, and no one knows it but the man who has believed in Jesus; but, having believed in Jesus, thousands of us who are not enthusiasts nor fanatics bear our witness that Jesus Christ is so precious, that if men did but know him, they would have to love him. If you did but know what delight it is to be a Christian, you would blame yourselves that you have lived so long without being one too. If you could but know the sweetness of having Christ to be yours, you would not wish another hour to pass over your heads before you could say, "Christ is mine." The way to have Christ is to trust him. There is life in a look at Jesus. There is nothing for you to do, nor even to feel, but simply to come just as you are, and trust Jesus.

This is the gospel: *He who has believed and has been baptized shall be saved.* Baptism is the outward expression of your faith. You are immersed in water to signify that you believe that you are buried with Christ, and that you rise again to life in him. But the saving matter is the believing – the trusting is the great soul-saving grace. Baptism follows as a test of obedience and a means of refreshment to the soul. *He who believes in the Son has eternal life. But as many as received Him, to them He gave the right to become children of God, even to those who believe in His name.*

This night, eternal Father, give your Son to understand his soul's toil. This night, we implore you, grant that some may no longer reject your Son, but may the eternal Spirit, who can plead as we cannot, work effectually with the wills and consciences of men, and compel those to come in who up to this time have stood outside, that your house of mercy may be filled. The Lord answer the desire of our hearts, for Jesus' sake. Amen.

Chapter 2

Christ's Curate in Decapolis

> *And they began to implore Him to leave their region. As He was getting into the boat, the man who had been demon-possessed was imploring Him that he might accompany Him. And He did not let him, but He said to him, "Go home to your people and report to them what great things the Lord has done for you, and how He had mercy on you."* (Mark 5:17-19)

That is a striking name for a man: he *who had been demon-possessed*. It would stick to him as long as he lived, and it would be a standing sermon wherever he went. He would be asked to tell the story of what he used to be, and how the change came about. What a story for any man to tell! It would not be possible for us to describe his life while he was a demoniac – the midnight scenes among the tombs, the cutting of himself with stones, the howling, the frightening away of all the travelers that went near him, the binding with chains, the snapping of the manacles, the breaking of the fetters, and a great many details that he alone could enter into when he told the story among his own familiar friends. With what emotion of pity would he tell how Jesus came that way, and how the evil spirit forced him to confront him! He would say, "That was the best thing that could have happened to me, to be brought to the Master of that desperate legion of demons, which had encamped within my nature and made my soul to be its barracks." He would tell how, in a moment, out went the whole legion at the word of Christ.

There are some people who could tell a story very like this man's, a story of slavery to Satan, and deliverance by the power of Christ. If you can tell such a story, do not keep it to yourself. If Jesus has done great things for you, be ever ready to speak of it, till all men shall know what Christ can do. I think that great sinners who have been saved are specially called upon to publish the good news, the gospel of the grace of God. If you have been valiant *against* the truth, be valiant now *for* the truth. If you were not lukewarm when you served Satan, be not lukewarm now that you have come to serve Christ. There are some of us here who might bear the name of "the man that was born blind," or "the leper that was healed," or "the woman that was a sinner"; and I hope that we shall all be willing to take any name or any title that will glorify Christ. I do not find that this man ever prosecuted Mark for libel because he wrote of him as *the man who had been demon-possessed*. Oh no! He admitted that he was possessed with the devil once; and he glorified God that he had been delivered by the Lord Jesus.

> If you have been valiant against the truth, be valiant now for the truth.

I am going to make a few observations upon the passage I have chosen for a text, and the first observation is this: see how men's desires differ. We find in the seventeenth verse that *they began to implore Him to leave their region*. In the eighteenth verse it says, *The man who had been demon-possessed was imploring Him that he might accompany Him*. The people wanted Christ to go away from them; the man whom he had cured wanted to go wherever he might go. To which class do you belong, my dear friend?

I hope you do not belong to the first class, the class of *the many who implored Jesus to depart from them*. Why did they want him to go?

I think it was, first, because they loved to be quiet and to dwell at ease. It was a great calamity that had happened; the swine had run into the sea. They did not want any more such calamities, and evidently the Person who had come among them possessed extraordinary power. Had he not healed the demoniac? Well, they did not want him; they did not want anything extraordinary. They were easygoing men, who would like to go on the even tenor of their way, so they asked him to be good enough to go away. There are some people of that kind still living. They say, "We do not want a revival here; we are too respectable. We do not want any stirring preaching here; we are very comfortable. Do not break up our peace." Such men, when they think that God is at work in any place, are half inclined to go elsewhere. They want to be quiet; their motto is, "Anything for a quiet life." "Leave us alone, let us go on our old way" is the cry of these foolish people, as it was the cry of the Israelites when they said to Moses, *"Let us alone, that we may serve the Egyptians."*

Possibly these people wanted the Savior gone because they had an eye to business. That keeping of swine was a bad business. As Jews, they should have had no business with it. They may have said they did not eat them themselves, they only kept them for other people to eat; and now they had lost the whole herd. I wonder what all those swine would have brought to their owners. As they began calculating how much they had lost, they resolved that the Savior must go out of their region before they lost anything more. I do not wonder that when men sell intoxicating liquors, for instance, or when they follow any trade in which they cannot make money except by injuring their fellow men, they do not want Christ to come that way. Perhaps some of you would not like him to see you pay those poor women for making shirts. I am afraid, if Jesus Christ were to come around and go into some people's business houses, the husband would say to his wife, "Fetch down that book where I enter the wages, and hide it away; I do not want him to see that."

Oh, dear friend, if there be any such reason why you do not want Christ to come your way, I pray that his Holy Spirit may convince you that you do need him to come your way. He who has the most objection to Christ is the man who most needs Christ. Be sure of this, that if you do not desire to be converted, if you do not wish to be born again, you are the person above all others needing to be converted and to be born again. Is it not a most unwise decision when, for the sake of swine, we are willing to part with Christ? *"For what does it profit a man to gain the whole world, and forfeit his soul?"* He will get a corner in the newspaper, saying that he died worth so many thousands of pounds; and that will not be true, for he was never worth a penny himself. Who would give a penny for him now that he is dead? He will spend money to get rid of himself, but he cannot take it with him. He was not worth anything; he used his money for selfish purposes, and never used it for the glory of God. Oh, the poverty of an ungodly rich man!

I do not wonder that these people, taken up with themselves and with the world, prayed Christ *to leave their region.* May he not, even though you may not care to hear him, stop somewhere on the shore? No; when men get excited against religion, they go to great lengths in trying to drive it away from their midst. Many a poor man has lost his cottage, where he had a few prayer meetings, because his landlord not only did not want Christ himself, but, like the dog in the manger, would also not let others have him who did want him. Are any of you in that condition?

I hope that I have some here who are of another kind, like *this poor man, who prayed him that he might be with him.* Why did he want to be with Jesus? I think he wanted to be his attendant to show his gratitude. If he might but wait on Christ, loose the latchets of his shoes, and wash his feet, or prepare his meals, he would feel himself the happiest man on earth. He would love to be doing something for the One who had cast a legion of devils out of him.

Next, he wished not only to be an attendant to show his gratitude, but also to be a disciple so that he might learn more of him. What he did know of Christ was so precious, he had personally had such an experience of his gracious power, that he wanted to be always learning something from every word of those dear lips, and from every action of those blessed hands. He prayed him that he might be with him as a disciple who wished to be taught by him.

He wanted also to be with him as a comrade, for now that Christ must go, exiled from Decapolis, he seemed to feel that there was no reason why he should remain there himself. "Lord, if you must leave these Gadarenes, let me leave the Gadarenes too! Do you go, O Shepherd? Then let me go with you. Must you cross the sea and be gone, I know not where? I will go with you to prison and to death." He felt so linked with Christ that he prayed to him that he might be with him.

I think that there was this reason also, one of fear, at the back of his prayer. Perhaps one from that legion of devils might come back again, and if he could stay with Christ, then Christ would turn the devil out again. I should not wonder but that he felt a trembling about him, as if he could not bear to be out of the sight of the Great Physician who had healed him of so grievous an ill. I would say to all here that we are never safe except when we are with Christ. If you are tempted to go where you could not have Christ with you, do not go. Did you ever hear the story of the devil running away with a young man who was at the theater? It is said that John Newton sent after Satan, and said, "That young man is a member of my church."

"Well," replied the devil, "I do not care where he is a member; I found him on my premises, and I have a right to him"; and the preacher could not give any answer to that. If you go on the devil's premises, and he takes you down, I cannot say anything against it. Go nowhere where you cannot take Christ with you. Be like this man, who longs to go wherever Christ goes.

> Go nowhere where you cannot take Christ with you.

Now, secondly, see how Christ's dealings differ, and how extraordinary they are. Here is an evil prayer: "Leave our region." He grants it. Here is a devout prayer: "Lord, let me be with you." *And He did not let him.* Is that his way, to grant the prayer of his enemies, and refuse the petition of his friends? Yes, it is so sometimes.

In the first case, *when they implored him to depart, he left.* Oh, dear friends, if Christ ever comes near you, and you get a little touched in your conscience, and feel a throb of something like spiritual life, do not implore him to go away; for if he does go, if he should leave you to yourself and never come again, your doom is sealed! Your only hope lies in his presence, and if you plead against your one hope, you are a suicide; you are guilty of murdering your own soul.

Jesus went away from these people because it was useless to stop. If they wanted him to go, what good could he do to them? If he spoke, they would not listen. If they heard his message, they would not heed it. When men's minds are set against Christ, what else is to be done but to leave them?

He could spend his time better somewhere else. If you will not have my Lord, somebody else will. If you sit there in your pride, and say, "I do not want the Savior," there is a poor soul in the gallery longing for him, and crying, "Oh, that I might find him to be my Savior!" Christ knew that if the Gadarenes refused him, the people on the other side of the sea would welcome him on his return.

By going away, he even saved them from still greater sin. If he had not gone away, they might have tried to plunge him into the sea. When men begin to implore Christ to leave their region, they are bad enough for anything. There might have followed violence to his blessed person, so he took himself away from them. Is it not an awful thing that if the gospel ministry does not save you, it is helping to damn you? We are a savor to God, always sweet; but in some men we are a savor of death unto death, while in others we are a savor of life unto life. O my hearers, if you will not come to Christ, the seat you occupy is misappropriated! There might be another person sitting there to whom the gospel might be very precious, and our opportunities for preaching it are none too many. We do not like to waste our strength on stony ground, on hard bits of rock that repel the seed. Rock, rock, rock, will you never break? Must we continue to sow you, though no harvest comes from you? God change you, rock, and make you good soil, that yet the truth may grow upon you! The evil prayer, then, was answered.

The good prayer was not answered. Why was that? The chief reason was because the man could be useful at home. He could glorify God better by going among the Gadarenes, and among his own family, and telling what God had done for him, than he could by any attention he could pay to Christ. It is remarkable that Christ took nobody to be his body servant, or personal attendant, during his earthly ministry. He came not to be ministered unto, but to minister. He did not desire this man to be with him to make him comfortable; he bid him to go back to his family, and make known the power of Jesus Christ, and seek to win them for God.

Perhaps, too, his prayer was not answered lest his fear should have been thereby sanctioned. If he did fear, and I feel morally certain that he did, that the devils would return, then, of course, he longed to be with Christ. But Christ takes that fear from him and as good as says to him, "You do not need to be near me; I have so healed you that you will never be sick again." A patient might say to his doctor, "I have been so very ill, and through your skill have been restored to health; I would like to be near you so that, if there should be any recurrence of my sickness, I might come to you at once." If the doctor should reply, "You may go to Switzerland or to Australia, if you like," it would be the best evidence that the doctor had no fears about him, and it ought to discharge his doubts.

You see, then, how Christ's dealings differ with different men. Have I not known some who continue in sin, and yet prosper in business, heaping up wealth, and having all that a heart could wish? Have I not known others who repent, and turn to God, and from that very day they have had more trouble than they ever had before, and their way has been strangely rough? Yes, I have seen them too, and I have not envied the easy ways of the wicked, neither have I felt that there was anything very wonderful about the rough ways of the righteous. For, after all, it is not the way that is the all-important matter, it is the end of the way; and if I could travel smoothly to hell, I would not choose to do so; and if the way to eternal life is rough, I take it with all its roughness. At the foot of the Hill Difficulty, Bunyan makes his pilgrim sing,

> The hill, though high, I covet to ascend,
>   The difficulty will not me offend;
> For I perceive the way to life lies here.

My third point is this: see how good a thing it is to be with Jesus. This man begged the Lord that he might be with him.

If you have been saved recently, I expect you have a longing in your heart to be with Christ always. I will tell you what shape that longing is likely to take. You were so happy, so joyful, and it was such a blessed meeting, that you said to yourself, "I am sorry it is over; I would have liked this meeting to have been kept on all night, and the next day, and never to end." Yes, you were of the mind of Peter, when he wanted to build three tabernacles on the holy mount, and to stop there the rest of his days; but you cannot do it, so it is no use wishing for it. You must go home to that drinking husband or that scolding wife, to that ungodly father or that unkind mother. You cannot stay in that meeting always.

Perhaps you have another idea of what it is to be with Christ. You are so happy when you can get alone, and read your Bible, and meditate, and pray, and you say, "Lord, I wish I could always do this; I would like to be always upstairs in this room, searching the Scriptures, and having communion with God." Yes, yes, yes, but you cannot do it. There are the children's socks to be mended; there are buttons to be put on the husband's shirts. There are all sorts of odds and ends to be done, and you must not neglect any one of them. Whatever household duties come upon you, attend to them. You wish that you did not have to go to the city tomorrow. Would it not be sweet to have an all-night prayer meeting, and then to have an all-day searching of the Scriptures? No doubt it would, but the Lord has not so arranged it. You have to go to business, so just put on your weekday clothes, and think yourself none the less happy because you have to show your religion in your daily life.

"Ah, well!" says one, and this I very often hear, "I think that I could always be with Christ if I could get right out of business, and give myself up to the service of the Lord." Especially do you think that it would be so if you were a minister. Well, I have nothing to say against the ministry of the gospel. If the Lord calls you to it, obey the call, and be thankful that he has counted you faithful, putting you into the ministry. But if you suppose that you will be nearer to Christ simply by entering the ministry, you are very much mistaken. I daresay that I had about as many of other people's troubles brought to me this morning, after I was done preaching, as would last most men a month. We have to bear with everybody's trouble, and everybody's doubt, and everybody's need of comfort and counsel. You will find yourself burdened with much serving, even in the service of the Lord; and it is very easy to lose the Master in the Master's work. We want much grace lest this insidious temptation should overcome us even in our ministry.

You can walk with Christ and keep a cloth dealer's shop. You can walk with Christ and sell groceries. You can walk with Christ and be a working man, a dock laborer. You can walk with Christ and be a chimney sweep. I do not hesitate to say that by the grace of God, you can walk with Christ as well in one occupation as in another, if it is a rightful one. It might be quite a mistake if you were to give up your business under the notion that you would be more with Christ if you became a city missionary, or a Bible woman, or a seller of religious books, or a captain in the Salvation Army, or whatever other form of holy service you might desire. Keep on with your business. If you can blacken shoes well, do that. If you can preach sermons badly, do not do that.

"Ah!" says one, "I know how I would like to be with Christ." Yes, yes, I know; you would like to be in heaven. Oh yes, and it is a laudable desire to wish to be with Christ, for it is far better than being here! But, mind you, it may be a selfish desire, and it may be a sinful desire, if it be pushed too far. A holy man of God was once asked by a fellow servant of Christ, "Brother So-and-so, do you not want to go home?" He said, "What?" "Do you not want to go home?" He said, "I will answer you by another question. If you had a man working for you, and on Wednesday he said, 'I wish that it was Saturday,' would you keep him on?" The other thought that he would need a large stock of patience to do so. Why, you know what a fellow is who is always looking for Saturday night, do you not? You will be glad to see the back of him before Saturday comes, for he will be no good for work. Have I a right to be wanting to go to heaven if I can do any good to you here? Is it not more of a heaven to be outside of heaven than inside, if you can be doing more for God outside than in? Long to go when the Lord wills; but if to remain in the flesh be more for the good of the church and the world, and more for the glory of God, waive your desire, and be not vexed with your Master when, after having prayed that you may be with him, it has to be written of you as it was of this man: *He did not let him.*

Still, it is a very delightful thing to be with Jesus.

But now, in the fourth place, see that there may be something even better than this. In the sense which I have mentioned, there is something even better than being with Christ.

What is better than being with Christ? Why, to be working for Christ! Jesus said to this man, *"Go home to your people and report to them what great things the Lord has done for you, and how He had mercy on you."*

This is *more honorable*. It is very delightful to sit at Jesus' feet, but if the most honorable post on the field of battle is the place of danger; if the most honorable thing in the state is to have royal service allotted to you, then the most honorable thing for a Christian is not to sit down, and sing, and enjoy himself, but to get up, and risk reputation, life, and everything for Jesus Christ's sake. Dear friend, aspire to serve your Lord; it is a more honorable thing even than being with him.

It is also *better for the people*. Christ is going away from the Gadarenes; they have asked him to go, and he is going; but he seems to say to this man, "I am going because they have asked me to go. My leaving them looks like a judgment upon them for their rejection of me; but yet I am not going away altogether. I am going to stay with you; I will put my Spirit upon you, and so will continue with you. They will hear you though they will not hear me." Christ, as it were, resigns the pastorate of that district; but he puts another in his place, not so good as himself, but one whom they will like better; not so powerful and useful as himself, but one better adapted to them. When Christ was gone, this man would be there, and the people would come to him to hear about those swine, and how they ran down into the sea; and if they did not come to him, he would go and tell them all about it; and so there would be a permanent curate left there to discharge the sacred ministry, now that the great Bishop had gone.

I like that thought. Christ has gone to heaven, for he is needed there, and so he has left you here, dear brother, to carry on his work. You are not equal to him in any respect; but yet remember what he said to his disciples: *"He who believes in Me, the works that I do, he will do also; and greater works than these he will do; because I go to the Father."* That is why Christ does not permit you to be with him at present. You must stay for the sake of the people among whom you live, as *the man who had been demon-possessed* had to remain for the sake of the Gadarenes, to whom he might testify concerning Christ.

His remaining, also, was *better for his family*; and do you not think that, oftentimes, a man of God is kept out of heaven for the sake of his family? You must not go yet, father; those boys still need your example and your influence. Christian mother, you must not go yet; I know that your children are grown up, and they are grieving you very much; but still, if there is any restraint upon them, it is their poor old mother, and you must stay till you have prayed them to God, and you will do so yet. Be of good courage. I believe that there are many here who might be in heaven, but that God has some whom he intends to bring in by them, so they must stay here a little longer. Though infirm in body, shattered in nerve, and often racked with acute pain, perhaps with a deadly disease upon you, and wishing to be gone, you must not go till your work is done.

And He did not let him. This demoniac had to go home, and tell his wife and his children what great things the Lord had done for him. Many eminent preachers have pictured the scene of his going home, so I will not try to do it. You may only imagine what it would be if it were your case, and you had been shut up in an asylum, or had been almost too bad even for that. How glad your friends were to have you taken away, and then how much more glad to find you coming back perfectly well! I can imagine how the man's wife would look through the window when she heard his voice. Has he come back in a mad fit? How the children would be filled with terror at the sound of their father's voice until they were assured that there was indeed a change in him!

Ah, poor sinner, you have come here today! Perhaps you forget that your children often have to hide away under the bed when Father comes home. I know that there are such persons around, and they may even find their way into the tabernacle. The Lord have mercy upon the drunkard, and turn his cups bottom upwards, and make a new man of him! Then, when he goes home to tell of free grace and dying love, and of the wonderful change that God has worked in him, he will be a blessing to his family and to all those around him. It may be, dear friend, that you have to stop here till you have undone some of the mischief of your early life. You have to bring to God some of those whom you tempted, and led astray, and helped to ruin.

So you see, dear friends, there is something better even than being with Christ, and that is, working for Christ.

But lastly, consider that there is yet a case which is best of all. We must always have three degrees of comparison. What is the best state of all? To be with Christ is good; to be sent by Christ on a holy errand is better; but here is something that is best of all, namely, to work for him, and to be with him at the same time. I want every Christian to aspire to that position. Is it possible to sit with Mary at the Master's feet, and yet to run about like Martha and get the dinner ready? It is; and then Martha will never be burdened with much serving if she does that, and she will never find fault with her sister Mary. "But sir, we cannot sit and stir at the same time." No, not as to your bodies, but you can as to your souls. You can be sitting at Jesus' feet, or leaning on his breast, and yet be fighting the Lord's battles and doing his work.

In order to do this, *cultivate the inner as well as the outer life.* Endeavor not only to do much for Christ, but also to be much with Christ, and to live wholly upon Christ. Do not, for instance, on the Sabbath day, go to a class, and teach others three times, as some whom I know do; but come once and hear the Master's message, and get your soul fed; and when you have had a spiritual feast in the morning, give the rest of the day to holy service. Let the two things run together. To be always eating and never working will bring on excess, and spiritual indigestion; but to be always working and never eating – well, I am afraid that you will not bear that trial so well as the gentleman who yesterday ate his first meal after forty days' fasting. Do not try to imitate him. It is not a right or wise thing to do, but very dangerous. Get spiritual food as well as do spiritual work.

> **Get spiritual food as well as do spiritual work.**

Let me say to you, again, *grieve very much if there is the least of a cloud between you and Christ.* Do not wait until it is as thick as a November fog; be full of sorrow if it is only like a tiny, fleecy cloud. George Müller's observation was a very wise one: "Never come out of your chamber in the morning until everything is right between you and God." Keep up perpetual fellowship with Jesus, and thus you can be with him, and yet be serving him at the same time.

And mind this: *before you begin Christ's service, always seek his presence and help.* Do not enter upon any work for the Lord without having first seen the face of the King in his beauty; and in the work, often recall your mind from what you are doing, to him for whom you are doing it, and by whom you are doing it; and when the work is completed, do not throw up your cap and say, "Well done, self!" Another will say to you, by-and-by, "Well done!" if you deserve it. Do not take the words out of his mouth. Self-praise is no recommendation. Solomon said, *Let another praise you, not your own mouth; a stranger, and not your own lips.* When we have done all, we are still unprofitable servants; we have only done that which it was our duty to do. So, if you are as humble as you are active, as lowly as you are energetic, you may keep with Christ, and yet go about his errands to the ends of the earth; and I reckon this to be the happiest experience that any one of us can reach this side of the gates of pearl. The Lord bless you, and bring you there, for Christ's sake! Amen.

Chapter 3

Going Home

"Go home to your people and report to them what great things the Lord has done for you, and how He had mercy on you." (Mark 5:19)

The case of the man referred to here is a very extraordinary one. It occupies a place among the memorabilia of Christ's life, perhaps as high as anything which is recorded by either of the Gospel writers. This poor wretch, being possessed with a legion of evil spirits, had been driven to something worse than madness. He fixed his home among the tombs, where he dwelt by night and day, and was the terror of all those who passed by. The authorities had attempted to curb him; he had been bound with shackles and chains, but in the outbursts of his madness he had torn the chains apart, and had broken the shackles in pieces. Attempts had been made to reclaim him, but no man could tame him. He was worse than the wild beasts, for they might be tamed, but his fierce nature would not yield. He was a misery to himself, for he would run upon the mountains by night and day, crying and howling fearfully, cutting himself with the sharp flints, and torturing his poor body in the most frightful manner. Jesus Christ passed by; he said to the devils, *"Come out of the man."* The man was healed in a moment; he fell down at Jesus' feet; he became a rational being – an intelligent man, yes, and what is more, a convert to the Savior. Out of gratitude to his deliverer, he said, "Lord, I will follow you wherever you go; I will be your constant companion and your servant; permit me to be so." "No," said Christ, "I esteem your motive, it is one of gratitude to me; but if you would show your gratitude, *go home to your people and report to them what great things the Lord has done for you, and how He had mercy on you.*"

Now, this teaches us a very important fact, namely, that true religion does not break apart the bonds of family relationship. True religion seldom encroaches upon that sacred – I would almost say divine – institution called *home;* it does not separate men from their families, and make them aliens to their flesh and blood. Superstition has done that; an awful superstition, which calls itself Christianity, has torn men from their kind, but true religion has never done so. Why, if I might be allowed to do such a thing, I would seek out the hermit in his lonely cavern, and I would go to him and say, "Friend, if you are what you profess to be, a true servant of the living God, and not a hypocrite, as I guess you are – if you are a true believer in Christ, and would show forth what he has done for you, then upset that pitcher, eat the last piece of your bread, leave this dreary cave, wash your face, untie your hemp girdle; and if you would show your gratitude, go home to your friends, and tell them what great things the Lord has done for you. Can you edify the dry leaves of the forest? Can the beasts learn to adore that God whom your gratitude should strive to honor? Do you hope to convert these rocks, and wake the echoes into songs?

> **True religion does not break apart the bonds of family relationship.**

No, go back; dwell with your friends, reclaim your kinship with men, and unite again with your fellows, for this is Christ's approved way of showing gratitude." And I would go to every monastery and every convent of nuns, and say to the monks, "Come out brethren, come out! If you are what you say you are, servants of God, go home to your friends. No more of this absurd discipline; it is not Christ's rule; you are acting differently from what he would have you; go home to your friends!" And to the sisters of mercy we would say, "Be sisters of mercy to your own sisters; go home to your friends; take care of your aged parents; turn your own houses into convents; do not sit here nursing your pride by a disobedience to Christ's rule, which says, 'Go home to your friends.' *Go home to your people and report to them what great things the Lord has done for you, and how He had mercy on you.*" The love of a solitary and ascetic life, which is by some considered to be a divine virtue, is neither more nor less than a disease of the mind. In the ages when there was but little benevolence, and consequently few hands to build lunatic asylums, superstition supplied the lack of charity, and silly men and women were allowed the indulgence of their fancies in secluded haunts or in easy laziness. Young has most truly said,

> The first sure symptoms of a mind in health
> Are rest of heart and pleasure found at home.

Avoid, my friends, above all things, those romantic and absurd conceptions of virtue which are the offspring of superstition and the enemies of righteousness. Be not without natural affection, but love those who are knit to you by ties of nature.

True religion cannot be inconsistent with nature. It can never demand that I should abstain from weeping when my friend is dead. *Jesus wept.* It cannot deny me the privilege of a smile, when Providence looks favorably upon me; for once Jesus *rejoiced greatly in the Holy Spirit, and said, "I praise You, O Father."* It does not make a man say to his father and mother, "I am no longer your son." That is not Christianity, but something worse than what beasts would do, which would lead us to be entirely severed from our fellows, to walk among them as if we had no kinship with them. To all who think a solitary life must be a life of devotion, I would say, "It is the greatest delusion." To all who think that those must be good people who snap the ties of relationship, let us say, "Those are the best who maintain them." Christianity makes a husband a better husband; it makes a wife a better wife than she was before. It does not free me from my duties as a son; it makes me a better son, and my parents better parents.

Instead of weakening my love, it gives me fresh reason for my affection; and he whom I loved before as my father, I now love as my brother and co-worker in Christ Jesus; and she whom I reverenced as my mother, I now love as my sister in the covenant of grace, to be mine forever in the state that is to come. Oh! suppose not, any of you, that Christianity was ever meant to interfere with households; it is intended to cement them, and to make them households which death itself shall never sever, for it binds them up in the bundle of life with the Lord their God, and reunites the several individuals on the other side of the flood.

Now, I will just tell you the reason why I selected my text. I thought within myself, there are a large number of young men who always come to hear me preach; they always crowd the aisles of my chapel, and many of them have been converted to God. Now, here is Christmas Day come around again, and they are going home to see their friends. When they get home they will want a Christmas carol in the evening; I think I will suggest one to them – more especially to those who have been lately converted. I will give them a theme for their discourse on Christmas evening; it may not be quite so amusing as "The Wreck of the Golden Mary," but it will be quite as interesting to Christian people. It shall be this: *"Go home to your people and report to them what great things the Lord has done for you, and how He had mercy on you."*

For my part, I wish there were twenty Christmas days in the year. It is seldom that young men can meet with their friends; it is rare that they can all be united as happy families; and though I have no respect to the religious observance of the day, yet I love it as a family institution, as one of England's brightest days, the great Sabbath of the year, when the plow rests in its furrow, when the din of business is hushed, and when the mechanic and the working man go out to refresh themselves upon the green, grassy land of the glad earth.

If any of you are masters you will pardon me for the digression, when I most respectfully beg you to pay your servants the same wages on Christmas Day as if they were at work. I am sure it will make their houses glad if you will do so. It is unfair for you to make them feast or fast, unless you give them the wherewithal to feast and make themselves glad on that day of joy.

But now to come to the subject. We are going home to see our friends, and here is the story some of us have to tell. *"Go home to your people and report to them what great things the Lord has done for you, and how He had mercy on you."* First, *here is what they are to tell;* then, secondly, *why they are to tell it;* and then thirdly, *how they ought to tell it.*

First, then, here is what they are to tell. It is to be a story of *personal experience*. "Go home to your people and report to them what great things the Lord has done for you, and how He had mercy on you." You are not to return to your houses and immediately begin to preach. That you are not commanded to do. You are not to begin to take up doctrinal subjects and lecture on them, and endeavor to bring persons to your peculiar views and sentiments. You are not to go home with various doctrines you have lately learned, and try to teach these. At least you are not commanded to do so; you may, if you please, and none shall hinder you. But you are to go home and tell not what you have believed, but what you have *felt* – what you really know to be your own; not what great things you have read, but what great things the Lord has *done for you*; not alone what you have seen done in the great congregation, and how great sinners have turned to God, but what the Lord has done for *you*. And mark this: there is never a more interesting story than that which a man tells about himself.

> There is never a more interesting story than that which a man tells about himself.

The Rime of the Ancient Mariner derives much of its interest because the man who told it was himself the mariner. He sat down, that man whose finger was skinny, like the finger of death, and began to tell that dismal story of the ship at sea in the great calm, when slimy things crawled with legs over the shiny sea. The Wedding Guest sat still to listen, for the old man was himself a story. There is always a great deal of interest excited by a personal narrative. Virgil, the poet, knew this, and therefore he wisely makes Aeneas tell his own story, and makes him begin it by saying, "In which I also had a great part myself." So if you would interest your friends, tell them what you felt yourself. Tell them how you were once a lost, abandoned sinner, how the Lord met with you, how you bowed your knees, and poured out your soul before God, and how at last you leaped with joy, for you thought you heard him say within you, *"I, even I, am the one who wipes out your transgressions for My own sake."* Tell your friends a story of your own personal experience.

Note, next, it must be a story of *free grace*. It is not, "Tell your friends what great things you have done for yourself," but "what great things *the Lord* has done for you." The man who always dwells upon free will and the power of the creature, and denies the doctrines of grace, invariably mixes up a great deal of what he has done himself in telling his experience. But the believer in free grace, who holds the great cardinal truths of the gospel, ignores this, and declares, "I will tell what the Lord has done for me. It is true I must tell how I was first made to pray; but I will tell it thus –

> Grace taught my soul to pray,
> Grace made my eyes o'erflow.

It is true, I must tell in how many troubles and trials God has been with me; but I will tell it thus–

> 'Twas grace which kept me to this day,
> And will not let me go.

He says nothing about his own doings, or willings, or prayings, or seekings, but he ascribes it all to the love and grace of the great God who looks on sinners in love and makes them his children, heirs of everlasting life. Go home, young man, and tell the poor sinner's story; go home, young woman, and open your diary, and give your friends stories of grace. Tell them of the mighty works of God's hand which he has worked in you from his own free, sovereign, and undeserved love. Make it a free grace story around your family fire.

In the next place, this poor man's tale was a *grateful* story. I know it was grateful, because the man said, "I will tell you what great things the Lord has done for me"; and (not meaning a pun in the least degree) I may observe, that a man who is grateful is always full of the greatness of the mercy which God has shown him; he always thinks that what God has done for him is immensely good and supremely great. Perhaps when you are telling the story one of your friends will say, "And what of that?" And your answer will be, "It may not be a great thing to you, but it is to me. You say it is little to repent, but I have not found it so; it is a great and precious thing to be brought to know myself to be a sinner, and to confess it; do you say it is a little thing to have found a Savior?"

Look them in the face and say, "If you had found him too, you would not think it little. You think it little that I have lost the burden from my back; but if you had suffered with it, and felt its weight as I have for many a long year, you would think it no little thing to be emancipated and free, through a sight of the cross." Tell them it is a great story, and if they cannot see its greatness, shed great tears, and tell it to them with great earnestness, and I hope they may be brought to believe that you at least are grateful, if they are not. May God grant that you may tell a grateful story. No story is more worth hearing than a tale of gratitude.

And lastly, upon this point: it must be a tale told by a poor sinner who feels himself *not to have deserved* what he has received. *"How He had mercy on you."* It was not a mere act of kindness, but an act of free compassion towards one who was in misery. Oh! I have heard men tell the story of their conversion and of their spiritual life in such a way that my heart has loathed *them* and their story too, for they have told of their sins as if they boasted in the greatness of their crime, and they have mentioned the love of God not with a tear of gratitude, not with the simple thanksgiving of the really humble heart, but as if they as much exalted themselves as they exalted God. Oh! when we tell the story of our own conversion, I would have it done with deep sorrow, remembering what we used to be, and with great joy and gratitude remembering how little we deserve these things.

> No story is more worth hearing than a tale of gratitude.

I was once preaching upon conversion and salvation, and I felt within myself, as preachers often do, that it was but dry work to tell this story, and a dull, dull tale it was to me. But all of a sudden the thought crossed my mind, "Why, you are a poor, lost, ruined sinner yourself. Tell it, tell it, as you received it; begin to tell of the grace of God as you trust you feel it yourself." Why, then my eyes began to be fountains of tears; those hearers who had nodded their heads began to brighten up, and they listened, because they were hearing something which the man felt himself, and which they recognized as being true to him, if it was not true to them.

Tell your story, my friends, as lost sinners. Do not go to your home, and walk into your house with a pompous air, as much as to say, "Here's a saint come home to the poor sinners, to tell them a story." But go home like a poor sinner yourself; and when you go in, your mother remembers what you used to be, so you need not tell her there is a change – she will notice it, if it is only one day you are with her; and perhaps she will say, "John, what is this change that is in you?" If she is a devoted mother, you will begin to tell her the story, and I know, man though you are, you will not blush when I say it, she will put her arms around your neck, and kiss you as she never did before, for you are her twice-born son, hers from whom she shall never part, even though death itself shall divide you for a brief moment. *"Go home to your people and report to them what great things the Lord has done for you, and how He had mercy on you."*

But now, in the second place, why should we tell this story? For I hear many of my congregation say, "Sir, I could relate that story to anyone sooner than I could to my own friends. I could come to your vestry, and tell you something of what I have tasted and handled of the Word of God; but I could not tell my father, nor my mother, nor my brothers, nor my sisters." Come, then; I will try and argue with you, to induce you to do so, that I may send you home this Christmas Day to be missionaries in the localities to which you belong, and to be real preachers, though you are not so by name. Dear friends, do tell this story when you go home.

First, do it for *your Master's sake*. Oh! I know you love him; I am sure you do, if you have proof that he loved you. You can never think of Gethsemane and of its bloody sweat, of Gabbatha and of the mangled back of Christ, flayed by the whip, and you can never think of Calvary and his pierced hands and feet, without loving him; and it is a strong argument when I say to you, for his dear sake who loved you so much, go home and tell it. What! Do you think we can have so much done for us, and yet not tell it? Our children, if anything should be done for them, do not stay many minutes before they are telling all the company, "Such a one has given me such a present, and bestowed on me such and such a favor." And should the children of God be backward in declaring how they were saved when their feet made haste to hell, and how redeeming mercy snatched them as brands from the burning?

You love Jesus, young man! I put it to you, then, will you refuse to tell the tale of his love for you? Shall your lips be silent when his honor is concerned? Will you not, wherever you go, tell of the God who loved you and died for you? This poor man, we are told, *went away and began to proclaim in Decapolis what great things Jesus had done for him; and everyone was amazed.* So with you. If Christ has done much for you, you cannot help it – you must tell it. My esteemed friend, Mr. Oncken, a minister in Germany, told us last Monday evening, that as soon as he was converted, the first impulse of his newborn soul was to do good to others. And where should he do that good? Well, he thought he would go to Germany. It was his own native land, and he thought the command was, *"Go home to your people and report to them."* Well, there was not a single Baptist in all of Germany, nor any with whom he could sympathize, for the Lutherans had swerved from the faith of Luther, and gone aside from the truth of God. But he went there and preached, and he now has seventy or eighty churches established on the continent. What made him do it? Nothing but love for his Master, who had done so much for him, could have forced him to go and tell his relatives the marvelous tale of divine goodness.

> If Christ has done much for you, you cannot help it – you must tell it.

But, in the next place, are your friends loyal? Then go home and tell them, in order *to make their hearts glad*. I received last night a short epistle written with a trembling hand by one who is past the natural age of man, living in the county of Essex. His son, under God, had been converted by hearing the Word preached, and the good man could not help writing to the minister, thanking him, and blessing most of all his God, that his son had been regenerated. "Sir," he begins, "an old rebel writes to thank you, and above all to thank his God, that his dear son has been converted." I shall treasure up that epistle. It goes on to say, "Go on! and the Lord bless you."

And there was another case I heard some time ago, where a young woman went home to her parents, and when her mother saw her, she said, "There! if the minister had made me a present of all London, I should not have thought so much of it as I do of this – to think that you have really become a changed character, and are living in the fear of God." Oh! if you want to make your mother's heart leap within her, and to make your father glad – if you would make that sister happy who sent you so many letters, which sometimes you read against a lamppost, with your pipe in your mouth – go home and tell your mother that her wishes are all accomplished, that her prayers are heard, that you will no longer tease her about her Sunday school class, and no longer laugh at her because she loves the Lord, but that you will go with her to the house of God, for you love God, and you have said, "Your people shall be my people, and your God shall be my God, for I have a hope that your heaven shall be my heaven forever." Oh! what a happy thing it would be if some here who had gone astray should thus go home!

It was my privilege a little while ago to preach for a noble institution for the reception of women who had led abandoned lives, and before I preached the sermon I prayed to God to bless it, and in the printed sermon you will notice that at the end of it there is an account of two persons who were blessed by that sermon and restored.

Now, let me tell you a story of what once happened to Mr. Vanderkist, a city missionary who toils all night long to do good in that great work. There had been a drunken brawl in the street; he stepped between the men to part them, and said something to a woman who stood there concerning how dreadful a thing it was that men should be so intemperate. She walked with him a little way, and he with her, and she began to tell him such a tale of woe and sin too – how she had been lured away from her parents' home in Somersetshire, and had been brought up here to her soul's eternal hurt. He took her home with him, and taught her the fear and love of Christ; and what was the first thing she did when she returned to the paths of godliness and found Christ to be the sinner's Savior? She said, "Now, I must go home to my friends." Her friends were written to; they came to meet her at the station at Bristol, and you can hardly conceive what a happy meeting it was. The father and mother had lost their daughter, they had never heard from her; and there she was, brought back by the agency of this institution,[1] and restored to the bosom of her family. Ah! if such a one be here! I know not; among such a multitude there may be such a one. Woman! have you strayed from your family? Have you left them for long? "Go home to your friends," I beg you, before your father totters to his grave, and before your mother's gray hairs sleep on the snow-white pillow of her coffin. Go back, I beg

---

[1] The London Female Dormitory

you! Tell her you are repentant; tell her that God has met with you – that the young minister said, "Go back to your friends."

And if so, I shall not blush to have said these things, though you may think I ought not to have mentioned them; for if I may but win one such soul, I will bless God to all eternity. *"Go home to your people and report to them what great things the Lord has done for you, and how He had mercy on you."* Can you not imagine the scene, when the poor demoniac mentioned in my text went home to his people? He had been a raving madman; and when he came and knocked at the door, don't you think you see his friends calling to one another in terror, "Oh! there he is again," and the mother running upstairs and locking all the doors, because her son had come back who was raving mad; and the little ones crying because they knew what he had been before – how he cut himself with stones, because he was possessed with devils. And can you picture their joy when the man said, "Mother! Jesus Christ has healed me. Let me in; I am no lunatic now!" And when the father opened the door, he said, "Father! I am not what I was. All the evil spirits are gone; I shall live in the tombs no longer. I want to tell you how the glorious man who brought about my deliverance accomplished the miracle – how he said to the devils, 'Go away from here,' and they ran down a steep place into the sea, and I have come home healed and saved." Oh! if such a one, possessed with sin, were here today, and would go home to his friends to tell them of his release, I think the scene would be somewhat similar.

Once more, dear friends. I hear one of you say, "Ah! sir, wish to God I could go home to loyal friends! But when I go home I go into the worst of places; for my home is among those who never knew God themselves, and consequently never prayed for me, and never taught me anything concerning heaven." Well, young man, go home to your friends. If they are ever so bad, they are still your friends. I sometimes meet with young men wishing to join the church, who say, when I ask them about their father, "Oh, sir, I am parted from my father." Then I say, "Young man, you must go and see your father before I have anything to do with you; if you are at ill will with your father and mother I will not receive you into the church; if they are ever so bad, they are still *your parents*." Go home to them, and tell them, not to make them glad, for they will very likely be angry with you; but tell them *for their soul's salvation.* I hope, when you are telling the story of what God did for you, that they will be led by the Spirit to desire the same mercy themselves. But I will give you a piece of advice. Do not tell this story to your ungodly friends when they are all together, for they will laugh at you. Take them one by one, when you can get them alone, and begin to tell it to them, and they will hear you seriously.

There was once a very faithful lady who kept a lodging house for young men. All the young men were very vivacious and giddy, and she wanted to say something to them concerning religion. She introduced the subject, and it was passed off immediately with a laugh. She thought within herself, "I have made a mistake." The next morning, after breakfast, when they were all going, she said to one of them, "Sir, I would like to speak with you a moment or two," and taking him aside into another room she talked with him. The next morning she took another, and the next morning another, and it pleased God to bless her simple statement when it was given individually; but, without doubt, if she had spoken to them altogether, they would have backed each other up in laughing her to scorn. Reprove a man alone. A verse may hit him at whom a sermon flies. You may be the means of bringing a man to Christ who has often heard the Word and only laughed at it, but who cannot resist a gentle admonition.

In one of the states of America there was an infidel who was a great despiser of God, a hater of the Sabbath and all religious institutions. What to do with him the ministers did not know. They met together and prayed for him. But among the rest, one Elder B—— resolved to spend a long time in prayer for the man; after that he got on horseback and rode down to the man's forge, for he was a blacksmith. He left his horse outside, and said, "Neighbor, I am under very great concern about your soul's salvation; I tell you I pray day and night for your soul's salvation." He left him and rode home on his horse. The man went inside to his house after a minute or two, and said to one of his faithful friends, "Here's a new argument: here's Elder B—— been down here; he did not dispute, and he never said a word to me except this, 'I say, I am greatly concerned about your soul; I cannot bear you should be lost.' Oh! that

> You may be the means of bringing a man to Christ who has often heard the Word and only laughed at it.

fellow," he said, "I cannot answer him"; and the tears began to roll down his cheeks. He went to his wife and said, "I can't make this out. I never cared about my soul, but here's an elder, who has no connection with me, but I have always laughed at him, and he has come five miles this morning on horseback just to tell me he is concerned about my salvation." After a little while he thought it was time he should be concerned about his salvation too. He went in, shut the door, began to pray, and the next day he was at the deacon's house, telling him that he too was concerned about his salvation, and asking him to tell him what he must do to be saved.

Oh! that the everlasting God might make use of some of those now present in the same way, that they might be induced to

> Tell to others round
> What a dear Savior they have found;
> To point to his redeeming blood,
> And say, Behold the way to God!

I shall not detain you much longer; but there is a third point upon which we must be very brief. How is this story to be told?

First, *tell it truthfully*. Do not tell more than you know; do not tell John Bunyan's experience, when you ought to tell your own. Do not tell your mother you have felt what only Rutherford felt. Tell her no more than the truth. Tell your experience truthfully, for perhaps one single fly in the pot of ointment will spoil it, and one statement you may make which is not true may ruin it all. Tell the story truthfully.

In the next place, *tell it very humbly*. I have said that before. Do not intrude yourselves upon those who are older and know more; but tell your story humbly, not as a preacher, not *ex cathedra,* but as a friend and as a son.

Next, *tell it very earnestly*. Let them see you mean it. Do not talk about religion flippantly; you will do no good if you do. Do not make puns on texts; do not quote Scripture by way of a joke, for if you do, you may talk till you are dumb, but you will do no good if in the least degree you give them occasion to laugh by laughing at holy things yourself. Tell it very earnestly.

And then, *tell it very devoutly.* Do not try to tell your tale to man till you have told it first to God. When you are at home on Christmas Day, let no one see your face till God has seen it. Be up in the morning, wrestle with God; and if your friends are not converted, *wrestle with God for them;* and then you will find it easy work to *wrestle with them for God.* Seek, if you can, to get them one by one, and tell them the story. Do not be afraid; only think of the good you may possibly do. Remember, he that saves a soul from death has covered a multitude of sins, and he shall have stars in his crown forever and ever. Seek to be under God as saviors in your family, to be the means of leading your own beloved brethren and sisters to seek and to find the Lord Jesus Christ, and then one day, when you shall meet in paradise, it will be a joy and blessedness to think that you are there, and that your friends are there too, whom God will have made you the instrument of saving. Let your reliance in the Holy Spirit be entire and honest. Trust not yourself, but fear not to trust him. He can give you words. He can apply those words to their heart, and so enable you to *give grace to those who hear.*

To close up, by a short, and I think, a pleasant turning of the text, I will suggest another meaning to it. Soon, dear friends, very soon with some of us, the Master will say, *"Go home to your people."* You know where the home is; it is up above the stars,

> Where our best friends, our kindred dwell,
> Where God our Savior reigns.

Yonder gray-headed man has buried all his friends. He has said, "I shall go to them, but they will not return to me." Soon his Master will say, "You have had enough waiting here in this vale of tears: go home to your friends!" Oh! happy hour! Oh! blessed moment, when that shall be the word – "Go home to your friends!" And when we go home to our friends in paradise, what shall we do? Why, first we will return to that blessed seat where Jesus sits, take off our crown and cast it at his feet, and crown him Lord of all. And when we have done that, what shall be our next occupation? Why, we will tell the blessed ones in heaven what the Lord has done for us, and how he has had compassion on us. And shall such a tale be told in heaven? Shall that be the Christmas carol of the angels? Yes, it shall be. It has been published there before – blush not to tell it yet again – for Jesus has told it before. *"When he comes home, he calls together his friends and his neighbors, saying to them, 'Rejoice with me, for I have found my sheep which was lost!'"* And you, poor sheep, when you shall be gathered in, will you not tell how your Shepherd sought you, and how he found you? Will you not sit in the grassy meadows of heaven, and tell the story of your own redemption? Will you not talk with your brothers and your sisters, and tell them how God loved you and has brought you there?

Perhaps you say, "It will be a very short story." Ah! it would be if you could write it now. A little book might be the whole of your biography; but up there when your memory shall be enlarged, when your passion shall be purified and your understanding clear, you will find that what was but a tract on earth will be a huge book in heaven. You will tell a long story there of God's sustaining, restraining, and constraining grace, and I think that when you pause to let another tell his tale, and then another, and then another, you will at last, when you have been in heaven a thousand years, break out and exclaim, "O saints, I have something else to say." Again they will tell their tales, and again you will interrupt them with "Oh, beloved, I have thought of another case of God's delivering mercy."

And so you will go on, giving them themes for songs, finding them the material for the warp and woof of heavenly sonnets. "Go home," he will soon say. *"Go home to your people and report to them what great things the Lord has done for you, and how He had mercy on you."* Wait a while; wait at his leisure, and you shall soon be gathered to the land of the hereafter, to the home of the blessed, where endless bliss shall be your portion. God grant a blessing for his name's sake!

Chapter 4

The Physician Pardons His Paralyzed Patient

And they brought to Him a paralytic lying on a bed. Seeing their faith, Jesus said to the paralytic, "Take courage, son; your sins are forgiven." And some of the scribes said to themselves, "This fellow blasphemes." And Jesus knowing their thoughts said, "Why are you thinking evil in your hearts? Which is easier, to say, 'Your sins are forgiven,' or to say, 'Get up, and walk'? But so that you may know that the Son of Man has authority on earth to forgive sins,"—then He said to the paralytic, "Get up, pick up your bed and go home." And he got up and went home. (Matthew 9:2-7)

I remarked in the reading that the Gospel of Matthew is especially the gospel of the kingdom and of the King. All through Matthew's writing, the title of *King* constantly occurs in connection with Christ, and his kingliness is prominent from the opening chapter to the close. Here we see the King exercising his royal prerogatives. In this passage we have several instances of Christ acting as he could not have acted if he had not possessed a royal and divine power.

I will go at once to my text, and note, first, that Jesus dealt with the paralyzed man in a truly royal and divine way.

The bearers of the paralyzed man had broken through the tiling, whatever that may have been, to get him near the Savior. They had dropped him down over the heads of the eager throng, and there he lay upon his pallet before Christ, unable to stir hand or foot, but looking up with that gaze of eager expectancy which Christ so well understood.

You will notice that our Lord did not wait for a word to be spoken; he simply looked, and *he saw their faith*. Matthew writes, *Seeing their faith, Jesus*.... Who can see faith? It is a thing whose effects can be seen, its signs and tokens are discoverable, and they were eminently so in this case, for breaking up the roof, and putting the man down before Christ in so strange a way, were evidences of their belief that Jesus would cure him. Still, Christ's eyes saw not only the proofs of their faith, but also faith itself. There stood the four men, speaking with their eyes, and saying, "Master, see what we have done! We are persuaded that we have done the right thing, and that you will heal him." There was the man, lying on his bed, looking up, and wondering what the Lord would do, but evidently cheered by the belief that he was now in a position of hope where, in all probability, he would become a man favored beyond everyone else. Christ not merely saw the looks of this man and his bearers, but he also saw their faith.

Ah, friends, *we* cannot see one another's faith! We may see the fruit of it. Sometimes we think that we can discern the lack of it; but to see the faith itself, this needs divine sight, this needs the glance of the eye of the Son of Man. Jesus saw their faith; and now, today, that same eye is looking upon all in this audience, and he sees your faith. Have you any faith that he can see? "Oh yes!" some of you can reply. "We have a humble, trembling faith, not such as it ought to be, but such as we are very thankful to possess." Some of you, it may be, are conscious of your sin tonight; and all the faith you have is just a faint hope, a feeble belief that if he will but speak to you, you shall be forgiven. You believe that he is able to save to the uttermost them that come unto God by him, but you have in the background a fear that you cannot come, or that you may not come in a right way. Still, if it is ever so little faith in him that you have, my Master sees it; and, as in our early days we used to look for a single spark in the tinder that we might get a light on the cold mornings, so does the Lord look for the tiniest gleam of faith in any human heart, that out of it may come a flame of spiritual life. *Seeing their faith, Jesus . . . .* Now then, my dear hearer, Christ's eye is looking at you today. Whatever faith you have, exert it now; believe in Jesus. He is the Son of God. Believe in him as able to save you, for he is able, and he is willing as well as able; and now trust your soul to him, sink or swim. Determine that if you must die, you will die at the foot of Christ's cross, but you will go nowhere else for salvation. *Seeing their faith, Jesus . . . .* His royal and divine sight could perceive that which was hidden from all mere mortal men.

But then, when Jesus saw their faith, observe next that *he dealt first with the chief evil which afflicted this man*. He did not begin by curing him of the paralysis. That was bad enough, but sin is worse than the paralysis; sin in the heart is worse than paralysis of every single muscle. Sin is death, and even something worse than death itself; therefore, Christ, at the very beginning of this miracle, to show his lordship, his royal and divine power, said to the man, *"Take courage, son; your sins are forgiven."* This was laying the axe at the root of the man's evil nature. This was hunting the lion, the biggest beast of all the foul creatures that lurked in the densest forest of the man's being. Christ's words drove the unclean animal from his lair, and by his almighty power tore him as though he had been a young goat.

Now, at this time, you may have many troubles, and perhaps you are eager to spread them before the Lord. That sick child, your dear husband who is at home ill, that business which is dwindling and likely to fail, that disease of yours which is weakening you and makes you scarcely fit to be in the Lord's house today. Now, waive all those things, for heavy as they are, they are trivial compared with sin. There is no venom as poisonous as that of sin; this is the wormwood and the gall; this is the deadly fang of the serpent whose sting infects and inflames our whole being. If this evil be removed, then every ill has gone; therefore, Christ begins with this: *"Your sins are forgiven."* Breathe a prayer to him now for the forgiveness of your sin: "Jesus, Master, forgive me! With a word you can pardon all my sin; you have but to pronounce the pardon, and all my iniquities will be put away at once and forever. O my Lord, will you not put them away today?"

Notice, also, that *Jesus did absolutely forgive that man*. *"Take courage, son; your sins are forgiven."* He did not say, "Your sins shall be forgiven," but *"Your sins are forgiven;* I absolve you from them all. Whatever they may have been, your youthful sins, your manhood sins, your sins before the paralysis laid hold upon you, your sins of grumbling since you have been upon that bed, put them all together into one great mass, and though they be multitudinous as the stars of heaven, or as the sands on the seashore, son, your sins are forgiven." And the man felt that it was so, he believed that it was so, a load was taken from his heart; his whole spirit was lifted up by that gracious word, *"Take courage, son; your sins are forgiven."* I pray my Master to deal thus with some who are sitting in these pews very heavy at heart. May he speak right into the depths of your spirit and say, "Son, daughter, your sins are forgiven! They are blotted out, they are all gone." Oh, what a dreadful time that is to a man when first he sees his sin! It is the darkest moment of his life; but it is a blessed moment when he sees that Christ has put away his sin and has said to him, "You shall not die in your iniquities; for they are all forgiven." Everything grows light and bright round about him; he himself is like one who comes up out of a well, or out of a horrible pit, out of the miry clay, yes, out of the very belly of hell. He seems to leap all at once up to the throne of heaven as he sings, "My sins are all forgiven. I am a miracle of grace." Wonder not if the man can scarcely contain himself; marvel not if he runs, and leaps, and dances for sheer joy.

This is how Christ behaves towards poor, paralyzed, sin-bound men and women. He sees their faith, and then puts their sin away where it shall be seen no more forever, for he is a King, he is God, and he is able to forgive and blot out all iniquity. I have heard of one who, having been under a great sense of sin, and being relieved of it, could for a long time only cry out, "He is a great Forgiver." When there were other things to be attended to, he could not see to them, nor speak of any other kind of business but this: "He is a great Forgiver." I do not feel as if, today, I wanted to say anything else to you but this: "He is a great Forgiver. I have found him so; many here have found him so; and all who will trust his great atoning sacrifice shall also know that he is a great Forgiver."

The second division of my subject diverges a little from the first, but it follows the text, and so it is no real divergence. By his royal and divine power, Christ read and judged men's thoughts.

See those scribes, those students of the letter of the Word, who know how many letters there are in every book of the Old Testament, and have counted them so accurately that they can tell which is the middle letter. Wonderfully wise men those! Do you see them? They are very vexed and angry, and they think hard thoughts of Christ. They did not dare to speak out what they thought; the people would not have listened to them just then if they had spoken, so they held their tongues. But they did not hold their hearts, and there was a Thought-reader there – not one who professed the art, but One who possessed it – and he heard where the quickest ear would have failed to detect the faintest sound. Jesus heard the scribes mentally say, "This." If you look at your Bibles, you will find that the word *fellow* is printed in italics, and that the scribes said within themselves, *"This fellow."* By this, they meant any wicked name that you would like to put in: "This blasphemer." They would not say what they thought of him; they did not like to call him anything but just "This riffraff."

Thus, *Christ read their contempt of him*. They had not uttered it, but he had heard it. It is an awful thing to have a silent contempt of Christ. You may pride yourself on saying, "I have never spoken anything against religion; I have never used a profane expression." No; but if you do not call Jesus your Lord, if you do not own him as your Savior, he knows what the contemptuous omission means. What you do not say, though you only say, "This ——," and leave a blank space – he reads it all. If there are any here who have such thoughts of my Lord and Master, I do not wish to know them, and I hope that they will never let any other creature know them; but let them remember that Jesus knows all about them, for he is a King who reads the secrets of all hearts, and in due time he will lay them bare.

But next, *Jesus marked their charge of blasphemy*. They said in their heart that he blasphemed because he had taken to himself the prerogative of God. According to Mark's and Luke's accounts, they asked,

"*Who is this man who speaks blasphemies? Who can forgive sins, but God alone?*" Now, mark you, we who worship Christ as God can never have any fellowship with those who deny his Godhead, nor can they have any fellowship with us; for if he is indeed the Son of God, then they who deny it blaspheme him; and if he is only a man, then we are clearly idolaters and man-worshippers, and he *did* blaspheme. We are obliged to confess that, and we do confess it; if he was not the Son of God, if he had not power to forgive sins, then they rightly judged that he was a blasphemer. Ah, my hearer, when you are afraid that Jesus cannot forgive your sins, you are trembling on the very verge of blasphemy! There is such a crime as constructive treason, and there is such a sin as constructive blasphemy. To deny Christ's power to save is to make him but a man; and if you put him down as only man, you blaspheme. Even though you may not intend to utter blasphemy, there is the shadow of its dark presence even in that unbelief of yours.

Notice, also, how *Jesus judged their thoughts*. He said to them, "*Why are you thinking evil in your hearts?*" It was their hearts rather than their thoughts that were evil. Intellectual error generally springs from an unrenewed heart. And what evil had these men thought? They had thought him a blasphemer, and they had also thought contemptuously of him. But the greatest evil of all was that they had limited his power; they did not believe that he could forgive. They thought it blasphemy on his part to profess to have the power to forgive the sins of men.

Now, my dear hearer, I know that you would shrink from openly blaspheming Christ, that is, if you are the person I think you are. Then, however great your sin at present is, do not make it greater by insinuating that he cannot forgive you, for of all sins this must be the most cruel, to think that he is unable to forgive. This stabs at Christ's Saviorship, which is his very heart. If you say, "I am very guilty," say it again, for you say the truth; but if you say, "I am so guilty that he cannot forgive me," I pray you to withdraw that wicked word, lest you should limit the Holy One of Israel, and he should have to say to you, "*Why are you thinking evil in your hearts?*" It is thinking evil of Christ to imagine that he cannot forgive. I mean this word for the very worst man in the world. If you are now the blackest soul out of hell, if you are at this moment the most guilty and the most condemned of all the myriad offenders of our ruined race, yet I charge you not to add to your past sin this further evil of doubting Christ's power to save even you; but come as you are, and cast yourself at his feet, and say, "Let all your power to save be shown in me; I am the chief of sinners, and here you have an opportunity of showing the greatness of your power to pardon."

And observe, once more, that in dealing with these scribes, our Lord spoke very royally and divinely to them, for *he revealed the unreasonableness of their thoughts.* He said to them, *"Why are you thinking evil in your hearts?"* I ask you who are here today if you know any reason why Christ cannot forgive sin. Will anyone here, who doubts his power to pardon, find a reason for that doubt? If you believe (and I will assume that you do believe) that he is the Son of God, can he not forgive sin? If you believe that he did heal the lepers, and the paralyzed, and even raised the dead, can he not forgive sin? Further, if you believe that he died for sin, that on the cross he offered no less a victim than himself, why do you think that he cannot forgive? If you believe that he rose again from the dead – and I know that you believe this – if indeed he rose again from the dead for the justification of the ungodly, how is it that he cannot forgive? And if he has gone into glory, and you know that he is at his Father's right hand, and he is there making intercession for the transgressors, how can you say that he cannot forgive you? *"Why are you thinking evil in your hearts?"* in limiting my Master's power? He can forgive everyone here present; he can forgive every soul in whom he sees faith in himself, whoever he may be, and however extreme his guilt.

Now we come back to the paralyzed man and our Master again, and notice, in the third place, that very royally Jesus openly declared his commission. He seems to me to read the letters unobstructedly which his Father gave him when he sent him on his errand of love and mercy: *"The Son of Man has authority on earth to forgive sins."*

First, *Jesus is the Son of Man.* He does not conceal that fact. One would have thought that he would have said, "I am the Son of God"; but here he chooses still to hold his Godhead in abeyance, so he says, *"The Son of Man has authority on earth to forgive sins.* I, the Son of Mary, I, the carpenter's Son, I, who dwelt in Nazareth for thirty years, I, who have gone up and down among you, worn with sufferings, pained by your hostility, wearied by labor for you, I, the Son of Man, have authority to forgive sins." Think of that. He puts himself on his very lowest standing, and declares that, as the Son of Man, there is bestowed upon him, by reason of his Godhead, the authority – or power – to forgive sins.

And having thus declared his title, he goes on to say that *he forgives sins as the Son of Man on earth.* He was on earth, and he had power on earth, that is, in his earthly life, in his humiliation, when he had made himself for a while to be less than the Father, so that he could say, "My Father is greater than I" – higher in office just then – when he had humbled himself, and taken upon himself the form of a servant, he could say, "The Son of Man has power on earth, at his lowest, divested of glory, here as a Man among men, the Son of Man has power on earth to forgive sins." Oh, how I love this word, for if he had power on earth, what power he has in heaven; and if he had power as the Son of Man, what power he has as God and Man in one person! Oh, how fully you may trust him! Even the Christ whom they could see, the Son of Man – for you know that there was a Christ whom they could not see, that Son of God whom carnal eyes could not behold, who must reveal himself spiritually or be unperceived by mortal sense; even he whom they could see, the Christ whom you poor weeping ones can see, though you cannot see the half of Christ, no, you cannot see the hundredth part of Christ; the Christ whom you poor doubters can see, the Christ whom you who are all but blind can only see out of the corners of those eyes of yours when you see men as trees walking – even that Christ, the Son of Man, in his weakness on earth, was able to forgive sins. I do not seem as if I ought to try to preach about this glorious truth; but I feel that I ought to state it, and leave it as a solemn fact for you to reject at your peril if you dare, or to receive with gladdest joy, for, believe me, your only hope lies here. O guilty sons of Adam, here is the way of escape for you! Your father Adam has ruined you, but the Son of Man has come to seek and to save you, and he declares that he has power on earth to forgive sins.

Now, notice, in this blessed unrolling of his commission as the Son of Man, how *Jesus cheers the sad.* He said to the poor paralyzed man, *"Take courage, son; your sins are forgiven."* How this should comfort you who are sad on account of sin! It is the Son of Man who can forgive you. You tremble at the greatness of God, you are afraid of his majesty; but this Son of Man, your Brother, whose hands were pierced with the nails, and whose feet still wear the nail-prints, whose side has the gash that the spear of the soldier made, he it is who can forgive sins. How tenderly he comes to you! How gently does he deal with you! Here is a hand fit for a surgeon, of whom it is said that he must have an eagle's eye, and a lion's heart, but a lady's hand. Here is a hand of flesh, a dainty, tender hand of love that brings to you pardon. You do not have to encounter God absolutely; but the one Mediator comes in between God and men. He who is bone of your bone, and flesh of your flesh, says to you, *"The Son of Man has authority on earth to forgive sins."* And this makes our hearts cheer up when they are sorrowing on account of sin.

Besides that, *Jesus assures the forgiven that he has forgiven them.* How I love to think of that blessed fact, that Christ does not forgive us and keep his forgiveness in the dark; but he says, *"Take courage, son; your sins are forgiven,"* giving the assurance of forgiveness to the sinner whom he forgives! The realization of pardon is a delightful feeling. It is not worthwhile to sin, whatever comes of it. I cannot say, with Augustine, *"Beata culpa!* Blessed fault!" But oh, if there is a joy outside of heaven that is higher than all others, it is the joy of a sinful soul when divine forgiveness is granted, making the forgiven one whiter than the driven snow, and fresher than the morning dew. I am a forgiven man, wonder of wonders! I, who have broken all God's laws, and have brought upon me The Lord's wrath, am pardoned for all my transgressions. God's Son has said it, and his word is sure and steadfast: *"Take courage, son; your sins are forgiven."*

I think that men would readily give up all the pleasures of this world, and count them as nothing, if they could but know the bliss of forgiven sin. Oh, if any man, who says that he loves a merry laugh, did but once know what it is to be reconciled to God, he would reckon that he never before enjoyed real merriment, or understood true cheer. Our Lord Jesus Christ, as I have said, makes us drink of the sweetness of forgiveness. It is not merely that he burns the books that recorded our indebtedness, but he also tells us that he has done so. He says, *"Your sins are forgiven."*

Thus it was that Christ publicly unrolled his divine commission, declaring that he had power on earth to forgive sins. He came here on purpose to forgive human guilt – not to condemn, no, not even to condemn her who was caught in the act of adultery. *"I do not condemn you,"* said he; *"Go. From now on, sin no more."* Jesus came not to condemn the thief who was dying on the cross, and confessing that he deserved so to die; no, but he said to him, *"Today you shall be with Me in Paradise."* It is Christ's business to pardon; it is his bliss to pardon; it is his glory to pardon. He came here on purpose that he might pardon the guilty. Oh, that all sinful ones would go to him for forgiveness!

After having thus declared his commission, let us note, in the fourth place, that Jesus exhibited his credentials.

Since the scribes disputed his power to pardon, he gave them a practical proof that he could forgive, and I want your special attention to this point. He said to them, in effect, "To forgive sin is a divine act. Now, *which is easier, to say, 'Your sins are forgiven,' or to say, 'Get up, and walk'?"* I put it to you, dear friends, which is the easier of the two? Mark that Jesus does not ask, "Which is the easier, to forgive sin, or to heal the paralysis?" No; he said, *"Which is easier, to say, 'Your sins are forgiven,' or to say, 'Get up, and walk'?"*

Well now, *the first is much the easier,* because there are a great many who can say, *"Your sins are forgiven,"* and you cannot see whether the sins are forgiven or not. Look at the number of those who call themselves priests, who say, after they have heard the repentant person's confession, "I absolve you." It is easy enough to say that, but who is to know whether that person who has professed repentance is absolved or not? There is no change apparent to the observer; the poor sinner who is told that he is absolved may credulously derive some delusive comfort from his fellow sinner's words; but those who look on cannot see any difference in the man or woman coming back from the confessional from what they were when they went there. It is very easy to say, *"Your sins are forgiven";* any fool can say it, any scoundrel can say it. But then, if you say, *"Get up, and walk,"* suppose they do not get up and walk, what then? Anybody can stand there and say to the paralyzed man, *"Get up, and walk,"* and the man may make an effort to rise, but fall back as helpless as ever; so that, although both miracles are, in themselves, equally impossible to man, and equally require divine power, yet the saying of the one is easy enough, but the saying of the other is more difficult. Many an impostor would shrink from saying, *"Get up, and walk,"* for he would be mightily afraid that it would be found one thing to say it, and quite another thing for the patient really to get up and walk. Thus Christ said to the scribes, "I will prove to you that I am divine, and therefore that I have the power to forgive sins, for I will now perform a miracle which you shall see, and which you shall be quite unable to dispute. It shall be worked before you all, and then you shall know that as I could do what was evidently the harder thing, that is, to say, 'Get up, and walk,' I had the right to say what has become the easier thing: 'Your sins are forgiven.'"

Then He said to the paralytic, while he lay there, *"Get up, pick up your bed and go home."* Thus *Jesus marked out the miracle in detail.* It was necessary to pile up the argument to make it complete and overwhelming. First, "Get up, sit up, stand up." The man could not do that if the paralysis was still upon him; but at once, *he got up.* "Now roll up your mattress." He stoops down, and you can see him rolling it up; he has it now under his arm, or on his shoulder. "Now," is Christ's next command, *"Go home,"* and he walks straight away off to his home. Of course, in modern times, we make exhibitions of converts, and we would have taken this man up and down the streets to show him off as a trophy; but the Savior does much better than that. For him to go home was a clearer proof of being cured than for him to remain with Christ, for it might be supposed that while he was with the Savior, some strange influence emanating from the Great Physician kept him in a state of excitement and up to the mark. So Christ says, "Go home to your house, to everyday life, just as anybody else might do, go along with you, bed and all"; and off he goes. Every point of detail was necessary to make it clear that this was a real, radical, and complete cure, and that the Christ who could work such a miracle was able also to forgive sin.

I remark, next, that *change of nature is the best proof of the pardon of the sinner.* You may come to me today and say, "Sir, I am forgiven." I am glad to hear it, but how will you behave at home today? "I am forgiven," cries one, all of a sudden, under a sermon, as if electrified. Yes, yes; and you want to stay with us, do you, and never go home anymore? That will not do, because such a cure as that could not be a perfect, businesslike, commonsense cure. Go home to your house. Your moral actions, your moderation, your honesty, your purity, your obedience to parents, your good conduct as a servant, your generosity as a master – these will not save you; but unless we see them, how are we to know that Christ has worked a miracle upon you? And if he has not worked a miracle upon you in raising you up from the sickness of sin, how do we know that he has forgiven you? In fact, we do not know it, and we do not believe that he has, for these two things go together: the one as the evidence of the power that brought about the other. If you have been forgiven, you have been renewed. Sitting in this place today, you may be forgiven of all your sin; but if you are, you will not be tomorrow what you have been today. The drunkard's cup will not be lifted to your lips anymore; the company of the impure will not be pleasant to you again; no oath, no profane speech, no foolish talk will come out of your mouth hereafter. Christ forgives you outright, not because you are cured of your evil habits; but he forgives you while you are still paralyzed by sin; and the evidence that you are forgiven, the harder thing as the world will always judge it to be, is your taking up your bed and walking home, quitting all your former laziness, for it will be laziness from this time. The bed which you could not help lying upon once, will become the couch of laziness to you if you lie on it any longer. You will take that up, and you will walk back, and be a man of activity, at your daily labor, in your own house, hereafter as long as you live.

Do notice this, dear friends. We do not preach to you salvation by works; but when you are forgiven, then the good works come. The same Christ who makes you a new creature pardons your sin. You cannot have half a Christ; you must have Christ the Healer as well as Christ the Forgiver. If Christ could be cut up into lots, we could sell him off immediately; but if he is to be taken all at once as a Sin-killer as well as a Sin-forgiver, there are always some who will avoid facing him. I pray that not one of you may be of that kind.

> If you have been forgiven, you have been renewed.

I think, also, that *the detailed obedience that the Savior required was the best evidence that he had forgiven the man's sin.* "Get up, pick up your bed and go home." From this point on, to do everything that Christ bids you to do, in the order in which he bids you to do it, because he bids you to do it, to do it at once, to do it joyfully, to do it constantly, to do it prayerfully, to do it thankfully, this shall be the token that he has indeed dealt with you as a pardoning God. O my dear friends, I am afraid that there are some who profess to have been forgiven who are not as obedient to Christ as they ought to be! I have known them to neglect certain duties. I even knew a man once, who would not read some parts of the Word of God because they made him feel uneasy; but be sure of this, that when you and the Word of God fall out, the Word of God has right on its side. There is something rotten in the state of Denmark when you cannot read a chapter without feeling that you wish that it was not there. If there is any verse that you would like left out of the Bible, that is the verse that ought to stick to you like a blister, until you really pay attention to its teaching. There is something wrong with you whenever you quarrel with the Word of God. I say again, that detailed obedience is the surest evidence that the Lord has forgiven your sin. For instance, *"He who has believed and has been baptized shall be saved."* Do not omit any part of that precept; and if Christ bids you to come to his table and thus remember him, do not live in neglect of that command. At the same time, remember to live soberly, righteously, honestly, and godly in this present evil age; for if you do not, if there is not a detailed obedience, there may be a fear that, after all, the Lord has never said to you, *"Your sins are forgiven."*

And, last of all, *the best evidence is always seen at home.* "Get up, pick up your bed and go home." If there is a place where devotion is best seen and best judged, it is upon the family altar. What the man is at home, that he really is; what the woman is in her own house, that she is truly. It is very easy, you know, to masquerade in society, to seem to be something very wonderful upon the stage of the world's theater, and then not to be in reality the king that you seemed to be, but, after all, to be only a very sorry specimen of humanity. *"Get up, pick up your bed and go home."* Someone said to me this very day, of a certain man, "Do you think, sir, that he was a good man?" I said, "Well, brother, I think that he was a good man of a very bad sort." I did not know how to put the truth more lovingly. I remember an old woman who went to hear a minister of a certain creed that she did not like, though he preached uncommonly well; and when she came out, they asked her how she fared with the preacher. She replied, "Well, he is one of the best of a very bad brand." Now, I do not like to have to say that of anybody who professes to be a Christian; and it should not be so. No; and I do not want you to be the worst of a good brand either; though that, perhaps, is better than being the best or the worst of a bad brand. We want to be such that we can bear the fullest inspection.

"Ah!" says one, "I came here seeking the pardon of sin, and now, sir, you have got off to moral conduct." Quite so, and that is where I want you to get off to. Seek the pardon of sin today; it is to be had, as I have told you, by faith: *Seeing their faith, Jesus said to the paralytic, "Take courage, son; your sins are forgiven."* But if you want to make sure that Christ is really able to forgive your sin, the very best evidence to you, and the only evidence to the outside scribes, will be that you pick up your bed and walk. "Oh!" say you sometimes, "I have many sins still, but I am not what I used to be. I am a changed man at heart; I could not bear what I once enjoyed, I could not do what I once commonly did, and the things that I loathed and despised are now delightful to me." I am glad that it is so with you, and I pray that it may be so with all my hearers. May God work that great and gracious change in many who are in this tabernacle today, for our Lord Jesus Christ's sake! Amen.

Chapter 5

The New Fashion

And he got up and immediately picked up the pallet and went out in the sight of everyone, so that they were all amazed and were glorifying God, saying, "We have never seen anything like this." (Mark 2:12)

It is very natural that there should be many surprising things in the gospel, for it is beyond measure remarkable that there should be a gospel at all. As soon as I begin thinking of it I exclaim with Bunyan, "O world of wonders, I can say no less"; and I invite you all to join with the multitude in saying with the text, *"We have never seen anything like this."* When man sinned, God might instantly have destroyed our rebel race, or he might have permitted it to exist as the fallen angels do, in a state of hatred of all goodness, and in consequent misery. But he who passed the angels by took up the seed of Abraham and looked upon man – that insignificant item in the ranks of creatureship – and determined that man should experience salvation and show forth his divine grace. It was a wonderful thing, to begin with, that there should be a gospel for men; and when we remember that the gospel involved the gift of the only begotten Son of God, when we remember that it was necessary that God, the invisible Spirit, should be veiled in human flesh, that the Son of God should become the son of Mary, should be subject to pain and weakness, poverty and shame – when we remember all this, we may expect to find great wonders clustering around such a stupendous fact.

Beholding God in human flesh, miracles no longer strike us as being at all marvelous, for the incarnation of God outmiracles all miracles. But we must further remember that in order to bring the gospel to us it was needful that God should in our nature offer atonement for human sin. Think of it! The holy God making atonement for sin! When the angels first heard of it they must have been lost in astonishment, for they had *"never seen anything like this."* Shall the offended die for the offender? Shall the judge bear the chastisement of the criminal? Shall God take upon himself the transgression of his creature? Yet so it has been, and Jesus Christ has borne, that we might never bear, the consequences of sin – no, sin itself. *For the transgression of my people was he stricken* (KJV). Jesus was made a curse for us, as it is written, *"Cursed is everyone who hangs on a tree."* Now, a commonplace result could not be imagined as growing out of a gospel sent to rebellious men, and a gospel involving the incarnation and the death of the Son of God. Everything in God's creation is made to scale. There is a balance between the dewdrop on the rose and the most majestic of yonder orbs that adorn the brow of night. Law regulates everything, from a single drop of water to the ocean itself. Everything is proportionate, and therefore we are persuaded that in an economy in which we start with an incarnate God and an infinite atonement, there must be something very striking; and we ought to be prepared frequently to exclaim, *"We have never seen anything like this."* Commonplaces are foreign to the gospel; we have entered the land of wonders when we behold the love of God in Christ Jesus. Romance is out-romanced in the gospel. Whatever marvels men are able to imagine, the *facts* of God's amazing grace are more extraordinary than anything imagination has ever conceived.

> The facts of God's amazing grace are more extraordinary than anything imagination has ever conceived.

I desire at this time to say two or three things to those who are not familiar with the gospel. Some have dropped in here to whom the gospel, as we believe it, is quite a new thing. I want to say to them, first, *do not disbelieve it because it strikes you as being something very strange.* In the second place, remember that *in the gospel there must be amazing and surprising things;* and we shall try to set them out before you, hoping that so far from your disbelieving them, faith may be worked in your soul as you hear them. And thirdly, *if any of these strange things should have happened to you, and you should have to say, "We have never seen anything like this,"* then glorify God and give new honors to his name.

First, then, do not disbelieve the gospel because it surprises you. Remember, in the first place, that *nothing stands so much in the way of real knowledge as prejudice.* Our race might have known a great deal more of scientific fact if it had not been so largely occupied and captivated with scientific supposition. Take up books upon most sciences, and you will find that the main part of the material is an answer to diverse theories that have been set up in ages gone by, or originated in modern times. Theories are the nuisances of science, the rubbish which must be swept away so that the precious facts may be laid bare. If you go to the study of a subject, saying to yourself, "This is how the matter must shape itself," having beforehand made up your mind what the facts ought to be, you will have put in your own way a difficulty more severe than the subject itself could place there. Prejudice is the stumbling block of advance. To believe that we know before we do know is to prevent our really making discoveries and coming to right knowledge. When an observer first discovered that there were spots on the sun, he reported it, but he was called before his father confessor and scolded for having reported anything of the kind. The Jesuit father said that he had read Aristotle through several times, and he had found no mention in Aristotle of any spots on the sun, and therefore there could be no such things. When the offender replied that he had seen these spots through glasses, the father told him that he must not believe his eyes: he must believe *him,* because it was certain, to begin with, that if Aristotle had not indicated the spots, spots there could not be, and he must not believe it. Now, there are some who come to hear the gospel in that spirit. They have a notion of what the gospel ought to be – a pretty firm and strong cast-iron creed of their own manufacturing, or a hereditary one which they have received with the old family chest of drawers; and they are therefore unprepared candidly to hear and learn, and neither do they turn to Scripture to discover the mind of the Spirit of God, but to find some color for their prejudices. It is easy to show a man a thing if he will open his eyes, but if he shuts his eyes, and resolves not to see, the task is difficult. You may light a candle pretty readily, but you cannot do so if it has an extinguisher over it; and there are persons who have extinguished their souls and covered them over with prejudices. They act as judges of what the gospel ought to be; and so, if there is anything said that does not suit their preconceived notions, right away they are offended. This is very absurd, and in a matter in which our souls are concerned it is something worse than ridiculous: it is dangerous to the highest degree. We ought to come to the preaching of the Word praying, "Lord, teach me. Blessed Spirit, guide me into all truth. Let me see a doctrine to be in your Word and I will accept it, though it should shock all my prejudices. Though it should seem to me to be a totally new thing, yet, if clearly it be the word of God, I am willing to receive it and to rejoice in it." God give us such a spirit, so that when we have to say in the words of the text, *"We have never seen anything like this,"* our prejudices may not prevent our accepting the truth.

Let us remember, dear friends, that *many things which we know to be true would not have been believed by our fathers if they had been revealed to them.* I feel morally certain that there were many generations of Englishmen who, if they could have been informed that men would travel at forty or fifty miles an hour over the surface of the earth, drawn without horses by a steam engine, would have shaken their heads and laughed such a prediction to scorn. Even a little time ago, if someone had prophesied that we would be able to speak across the Atlantic in a single instant, and speedily obtain a reply by a cable that could be laid along the ocean's bottom, we ourselves could not have conceived it to be possible. How could it be? And yet these things are common, everyday facts with us now. Do let us, therefore, expect that when we come to deal with what is more wonderful than creation, and far more wonderful than any of the inventions of man, we should meet with things which will be hard to be believed. Let us willingly give up our heart and soul to receive the imprint of the truth, and constantly exercise a simple faith in what God reveals.

It is well known that *there are many things which are undoubted facts which certain classes of men find it hard to believe.* Some time ago a missionary had told his black congregation that in the wintertime the water in England became so hard that a man could walk upon it. Now, they believed a good deal that he had said, but they did not believe that, and they whispered to one another that the missionary was a great liar. One of them was brought over to England. He came over with the full conviction that it was a most ridiculous thing to suppose that any man could ever walk across a river. At last the frost came, the river was frozen over, and the missionary took his black friend down to it. The good man stood on the ice himself, but he could not persuade his convert to venture. "No," he said, "I cannot believe it."

"But you can *see* it, man!" said the missionary. "Come along with you! Come here!"

"No," he said, "for I never saw it so. I have lived fifty years in my own country, and I never saw a man walk on a river before."

"But here I am doing it," said the missionary. "Come along with you!" and he seized his hand and pulled so vigorously that at last the African tried the frozen water and found that it did support his weight. Thus a statement proved to be nonetheless true because it was contrary to experience; the same rule holds good in the case of the gospel. Yet you must expect to find in it certain things which you could not have believed to be true; but if some of us have proved them to be facts, and are living in the daily enjoyment of them, do not stubbornly refuse to try them yourself. If we get you by the hand affectionately and say, "Come on to this river of life; it will bear you; you can walk in safety here; we are doing so, and have done so for years," do not act towards us as if we were deceivers, and do not put us off with the absurd argument that the gospel cannot be true because you have not yet tried it, and therefore have no experience of its power. Why, my dear friend, it may be true for all that, just as the ice was a matter of fact, though the friend from Africa had never seen it. He did find the ice a reality when he ventured upon it, and you will find Jesus Christ and the precious things of the gospel to be sure and firm and true, as we have found them to be, if you will only venture your soul upon them.

I merely mention these things to prepare your mind for the full conviction that *the fact that a gospel statement seems new and astonishing ought not to create unbelief in the mind.* My beloved friend, it may be that you exclaim, "I cannot hope that my sin can be forgiven. I cannot imagine that my heart can be changed. I cannot suppose it be possible that by one simple act of faith, I could be a saved man." No; but do you not see that every man measures things according to his own standard? We measure other people's corn, but we always do it with our own bushel. We even try to measure God by our own standard, and there is a text which very sweetly rebukes us for it: *"For My thoughts are not your thoughts, nor are your ways My ways," declares the Lord.* What I consider it right to expect from God may, very naturally, be a very different thing from what God may be prepared to give me. Perhaps I judge his behavior towards me by what I deserve, and if I do so, what can I look for? Or perhaps I judge his mercy by my own, and considering whether I could forgive to seventy times seven – whether, if often provoked, I could still overlook the transgression; I find in my own heart no very great powers of forgiveness, and then I conclude that God is as hard and as unwilling to forgive as I am. But we must not so judge. Oh sinners, *you* must not do so! If you are longing for a great salvation you must not sit down and begin to calculate the Godhead by inches, and measure out the merit of Christ by ells (an English unit of length), and calculate whether he can do this or can do that. A God – what is there that he cannot do? Did Jesus make an atonement as boundless as his nature? Then what sin is there which that atonement cannot wash away? Judge not the Lord according to human judgment. Know you, O man, that he is no streamlet, or lakelet, which you can measure, and whose capacity you can calculate; he is a sea without a bottom and without a shore, and all your thoughts are drowned when you do attempt to measure him. Lift up your thoughts as high as ever you will, and think great things of God, and expect great things from God; and when you shall have enlarged your expectation, and your faith shall have grown to its very utmost, God is able to do far more abundantly above what you ask or even think. *"Can you discover the depths of God?"* Do you expect that you can exceed him, and desire more and hope for more than he is able to give? Oh, it cannot be. Consider this – that you are very liable to make a mistake as to what the gospel is, because your mode of estimating it must naturally be a false one, since you judge only from what you know

> **Judge not the Lord according to human judgment.**

and what you are capable of, while God is infinitely above all that you know or can conceive.

Further, let me remind you, dear friend, you who are a stranger to the gospel, that when we come to speak of it directly, *you must not disbelieve it on account of its strangeness, for it is clear that many have made a mistake as to what the gospel is.* The Jews who lived in our Savior's day heard the best preacher that ever preached, but they did not understand him. It was not from lack of an intelligible style, for *"never has a man spoken the way this man speaks";* but yet they mistook all that he said. They thought that they knew his meaning, but they did not. And even his own disciples and the apostles, until they were illuminated by the Spirit of God, mistook the meaning of their Master and knew but little, after all his teaching.

Should you feel at all astonished if you should have been mistaken, dear friend – you who have never found joy and peace in believing? Is it not possible that you may have been mistaken after all? The Jews heard the Savior himself and yet did not understand the truth. Some of them were men of genius, and well instructed. There was one especially who was a ruler – a doctor among the Jews – who did not understand these things; and when the Savior said to him, *"You must be born again,"* he took it literally; he could not understand the mystic change which the Savior meant to describe. Now, if Nicodemus did not know, and a great many like Nicodemus, may it not happen to be the case that you also have not found out the secret, and are at this moment without the possession of it? Possibly you may be a person of very considerable education, and of remarkable gifts and talents. My dear friend, if any people are liable to miss the true sense of the gospel, it is such as you are. It is strange, you will say, that I should make such a remark, but the observation is founded upon fact. *Consider your calling, brethren, that there were not many wise according to the flesh, not many mighty, not many noble.* Not many of the learned of this world ever learn of Christ. He teaches babes, but leaves wise men to boast in their own folly. The magi of the east went round about to find the Savior, and even with a star to guide them they missed their way; but the humble shepherds from the plains of Bethlehem, without a star, went immediately to the place where Jesus was. Ah, it was a good and true remark of Augustine, when he said, "While the learned are fumbling to find the latch, the simple and poor have entered into the kingdom of heaven." Simplicity of heart is more helpful to the understanding of the gospel than culture of mind. To be ready to be taught is a better function than to be able to teach, as far as the reception of the gospel is concerned. That degree in divinity may stand in your way of understanding divinity; and the very position that you have taken in the classical tripos may render it the more difficult for you to comprehend that which the wayfaring man, though he be a fool, knows by heart. Since it is certainly so, I am not offering you any insult when I say perhaps, dear friend, you may up to this time have labored under a mistake; and, therefore, if at any time the gospel should be spoken to you, it would well become you to give it a fair hearing, and not to reject it because it appears to be new.

One other remark, and I will go on to the next point, and it is this. The person I am now addressing, and I believe that there are such persons here, if he be the man I mean, must confess that *the religion he now possesses has not done much for him.* You think you know the gospel, but, say, could you die upon what you know? Could you die *now* – *now* – happily and contentedly with the hope you have? If you could, I thank God and congratulate you. Has your hope which you possess comforted your heart? Do you feel and know assuredly that your sins are forgiven you? Do you look upon God as your Father? Are you in the habit of speaking with him as a child speaks with his father, confiding in him, and telling all your cares and troubles to him? If it be so, my dear friend, I rejoice with you; but unless yours be the religion of Jesus Christ, I know you have not found such peace. There are many shapes of what is called "religion" – many, many shapes, but they amount to this: they put a man in a position in which he feels that he is about as good as other people, and as well to do in spiritual things as the average of others; and if he does his best, and acts up to his knowledge and light, he will get better, no doubt; and perhaps, when he comes to die, possibly by the assistance of a clergyman or a priest, or perhaps by some remarkable experience that he may undergo in the use of sacraments – he may get into heaven. It is the general religion of mankind that they are on a road which they have to follow, and by industriously and carefully pursuing it they will possibly save themselves by the gracious help of the Lord Jesus Christ; they generally tack that on, of course, to make their self-righteousness look a little more respectable. Now, I say deliberately, as in the sight of God, that such religion is not worth one solitary halfpenny. The religion of the Lord Jesus Christ gives a man a complete, full, free, and irreversible pardon of all his sins at once, together with the changing of his nature, the implantation of a new life, and the putting of him into the family of God; and it gives to him these things so that he knows that he has them, and consciously enjoys them, and lives in the power and spirit of them, humbly serving the Lord who has done such great things for him. This is the religion of Christ, and this is what we are now going to speak of more fully, while we mention some few things which lead men to say, "*We have never seen anything like this.*"

Our second point was to be that there are very singular and surprising things in the gospel. Let us mention some of them.

One is this – *that the gospel should come to people whom it regards as incapable.* In the narrative before us the wonder was that the Lord Jesus dealt with a crippled and paralyzed person so far gone that he could not crawl into Christ's presence, but had to be carried by four men. See him! He is incapable and incurable. All that he can do is lie on that bed on which the kindness of friends has placed him, and there he must remain; he can do nothing. Now, the gospel regards every man to whom it comes as unable to do anything good. It addresses you not merely as paralyzed, but it goes farther, and describes you also as dead. The gospel speaks to the dead. I have often heard it said that the duty of the Christian minister is to arouse the activities of sinners. I believe the very reverse: he should rather labor to strike their self-trusting activities dead, and to make them know that all that they can do of themselves is worse than nothing. They can do nothing, for how can the dead move in their graves? How can the dead in sin accomplish their own revival? The power which can save does not lie in the sinner, it lies in his God. And if any of you be unconverted, I do not come to tell you something which you are able to do, by the doing of which you can save yourselves, but I warn you that you are lost, ruined, and undone; you have power to stray like lost sheep, but if ever you come back, your shepherd must bring you back, for you will never come back of yourselves. You had power to destroy yourselves, and you have exercised that power; but now your help does not lie in you, it lies in your God. It is a strange thing that the gospel should represent a man to be in such a desperate condition, but it is a fact; and though it be astonishing, let it not be doubted.

An equally remarkable thing is that the gospel *calls upon men to do what they cannot do,* for Jesus Christ said to this paralyzed man, *"I say to you, get up, pick up your pallet and go home."* He could not rise, could not pick up his pallet, and could not walk, and yet he was bidden to do it. And it is one of the strange things of the way of salvation that

> The gospel bids the dead revive;
>   Sinners obey the voice and live.
> Dry bones are raised and clothed afresh,
>   And hearts of stone are turned to flesh.

We have to say, in the name of Jesus, to the man with the withered arm – whose arm is so withered that we know he has no power in it, *"Stretch out your hand";* and we do say it in God's name. Some of my brethren of a certain order of doctrine say, "It is ridiculous! If you admit that a man cannot do it, it is ridiculous to tell him to do it." But we do not mind being ridiculous; we care little for the rebuke of human judgment. If God gives us a commission, that commission will prevent our suffering very seriously from the ridicule of other people. "Ezekiel, do you not see before you that valley of dry bones?"

"Yes," says he, "I see them; they are very many and very dry. Lo! through many a summer the sun has scorched them, and through many a winter the fierce winds have dried them till they are as if they had passed through an oven."

"Prophet, what can *you* do with these bones? If God means to raise them to life they will be raised; therefore, let them alone. What can *you* do?"

Listen to him as he makes a solemn proclamation. "Thus says the Lord, You dry bones live!"

"Ridiculous, Ezekiel! They cannot live, so why speak to them?" He knows they cannot live of themselves, but he also knows that his Master bids him to tell them to live, and he does what his Master bids him. So, in the gospel, the minister is to command men to believe, and he is to say, "Repent, and believe the gospel." For this reason alone do we say, *"Believe in the Lord Jesus, and you will be saved."* The gospel bids you to believe, albeit that you are dead in trespasses and sins. "I cannot understand it," says somebody. No, and you never will till God reveals it to you. But when the Lord comes and dwells with you, you will perfectly understand, and see how the exercise of faith on the part of the preacher of the gospel is a part of the divine operation by which dead souls are raised.

Another and more remarkable thing is this – that while the gospel comes to men who are incapable and dead, and bids them to do what they cannot of themselves do, *they actually do it;* there is the marvel. In the name of Jesus we say to the paralyzed man, *"Pick up your pallet and go home,"* and he does pick up his pallet and goes home; for with the word faithfully spoken, in confidence in God, there comes the eternal power into the man who had no power of his own; and God's elect, called out by the preaching of the gospel, hear the message from heaven, and the power comes with it at the time they hear the message, so that they obey it and live. Dead as they were, they live. Oh, marvelous operation this – that out of this congregation, while I say, "Believe on the Lord Jesus Christ," there will be some who will believe and be saved. Those who will believe have no more power, naturally, to believe, than others have; they are by nature all in an equal state of death. But to God's own chosen, the Word comes with power, attended by the Holy Spirit, and they do believe and live.

Here are three singular things. It is a strange thing to have to tell you good church people and chapel people, who have always done everything so well, that unless you are converted you are dead in trespasses and sins, and all your good works are so many graveclothes in which your corpse is wrapped up, and nothing better. And it is strange that we should be bound to call upon you to believe in Jesus when we have already told you that you have no spiritual life. And it is remarkable that we should be commanded to warn you that you are living in great sin if you do not believe in Jesus. More singular still, you may judge it to be, that we are confident that the telling you these things, plainly and honestly in the name of God, will be blessed by the Spirit of God, and will lead you to believe and to trust in Jesus. It seems strange, but so it is.

More remarkable still to the crowd, no doubt, was this – that *this paralyzed man was healed at once*. If ever a cure of paralysis is worked at any time – and it is very rarely that such a thing occurs – I do not think that it is ever cured in an instant. This man is unable to move hand or foot, but Jesus says, *"Pick up your pallet and go home,"* and he gets up as if he had never been paralyzed. Every ligature is in its place; every muscle is ready for action in a moment. You would have thought it would take a month or two, and a good deal of rubbing and friction to bring the man's blood into healthy action, to get him up and about, and to warm him into life again; but it did not. He only heard that strange voice which told him to do what he could not do, and he did do what he could not do by a power that went with that message, and he rose up and was healed at once. And here is the marvel of the gospel. A sinner hears the gospel, and all the sins of his whole life are upon him, but he believes that gospel and all his sins are gone in a moment, and he is as clean before the throne of God as if never a sin had defiled him. He was, up to the time of his reception of the gospel, an enemy to God by wicked works; but he accepts the testimony of God concerning his Son Jesus, and he rests in Jesus, and his heart becomes as the heart of a little child. In a moment the stone is taken away, and the fleshy heart is given; he becomes a new creature in Christ Jesus. The darkness disappears as the primeval darkness fled before the decree which said, *"Let there be light."* It is done – done in a moment.

You will not comprehend this, I am sure, till you experience it. Oh, how I bless God that years ago when I heard the message of God – *Look unto me and be ye saved all ye ends of the earth* (KJV), I was enabled to look and live. I yearned and longed for salvation, and labored hard and prayed hard to get it, but I never got one inch the farther. But the message came – "Look!" How could I look? My eyes were sightless. But I did look, for the power to look came with the command to look, and the moment I looked I was as conscious that I was forgiven as I am conscious of my existence. There was life to me in a look at the Crucified One. Pardon – sure, certain, and sealed home to my conscience – was given to me in the selfsame moment when I looked to Jesus in the bloody sweat, Jesus on the cross, Jesus risen from the dead, and Jesus gone into glory. A look at him, and it was all done. You had not thought of that, you say, and even now it startles you. You thought you would have to take the sacrament, and keep on attending a place of worship, and gradually work yourself up out of your paralyzed condition. That is man's way of salvation; but Christ's way of salvation is an instantaneous change of heart, and an instantaneous forgiveness of sin.

Another thing which they had never seen like this was that *the man was healed without any ceremony.* The proper way to heal a paralyzed person would have been to fetch the priest down, and to bring water and oil, or to shed the blood of a young bull, and offer it, and then to go through no end of ceremonies, and by degrees, through the mysterious power of ceremonies, at last the man might be cleansed. But here was no one single ceremony. It was just this: *"Pick up your pallet and go home."* The man, though he cannot take up his pallet and walk, yet believes that he who told him to do it will give him power to do it, and he does take up his pallet and walks home: there is the whole of it in a nutshell. He believes and acts on that belief; and he is restored. And that is the whole plan of salvation. You believe the gospel and act upon the truth of it, and you are saved – saved the moment you accept the witness of God concerning his Son Jesus Christ. But is there not baptism? Yes, for the saved: but no baptism in order to be saved. When you *are* saved – when you are a believer in Jesus – then the instructive ordinances of God's house become useful to you; but God forbid that we should ever look to baptism as a means of salvation. God forbid that we should even look to the Lord's Supper for that purpose. May we be preserved from anything approximating trust in rites and forms. When you are saved, then the ordinances of the house into which you have come – the ordinances of the family of which you are a member – belong to you; but they do not belong to you, and can render to you no service whatever, until you are a saved man. Salvation from death in sin has nothing to do with ceremonies. "Believe and live" is the sole gospel precept.

> That is the whole plan of salvation. You believe the gospel and act upon the truth of it, and you are saved.

Another remarkable thing was that *this man was perfectly restored* – not merely restored in a moment, but perfectly so. A partial restoration would not have been one-tenth so memorable. I have known dear friends partially paralyzed who, after some time, in the good providence of God, have somewhat recovered; but a twist of the mouth, a weakness in the eye, or a feebleness of the hand has remained as a proof that the paralysis had been there. But this man was perfectly whole, and was so at once. The glory of salvation is that whosoever believes in the Lord Jesus is completely pardoned. It is not some of his sin that is put away, but all of it. I rejoice to look upon it as dear Kent does when he sings,

> Here's pardon for transgressions past,
>   It matters not how black their cast;
> And, O my soul, with wonder view,
>   For sins to come here's pardon too.

We are plunged into the fountain of redeeming blood and cleansed from every fear of ever being found guilty before the living God. We are accepted in the beloved through the righteousness of Jesus Christ, justified once for all and forever before the Father's face! Christ said, *"It is finished!"* and finished it is. And oh, what a bliss is this – one of the things that may well stagger those who have never heard it before; but let them not reject it because it staggers them, but rather let them say, "This wonderful system which saves and saves completely, in an instant, simply by looking out of self to Christ, is a system worthy of divine wisdom, for it magnifies the grace of God, and meets man's deep necessities."

One other thing, no doubt, astonished them about this man – *that his cure was done evidently.* There was no deception about it, for he rolled up the pallet that he had lain upon, put it upon his back, and walked away with it and went home to his house. There was no doubt about his being perfectly restored, for he was carrying a burden on his back. And here is the glory of it – that when a man believes in Jesus Christ there is no doubt about his conversion: you see it in his actions. They tell me that a child is born again in baptism. Very well, let me have a look at the child; is there any difference in him? Some of you, perhaps, have had children that were born again in the sacramental fashion. Mine were not, so I cannot, therefore, speak from experience. I wonder whether yours have turned out any better than mine – whether, indeed, the watery regeneration made any difference in them. I am persuaded that you could not pretend to having seen any result. It is a kind of regeneration that does not show itself in the life, and indeed, it produces no result; for these precious regenerate babies, and regenerate boys and girls, are just the same as the unregenerate boys and girls: there is not a pin to choose between them. Send them to the same school, and I will undertake very often to show you that some of those that never were baptismally regenerated are better than those who were; for probably they have had Christian parents who had taken more pains to instruct them than those superstitious parents who merely relied upon the outward ceremony. Now, that regeneration which produces no effect is nothing – less than nothing. It would be like saying, "That man is saved from the paralysis." "Well, but he lies on the bed." "Yes, he lies on the bed the same as he did before; but," you say, "he is – he is delivered from the paralysis." "But how do you know?" "Well, of course, it may not be an actual cure, but it is a virtual cure, because he has undergone a ceremony, and therefore it must be so; you are to believe it." This is fine talk; but when the man got up and picked up his pallet, and carried it on his back, that was a deal more convincing.

Now, when God's providence brings into this house a man who has been a drunkard, and he hears the gospel of Jesus Christ, and believes in Jesus, and turns his cups bottom upwards and becomes a sober man, there is something in that. If a man comes here who is proud, haughty, a hater of the gospel altogether, a man who can swear, and who has no regard for the Sabbath day, and he believes in Jesus, and becomes at home as gentle as a lamb so that his wife hardly knows that he is the same man, and on the Sabbath he delights to go to the house of God, there is something to be seen in that, is there not? There is something real and tangible. Here is a man that would cheat you, as soon as look at you, in his business, but the grace of God comes to him, and he becomes scrupulously honest. Here is a man that used to associate with the lowest of the low, and the gospel of Jesus Christ is received by him, and he seeks godly companions, and he loves only those whose talk is sweet and clean and holy. Why, you can *see* it; you can *see* it. And this is the kind of salvation we want in these days, a salvation that can be seen – which makes the paralyzed sinner pick up his pallet and carry it away, makes him a conqueror over depraved habits, delivers him from the enslavement of his sins, and shows itself in the outer life to all who care to look upon him. Yes, brethren, this is what the gospel has done for us; and if I address any here today who have looked upon religion as a kind of salve that they were to use while they continued in their sins, I want them to see what a very different thing it is. Christ has come to save you *from* your sins: not to keep you in the fire and prevent your burning, but to pluck you like a brand out of the burning. He has come to make you new creatures, and this he can do at this very moment, while you are sitting in your pews. If, while you hear the sound, "Believe in the Lord Jesus Christ," there be found in you a willing mind, given you of his grace, so that you do trust him, you shall be saved as surely as Christ lives.

These are strange things, but do not reject them because they are strange. They are things worthy of God.

So, lastly, if you have ever found out any of these things, and had to say, "*We have never seen anything like this,*" then go and glorify God. Magnify him from your inmost soul.

If salvation were by works, and we could fight our own way to heaven by our own merits, I for one, when I got up there, would throw up my cap and say, "Well done! I have deserved something, and I have gotten it." But since salvation is by grace from first to last, and not of man, neither by man, nor of the will of the flesh, nor by blood or birth – since the Lord begins and carries on and ends – let us give him all the glory. And if ever he gives us, as he will give us, a crown of life that fades not away, we will go and cast it at his feet and say, "*Not to us, O Lord, not to us, but to Your name give glory* forever and ever." Let us live in this spirit, dear friends. The man who believes in the doctrines of grace, and yet thinks much of himself, is highly inconsistent. A man who believes salvation to be all of grace, and yet does not glorify God continually, acts contrary to his own convictions. *O magnify the Lord with me, and let us exalt His name together.* He took us up out of the horrible pit, and out of the miry clay; and he set our feet upon a rock

> The man who believes in the doctrines of grace, and yet thinks much of himself, is highly inconsistent.

and established our goings. He put a new song into our mouths, even praise forevermore. Praise be unto him, for he has done it, and he shall be extolled.

Oh, you cannot praise him, you who do not know this salvation, and I do not exhort you to attempt to do so; but, first of all, may you know this salvation for yourselves. You *can* know it. Blessed be God, I trust that some of you will know it this very night by ceasing from yourselves, giving up all dependence upon anything you can do or be or feel, and by dropping into the arms of Jesus, resting in his finished work, and confiding in him. He will – he *must* save you if you trust him, and then you shall give him praise. God bless you, dear friends, for Christ's sake.

Chapter 6

Carried by Four

But Jesus Himself would often slip away to the wilderness and pray. One day He was teaching; and there were some Pharisees and teachers of the law sitting there, who had come from every village of Galilee and Judea and from Jerusalem; and the power of the Lord was present for Him to perform healing. And some men were carrying on a bed a man who was paralyzed; and they were trying to bring him in and to set him down in front of Him. But not finding any way to bring him in because of the crowd, they went up on the roof and let him down through the tiles with his stretcher, into the middle of the crowd, in front of Jesus. Seeing their faith, He said, "Friend, your sins are forgiven you." The scribes and the Pharisees began to reason, saying, "Who is this man who speaks blasphemies? Who can forgive sins, but God alone?" But Jesus, aware of their reasonings, answered and said to them, "Why are you reasoning in your hearts? Which is easier, to say, 'Your sins have been forgiven you,' or to say, 'Get up and walk?' But, so that you may know that the Son of Man has authority on earth to forgive sins,"—He said to the paralytic—"I say to you, get up, and pick up your stretcher and go home." Immediately he got up before them, and picked up what he had been lying on, and went home glorifying God. They were all struck with astonishment and began glorifying God; and they were filled with fear, saying, "We have seen remarkable things today."
(Luke 5:16-26)

You have this same narrative in the ninth chapter of Matthew, and in the second chapter of Mark. What is three times recorded by inspired pens must be regarded as three times as important, and well worthy of our earnest consideration. Observe the instructive fact that our Savior withdrew and spent a special time in prayer when he saw unusual crowds assembling. He withdrew into the wilderness to hold communion with his Father, and, as a consequence, to come forth clothed with an abundance of healing and saving power. Not but that in himself as God he always had that power without measure, but for our sakes he did it, that we might learn that the power of God will only rest upon us in proportion as we draw near to God. Neglect of private prayer is the locust which devours the strength of the church.

When our Lord left his retreat he found the crowd around him exceedingly great, and it was as motley as it was great; for while here were many sincere believers, there were still more skeptical observers. Some were anxious to receive his healing power, others equally desirous to find occasion against him. So in all congregations, however the preacher may be clothed with his Master's spirit and his Master's might, there will be a mixed gathering. There will come together your Pharisees and doctors of the law, your sharp critics ready to pick holes, your cold-blooded nitpickers searching for faults; and at the same time, chosen of God and drawn by his grace, there will be present some devout believers who rejoice in the power that is revealed among men, and earnest seekers who wish to feel in themselves the healing energy. It seems to have been a rule with our Savior to supply each hearer with food after his kind. The Pharisees soon found the matters to fuss over for which they were looking. The Savior so worded his expressions that they took hold of them eagerly and charged him with blasphemy; the enmity of their hearts was thus thrown out upon the surface that the Lord might have an opportunity of rebuking it; and had they been but willing, the power of the Lord was present to heal even them. Meanwhile, those poor trembling ones who were praying for healing were not disappointed; the Great Physician passed not by a single case, and at the same time his disciples who were looking for opportunities of praising him anew were also fully gratified, for with glad eyes they saw the paralytic restored, and heard sins forgiven.

The case which the narrative brings before us is that of a man stricken down with paralysis. This sad disease may have been of long continuance. There is a paralysis which gradually kills the body, binding it more and more surely in utter helplessness. The nerve power is almost destroyed; the power of motion is entirely suspended; and yet the faculties of the mind remain, though greatly weakened, and some of them almost extinguished. Some have thought that this man may have been stricken with what is called the universal paralysis, which very speedily brings on death, which may account for the extreme haste of the four bearers to bring him near the Savior. We do not know the details of his case, but certain is it that he was paralyzed; and, as I look at the case and study the three records, I think I perceive with equal clearness that this paralysis was in some way or other, at least in the man's own judgment, connected with his sin. He was evidently repentant, as well as paralyzed. His mind was as much oppressed as his bodily frame. I do not know that he could be altogether called a believer, but it is most probable that being burdened with a sense of sin he had a feeble hope in divine mercy, which, like a spark in smoking flax, had hard work to exist, but yet was truly there. The affliction for which his friends pitied him was in his body, but he himself felt a far severer trouble in his soul, and probably it was not so much with the view of being healed bodily, as in the hope of spiritual blessing, that he was willing to be subjected to any process by which he might come under the Savior's eye. I gather that from the fact that our Savior addressed him in these words: *"Take courage, son,"* implying that he was desponding, that his spirit sunk within him, and, therefore, instead of saying to him at once, *"Get up, and pick up your stretcher,"* our tenderhearted Lord said, *"Son; your sins are forgiven."* He gave him at the outset a blessing for which the patient's friends had not asked, but which the man, though speechless, was seeking for in the silence of his soul. He was a "son," though an afflicted one; he was ready to obey the Lord's bidding when power was given, though as yet he could lift neither hand nor foot. He was longing for the pardon of sin, yet could not stretch out his hand to lay hold upon the Savior.

I intend to use this narrative for practical purposes; may the Holy Spirit make it really useful. Our first remark will be this:

There are cases which will need the aid of a little band of workers before they will be fully saved.

This man needs to be carried by four men, so the Gospel writer Mark tells us; there must be a bearer at each corner of the pallet whereon he lay. The great mass of persons who are brought into the kingdom of Christ are converted through the general prayers of the church by the means of her ministry. Probably three out of four of the members of any church will owe their conversion to the church's regular teaching in some form or other; her school, her pulpit, her crowd have been the nets in which they were taken. Private personal prayer has, of course, in many instances been mingled with all this, but still most cases could not be so distinctly traced out as to be attributable mainly to individual prayers or exertions. This is the rule, I think, that the Lord will have the many brought to himself by the sounding of the great trumpet of jubilee in the dispensation of the gospel by his ministers. There are some, again, who are led to Jesus by the individual efforts of one person; just as Andrew found his own brother Simon, so one believer by his private communication of the truth to another person becomes instrumental, by the power of God's Spirit, in his conversion. One convert will bring another, and that other a third. But this narrative seems to show that there are cases which will neither be brought by the general preaching of the Word, nor yet by the instrumentality of one; they require that there should be two, or three, or four in holy combination who, with one consent, feeling one common agony of soul, shall resolve to band themselves together as a company for this one object, and never to cease from their holy confederation until this object is gained and their friend is saved. This man could not be brought to Christ by one; he needed to have four to lend their strength for his carrying, or he could not reach the place of healing.

Let us apply the principle. Yonder is a householder as yet unsaved. His wife has prayed for him long, but her prayers are yet unanswered. Good wife, God has blessed you with a son who with you rejoices in the fear of God. Have you not two Christian daughters also? O you four, take each a corner of this sick man's stretcher and bring your husband, bring your father, to the Savior. A husband and a wife are here, both happily brought to Christ; you are praying for your children; never cease from that supplication, but pray on. Perhaps one of your beloved family is unusually stubborn. Extra help is needed. Well, to you the Sunday school teacher will make a third; he will take one corner of the stretcher; and happy shall I be if I may join the blessed set of four by being the fourth. Perhaps when home discipline, the school's teaching, and the minister's preaching shall go together, the Lord will look down in love and save your child. Dear brother, you are thinking of one whom you have long prayed for; you have spoken to him also, and used all proper means, but as yet without effect. Perhaps you speak too comfortingly to him: it may be you have not brought that precise truth to bear upon him which his conscience requires. Seek yet more help. It may possibly be that a second brother will speak instructively, where you have only spoken consolingly; perhaps the instruction may be the means of grace. Yet may it possibly happen that even instruction will not suffice any more than consolation, and it may be needful for you to call in a third, who perhaps will speak impressively with exhortation, and with warning, which may possibly be the great requisite. You two, already in the field, may balance his exhortation, which might have been too pungent by itself, and might have raised prejudice in the person's mind if it had come alone. All three of you together may prove the suitable instruments in the Lord's hand. Yet when you three have happily combined, it may be that the poor paralyzed one is not yet affected savingly; a fourth may be needed, who, with deeper affection than all three of you, and perhaps with an experience more suited to the case than yours, may come in, and working with you, the result may be secured. The four fellow helpers together may accomplish, by the power of the Spirit, what neither one, nor two, nor three were competent to have done.

It may sometimes happen that a man has heard Paul preach, but his clear doctrine, though it has enlightened his intellect, has not yet convinced his conscience. He has heard Apollos, and the glow of the orator's eloquent appeals has warmed his heart but not humbled his pride. He has later still listened to Cephas, whose rough-cutting sentences have cut him down and convinced him of sin; but before he can find joy and peace in believing, he will need to hear the sweet, affectionate words of

John. Only when the fourth shall grasp the stretcher and give a hearty lift will the paralyzed person be laid in mercy's path.

I anxiously desire to see in this church little bands of men and women bound to each other by zealous love for souls. I would have you say to one another, "This is a case in which we feel a common interest: we will pledge each other to pray for this person; we will unitedly seek his salvation." It may be that one of our seatholders, after listening to my voice these ten or fifteen years, is not impressed; it may be that another has left the Sunday school unsaved. Let brotherly sets of four look after these by God's help. Moved by one impulse, form a square around these persons, surround them behind and before, and let them not say, "No man cares for my soul." Meet together in prayer with the definite object before you, and then seek that object by the most likely ways. I do not know, my brethren, how much blessing might come to us through this, but I feel certain that until we have tried it we cannot pronounce a verdict upon it; nor can we be quite sure that we are free from all responsibility for men's souls until we have tested every possible and probable method for doing them good.

I am afraid that there are not many, even in a large church, who will become sick-bearers. Many will say the plan is admirable, but they will leave it to others to carry it out. Remember that the four persons who join in such a labor of love ought all of them to be filled with intense affection for the persons whose salvation they seek. They must be men who will not shrink because of difficulty, who will put forth their whole strength to shoulder the beloved burden, and will persevere until they succeed. They need to be strong, for the burden is heavy; they need to be resolute, for the work will test their faith; they need to be prayerful, for otherwise they labor in vain; they must be believing, or they will be utterly useless – Jesus saw their faith, and therefore accepted their service; but without faith it is impossible to please him. Where shall we find "quartets" such as these? May the Lord find them, and may he send them to some of you poor dying sinners who lie paralyzed here today.

We now pass on to the second observation, that some cases thus taken up will need much thought before the design is accomplished.

The essential means by which a soul is saved is clear enough. The four bearers had no question with each other as to what was the way to effect this man's cure; they were unanimous in this – that they must bring him to Jesus; by some means or other, by hook or by crook, they must place him in the Savior's way. That was undoubted fact. The question was how to do this. There is an old worldly proverb, that "where there's a will there's a way"; and that proverb, I believe, may be safely imported into spiritual things, almost without a caution or grain of salt. "Where there's a will there's a way," and if men are called of God's grace to a deep anxiety for any particular soul, there is a way by which that soul may be brought to Jesus; but that way may not suggest itself till after much consideration. In some cases the way to impress the heart may be an out-of-the-way way, an extraordinary way – a way which ordinarily should not be used and would not be successful. I dare say the four bearers in the narrative thought early in the morning, "We will carry this poor paralytic to the Savior, passing into the house by the ordinary door"; but when they attempted to do so, the multitudes so blocked up the road that they could not even reach the threshold. "Make way; make way for the sick! Stand aside there, and give room for a poor paralyzed man. For mercy's sake, give a little space, and let the sick man reach the healing prophet!" In vain were their pleas and commands. Here and there a few compassionate persons back out of the crowd, but many neither can nor will move; besides, many of them are engaged upon a similar business, and have equal reasons for pressing in.

> If men are called of God's grace to a deep anxiety for any particular soul, there is a way by which that soul may be brought to Jesus.

"See," cries one of the four, "I will make way," and he pushes and elbows himself a little distance into the passage. "Come on, you three!" he cries. "Follow up, and fight for it, inch by inch." But they cannot do it, it is impossible. The poor patient is ready to die for fear; the stretcher is tossed about by the throng like a light, flimsy boat on the sea waves, the patient's alarm increases, the bearers are distressed, and they are quite glad to get outside again and consider. It is evidently quite impossible by ordinary means to get him in. What then? "*We* cannot burrow under the ground; can we not go over the heads of the people, and let the man down from above? Where is the staircase?" Frequently there is an external staircase to the top of an eastern house; we cannot be sure that there was one in this case; but if not, the next-door house may have had such a convenience, and so the resolute bearers reached the top and passed from one roof to another. Where we have no definite information, much may be left to conjecture; but this much is clear: by some means they elevated their unhappy burden to the housetop, and provided themselves with the necessary tackle with which to let him down.

The Savior was probably preaching in one of the upper rooms, unless the house was a poor one without an upper story. Perhaps the room was open to the courtyard, which was crowded. At any rate, the Lord Jesus was under the cover of a roof, and a substantial roof too. No one who carefully reads the original will fail to see that there was real roofing to be broken through. It has been suggested as a difficulty, that the breaking up of a roof might involve danger to those below, and would probably make a great smother of dust; and to avoid this, there have been various suppositions – such as that the Savior was standing under an awning, and the men rolled up the canvas; or that our Lord stood under a veranda with a very light covering, which the men could readily uncover; or others have even invented a trapdoor for the occasion. But with all due deference to eminent travelers, the words of the Gospel writers cannot be so readily disposed of.

According to our text, the man was let down through *tiles,* not canvas, or any light material; whatever sort of tile it was, it was certainly made of burnt clay, for that enters into the essence of the word. Moreover, according to Mark, after they had uncovered the roof, which, I suppose, means the removal of the *tiles,* they *dug an opening,* which looks exceedingly like breaking through a ceiling. The Greek word used by Mark, which is interpreted "breaking up," is a very emphatic word, and signifies digging through, or scooping up, which evidently conveys the idea of considerable labor for the removal of material. We are told that the roofs of Oriental houses are often made of big stones; that may be true as a general rule, but not in this case, for the house was covered with tiles; and as to the dust and falling rubbish, that may or may not be a necessary conclusion. But as clear as noonday is it that a substantial housetop, which required untiling and digging through, had a hole made in it, and through the opening the man on his stretcher was let down. Perhaps there was dust, and possibly there was danger too, but the bearers were prepared to accomplish their purpose at all risks. They must get the sick man in somehow. There is no need, however, to suppose either, for no doubt the four men would be careful not to inconvenience the Savior or his hearers. The tiles or plaster might be removed to another part of the flat roof, and the boards likewise, as they were broken up; and as for the poles, they might be sufficiently wide to admit the narrow stretcher of the sick man without moving any of them from their places. Mr. Hartley, in his "Travels," says,

When I lived at Aegina I used to look up not infrequently at the roof above my head, and contemplate how easily the whole transaction of the paralytic might take place. The roof was made in the following manner: A layer of reeds, of a large species, was placed upon the rafters; on these a quantity of heather was strewed; on the heather earth was deposited, and beaten down into a solid mass. Now, what difficulty would there be in removing first the earth, next the heather, and then the reeds? Nor would the difficulty be increased, if the earth had a pavement of tiling laid upon it. No inconvenience could result to the persons in the house, from the removal of the tiles and earth; for the heather and reeds would stop anything that might otherwise fall down, and would be removed last of all.

To let a man down through the roof was a device most strange and striking, but it only gives point to the remark which we have now to make here. If we want to have souls saved, we must not be too squeamish and delicate about conventionalities, rules, and proprieties, for the kingdom of heaven suffers violence. We must make up our minds to this: "Smash or crash, everything shall go to pieces which stands between the soul and its God. It matters not what tiles are to be taken off, what plaster is to be dug up, or what boards are to be torn away, or what labor, or trouble, or expense we may be at; the soul is too precious for us to stand upon nice questions. If by any means we may save some, is our policy. Skin for skin, yes, all that we have is nothing comparable to a man's soul." When four true hearts are set upon the spiritual good of a sinner, their holy hunger will break through stone walls or house roofs.

I have no doubt it was a difficult task to carry the paralyzed man upstairs; the breaking up of the roof, the removing of the tiles with all due care, must have been a laborious task, and must have required much skill; but the work was done, and the end was gained. We must never stop at difficulties; however stern the task, it must always be more difficult to us to let a soul perish than to labor in the most self-denying form for its deliverance.

It was a very singular action which the bearers performed. Who would have thought of breaking up a roof? Nobody but those who loved much, and much desired to benefit the sick. O that God would make us attempt singular things to save souls. May a holy ingenuity be excited in the church, a sacred inventiveness set at work for winning men's hearts. It appeared to his generation a singular thing when John Wesley stood on his father's tombstone and preached at Epworth. Glory be to God that he had the courage to preach in the open air. It seemed an extraordinary thing when certain ministers delivered sermons in the theaters; but it is a matter of joy that sinners have been reached by such irregularities who might have escaped all other means. Let us but feel our hearts full of zeal for God, and love for souls, and we shall soon be led to adopt means which others may criticize, but which Jesus Christ will accept.

After all, the method which the four friends followed was one most suitable to their abilities. They were, I suppose, four strong fellows to whom the load was no great weight, and the work of digging was comparatively easy. The method suited their capacity exactly. And what did they do when they had let the sick man down? Look at the scene and admire? I do not read that they said a single word, yet what they did was enough: abilities for lifting and carrying did the needful work. Some of you say, "Ah, we cannot be of any use; we wish we could preach." These men could not preach; they did not need to preach. They lowered the paralytic, and their work was done. They could not preach, but they could hold a rope. We want in the Christian church not only preachers, but also soul winners, who can bear souls on their hearts, and feel the solemn burden; men who, it may be, cannot talk, but who can weep; men who cannot break other men's hearts with their language, but who break their own hearts with their compassion. In the case before us there was no need to plead, "Jesus, son of David, look up, for a man is coming down who needs you."

There was no need to declare that the patient had been sick for so many years. We do not know that the man himself uttered a word. Helpless and paralyzed, he had not the vigor to become a pleader. They placed his almost lifeless form before the Savior's eye, and that was appeal enough; his sad condition was more eloquent than words. O hearts that love sinners, lay their lost estate before Jesus; bring their cases as they are before the Savior. If your tongues stammer, your hearts will prevail; if you cannot speak even to Christ himself, as you would desire, because you have not the gift of prayer, yet if your strong desires spring from the spirit of prayer, you cannot fail. God help us to make use of such means as are within our power, and not to sit down idly to regret the powers we do not possess. Perhaps it would be dangerous for us to possess the abilities we covet; it is always safe to consecrate those we have.

Now we must move on to an important truth. We may safely gather from the narrative that the root of spiritual paralysis generally lies in unpardoned sin.

Jesus intended to heal the paralyzed man, but he did so by first of all saying, *"Your sins are forgiven you."* There are some today who are spiritually paralyzed; they have eyes and they see the gospel; they have ears and they have heard it, and heard it attentively too; but they are so paralyzed that they will tell you, and honestly tell you, that they cannot lay hold upon the promise of God; they cannot believe in Jesus to the saving of their souls. If you urge them to pray, they say, "We try to pray, but it is not acceptable prayer." If you bid them to have confidence, they will tell you, though not in so many words perhaps, that they are given up to despair. Their mournful ditty is:

> I would, but cannot sing;
>   I would, but cannot pray;
> For Satan meets me when I try,
>   And frights my soul away.

I would, but can't repeat,
>   Though I endeavor oft;
This stony heart can ne'er relent
>   Till Jesus makes it soft.

I would, but cannot love,
>   Though woo'd by love divine;
No arguments have power to move
>   A soul so base as mine.

O could I but believe!
>   Then all would easy be;
I would, but cannot – Lord, relieve:
>   My help must come from thee.

The bottom of this paralysis is sin upon the conscience, working death in them. They are sensible of their guilt, but powerless to believe that the crimson fountain can remove it; they are alive only to sorrow, despondency, and agony. Sin paralyzes them with despair. I grant you that into this despair there enters largely the element of unbelief, which is sinful; but I hope there is also in it a measure of sincere repentance which bears in it the hope of something better. Our poor, awakened paralytics sometimes hope that they may be forgiven, but they cannot believe it; they cannot rejoice; they cannot cast themselves on Jesus; they are utterly without strength. Now, the bottom of it, I say again, lies in unpardoned sin, and I earnestly beg you who love the Savior to be earnest in seeking the pardon of these paralyzed persons. You tell me that *I* should be earnest; so I should, and so I desire to be; but brethren, their cases appear to be beyond the minister's sphere of action; the Holy Spirit determines to use other agencies in their salvation. They have heard the public word; they now need private consolation and aid, and that from three or four persons. Lend us your help, you earnest brethren; form your parties of four; grasp the stretchers of these who wish to be saved, but who feel they cannot believe. The Lord, the Holy Spirit, make you the means of leading them into forgiveness and eternal salvation. They have been lying a long time waiting; their sin, however, still keeps them where they are; their guilt prevents their laying hold on Christ; and there is the point, and it is for such cases that I earnestly invoke my brethren's aid.

Let us proceed to notice, fourthly, that Jesus can remove both the sin and the paralysis in a single moment. It was the business of the four bearers to bring the man to Christ, but there their power ended. It is our part to bring the guilty sinner to the Savior, but there our power ends. Thank God, when *we* end, Christ begins, and works right gloriously. Observe that he began by saying, *"Your sins are forgiven you."* He laid the axe at the root; he did not desire that the man's sins might be forgiven, or express a good wish in that direction, but he pronounced a pardon by virtue of that authority with which he was clothed as the Savior. The poor man's sins there and then ceased to be, and he was justified in the sight of God. Do you believe this, my hearer, that Christ did thus for the paralytic man? Then I charge you to believe something more, that if on earth Christ had power to forgive sins before he had offered an atonement, much more has he power to do this now that he has poured out his blood and has said, *"It is finished,"* and has gone into his glory, and is at the right hand of the Father. He is exalted on high, to give repentance and remission of sin. Should he send his Spirit into your soul to reveal himself in you, you would in an instant be entirely absolved. Does blasphemy blacken you? Does a long life of infidelity pollute you? Have you been sexually immoral? Have you been abominably wicked? A word can acquit you – a word from those dear lips which said, *"Father, forgive them; for they do not know what they are doing."* I charge you to ask for that word of acquittal. No earthly priest can give it to you; but the Great High Priest, the Lord Jesus, can utter it at once. You twos and fours who are seeking the salvation of men, here is encouragement for you. Pray for them now, while the gospel is being preached in their hearing; pray for them day and night, and bring the glad tidings constantly before them, for Jesus is still able *to save forever those who draw near to God through Him.*

After our blessed Lord had taken away the root of the evil, you observe that he then took away the paralysis itself. It was gone in a single moment. Every limb in the man's body was restored to a healthy state; he could stand, could walk, could lift his stretcher, and both nerve and muscle were restored to vigor. One moment will suffice, if Jesus speaks, to make the despairing happy, and the unbelieving full of confidence. What *we* cannot do with our reasonings, persuadings, and pleadings, nor even with the letter of God's promise, Christ can do in a single instant by his Holy Spirit, and it has been our joy to see it done. This is the standing miracle of the church, performed by Christ today even as formerly. Paralyzed souls who could neither do nor will, have been able to do valiantly, and to will with solemn resolution. The Lord has poured power into the faint, and to them that had no might he has increased strength. He can do it still. I say again to loving spirits who are seeking the good of others, let this encourage you. You may not have to wait long for the conversions you aim at. It may be before another Sunday ends that the person you pray for may be brought to Jesus; or if you have to wait a little, the waiting shall well repay you, and meanwhile, remember he has never spoken in secret in the dark places of the earth; he has not said to the seed of Jacob, "Seek my face in vain."

Passing on, and drawing to a conclusion: Wherever our Lord works the double miracle, it will be apparent. He forgave the man's sin and took away his disease at the same time. How was this apparent? I have no doubt the pardon of the man's sin was best known to himself; but possibly those who saw that gleaming countenance which had been so sad before, might have noticed that the word of pardon sank into his soul as the rain into the thirsty earth. *"Your sins are forgiven you"* fell on him as a dew from heaven; he believed the sacred declaration, and his eyes sparkled. He might almost have felt indifferent about whether he remained paralyzed or not; it was such joy to be forgiven, forgiven by the Lord himself. That was enough, quite enough for him; but it was not enough for the Savior, and therefore he bid him to take up his stretcher and walk, for he had given him strength to do so. The man's healing was proved by his obedience. Openly to all onlookers an active obedience became indisputable proof of the poor creature's restoration. Notice, our Lord commanded him to get up – he got up; he had no power to do so except that power which comes with divine commands. He got up, for

Christ said, *"Get up."* Then he folded up that miserable *palliasse* – the Greek word used shows us that it was a very poor, shabby, miserable thing, his stretcher – he rolled it up as the Savior bid him, he shouldered it, and went to his home. His first impulse must have been to throw himself down at the Savior's feet and say, "Blessed be your name"; but the Master said, *"Go home,"* and I do not find that he stayed to make one grateful bow to the Master, but elbowing the crowd, jostling the throng with his load on his back, he proceeded to his home just as he was told, and that without deliberation or questioning. He did his Lord's bidding, and he did it accurately, in detail, at once, and most cheerfully. Oh! how cheerfully; none can tell but those in similar cases restored. So, the true sign of pardoned sin, and of paralysis removed from the heart, is obedience. If you are really saved you will do what Jesus bids you; your request will be, *"Lord, what wilt thou have me to do?"* (KJV), and that once ascertained, you will be sure to do it. You tell me Christ has forgiven you, and yet you live in rebellion to his commands; how can I believe you? You say you are a saved man, and yet you willfully set up your own will against Christ's will; what evidence have I of what you say? Have I not, rather, clear evidence that you speak not the truth? Open, careful, prompt, and cheerful obedience to Christ becomes the test of the wonderful work which Jesus works in the soul.

Lastly, all this tends to glorify God. Those four men had been the indirect means of bringing much honor to God and much glory to Jesus, and they, I doubt not, glorified God in their very hearts on the housetop. Happy men to have been of so much service to their bed-ridden friend! Who else united in glorifying God? Why, first the man who was restored. Did not every part of his body glorify God? I think I see him! He sets one foot down to God's glory, he plants the other to the same note, he walks to God's glory, he carries his stretcher to God's glory, he moves his whole body to the glory of God, he speaks, he shouts, he sings, he leaps to the glory of God. When a man is saved his whole manhood glorifies God; he becomes infused with a newborn life which glows in every part of him – spirit, soul, and body. As an heir of heaven, he brings glory to the great Father who has adopted him into the family, he breathes and eats and drinks to God's praise. When a sinner is brought into the church of God we are all glad, but we are none of us so joyous and thankful as he; we would all praise God, but *he* must praise him the loudest, and he will.

But who next glorified God? The text does not say so, but we feel sure that his family did, for he went to his own home. We will suppose that he had a wife. That morning when the four friends came and put him on the stretcher and carried him out, it may be that she shook her head in loving anxiety, and I dare say she said, "I am half afraid to trust him to you. Poor, poor creature, I dread his encountering the throng. I am afraid it is madness to hope for success. I wish you Godspeed in it, but I tremble. Hold well the stretcher; be sure you do not let him fall. If you do let him down through the roof, hold fast the ropes, be careful that no accident occurs to my poor bedridden husband; he is bad enough as he is, do not cause him more misery." But when she saw him coming home, walking with the stretcher on his back, can you picture her delight? How she would begin to sing, and praise and bless the Lord Jehovah-Rophi, who had healed her beloved one. If there were little children around, playing in front of the house, how they would shout for glee, "Here's father! Here's father walking again, and coming home with the bed on his back! He is made whole again, as he used to be when we were very little." What a glad house! They would gather around him, all of them, wife and children, and friends and neighbors, and they would begin to sing, *Bless the Lord, O my soul, and all that is within me, bless His holy name. Bless the Lord, O my soul, and forget none of His benefits; who pardons all your iniquities, who heals all your diseases.* How the man would sing those verses, rejoicing in the forgiveness first, and the healing next, and wondering how it was that David knew so much about it and had put his situation into such proper words.

> The whole Christian church is full of sacred praise when a sinner is saved; even heaven itself is glad.

Well, but it did not end there. A wife and family utter but a part of the glad chorus of praise, though a very melodious part. There are other adoring hearts who unite in glorifying the healing Lord. The disciples who were around the Savior, they glorified God too. They rejoiced, and said one to another, *"We have seen remarkable things today."* The whole

Christian church is full of sacred praise when a sinner is saved; even heaven itself is glad.

But there was glory brought to God even by the common people who stood around. They had not yet entered into that sympathy with Christ which the disciples felt, but they were struck by the sight of this great wonder, and they too could not help saying that God had worked great marvels. I pray that onlookers, strangers from the commonwealth of Israel, when they see the desponding comforted, and lost ones brought in, may be compelled to bear their witness to the power of divine grace, and be led themselves to be partakers in it. There is *"Glory to God in the highest, and on earth peace among men with whom He is pleased"* when a paralyzed soul is filled with gracious strength.

Now, shall I need to stand here and plead for the four to carry poor souls to Jesus? Shall I need to appeal to my brethren who love their Lord, and say, Band yourselves together to win souls? Your humanity to the paralytic soul claims it, but your desire to bring glory to God compels it. If you are indeed what you profess to be, to glorify God must be the fondest wish and the loftiest ambition of your souls. Unless you be traitors to my Lord as well as inhuman to your fellow men, you will catch the practical thought which I have endeavored to bring before you, and you will seek out some fellow Christians and say, "Come, let us pray together for such a one," and if you know a desperate case you will make up a sacred foursome to deal with their salvation. May the power of the Highest abide upon you, and who knows what glory the Lord may gain through you? Never forget this strange story of the stretcher which carried the man, and the man who carried his stretcher.

Chapter 7

The Gospel's Healing Power

One day He was teaching; and there were some Pharisees and teachers of the law sitting there, who had come from every village of Galilee and Judea and from Jerusalem; and the power of the Lord was present for Him to perform healing. (Luke 5:17)

Luke, the writer of this Gospel, was a physician, and therefore had a quick eye for cases of disease and instances of cure; you can trace throughout the whole of his Gospel the hand of One who was skilled in surgery and medicine. From this I gather that whatever may be our calling, or in whatever art or science we may have attained proficiency, we should take care to use our knowledge for Christ; and that if we be called being physicians we may understand the work of the Lord Jesus all the better by what we see in our own work, and we may also do much for our Lord in real, substantial usefulness among our patients. Let no man despise his calling; whatever instrument of usefulness God has put into your hand, consider that the Great Captain knew what weapon it was best for you to wield. Covet not your neighbor's sword or spear, but use that which your Lord has given you, and go forth to the battle of life to serve according to your capacity. If you be placed in this corner of the vineyard or that, consider that you are in the best place for yourself, and the best place for your Master; and do not always be judging what your fellow servants ought to do in *their* place, nor what you could do if you were in another place; but see what it is that you can do where you are, and use such things as you have in glorifying your Lord and Master.

One is pleased to observe in the language of a true man how the man's self shows itself. David frequently sings like one who had been a shepherd boy, and though a king, he is not ashamed to own that he once grasped the shepherd's staff. There is a clear difference between the prophecies of Amos the herdsman and of Isaiah the royal seer. True men do not imitate one another; but each one, moved of God, speaks according to his native bias, and according to the circumstances in which Providence has cast him. It was destructive to Egyptian art when the great men of the land framed articles of taste, and laws of statuary and of painting by which every sculptor must be bound, for then everything like freshness and originality was driven away; the proportions of every colossal statue and of every figure upon the wall were rigidly fixed, and then the glory and excellence of art vanished from the land. To do the same in religion is even more unwise; to say, "You shall all speak after one fashion, and you all shall conform to this manner of talk and life" is folly at its height. Let each man speak after his own manner, every man in his own order, each revived soul bringing out its own individuality, and seeking in that individuality to magnify God and to show forth the riches of his grace. These remarks were suggested by the abundant record of cures in this chapter and elsewhere in Luke's Gospel. Luke does not write like John, nor copy the style of Matthew; he writes not as a fisherman or a publican, but as a physician. Luke did not cease to be Luke when he was called by grace, but he was the same man elevated and refined, and taught to consecrate to noblest ends the gifts which he had acquired in his earthly calling; he was a physician before, and he became *the beloved physician* after his conversion.

The text, as we read it, suggests in the first place, that the power of Christ in the gospel is mainly a power to heal. *The power of the Lord was present for Him to perform healing.* The power of the gospel, of which Christ is the sum and substance, is a healing power. My brethren, when Christ came on earth, he could have come with destroying power. Justly enough could God have sent his only Son with the armies of vengeance to destroy this rebellious world. But

> Thy hands, dear Jesus, were not arm'd
>   With an avenging rod;
> No hard commission to perform,
>   The vengeance of a God.
>
> But all was mercy, all was mild,
>   And wrath forsook the throne,
> When Christ on the kind errand came,
>   And brought salvation down.

"I have not come," said he, *"to destroy men's lives, but to save them."* Elijah calls down fire from heaven upon the captains of fifties, and their fifties, so that they are utterly consumed; but Christ brings fire from heaven for quite another purpose, namely, that by its power men might be saved from the wrath to come. The gospel is not intended to be a power to destroy. *"For God did not send the Son into the world to judge the world, but that the world might be saved through Him."* And if that gospel be made a savor of death unto death unto any, it is not on account of its own intrinsic qualities or design, but because of the perversity and wickedness of the human heart. If men perish by the gospel of life, it is because they make that to be a stumbling stone which was meant to be a foundation.

> One of the clearest exposures of man's fallen estate is the gospel of the grace of God.

The gospel does not even come into the world merely to reveal disease. It is true it does discover, detect, and describe the sicknesses of fallen man. One of the clearest exposures of man's fallen estate is the gospel of the grace of God; but it is rather the design of the law than of the gospel to show to man his ruin. It is by the glare of Sinai's lightnings that men tremblingly read the sentence of condemnation upon those who have broken God's law. By the gentler light of Calvary they *may* read the same truth, and *must* read it; but this is not the main design of Calvary. Calvary is the place for the healing balm rather than for the lancet and the knife. The work of Jesus, our heavenly physician, is not so much to point out disease as to indicate and to apply the remedy. Certain philosophers have made it their business and delight, with a grim, scathing smile upon their faces, to put forth the finger and mark out human wickedness and weakness as a theme for ridicule and sarcasm. The philosophy of the Stoics, the wisdom of such men as Diogenes, was but a heartless, unpitying showing up of human folly and sin; it knew no remedy, and cared not to search for one. They showed poor manhood to be blind, deluded, debased, and depraved, and there they left it, passing by on the other side as the priest and Levite did with the wounded man in the parable. But Jesus came upon no such fruitless errand; he *does* convince the world of sin by his Spirit, but it is not to leave the world hopelessly despairing of its restoration, but to recover it by his power. Jesus carries with him power to heal; this is his honor and renown. He has the eagle's eye to see our sicknesses, the lion's heart bravely to encounter them, and the lady's hand gently to apply the heavenly ointment; in him the three necessaries of a good surgeon meet in perfection.

Beloved, I trust you and I have known this power to heal in our own cases, and if it be so we know with certainty that it is *a divine power* which comes from our Lord Jesus because he is most surely God. It is the sole prerogative of God to heal spiritual disease. Natural disease may be instrumentally healed by men, but even then the honor is to be given to God who gives virtue unto medicine, and bestows power unto the human frame to cast off disease. But as for spiritual sicknesses, these remain with the Great Physician alone; he claims it as his prerogative: "I kill and I make alive, I wound and I heal." And one of the Lord's choice titles is *Jehovah-Rophi,* meaning "the Lord that heals." "*I will heal you of your wounds"* is a promise which could not come from the lips of man, but only from the mouth of the eternal God. On this account the psalmist cried unto the Lord, *"Heal me, O Lord, for my bones are dismayed,"* and again, *"Heal my soul, for I have sinned against You."* For this also, the godly ones praise the name of the Lord, saying, "He *heals all [our] diseases."* He who made man can heal man; he who was at first the Creator of our nature can create it new. What a transcendent comfort it is that in the person of Jesus Christ of Nazareth we have Deity

Incarnate! *For in Him all the fullness of Deity dwells in bodily form.* My soul, whatever your disease may be, this Great Physician can heal you. If he be God, there can be no limit to his infinite power; if he be truly divine, there can be no boundary to the majesty of his might. Come then with the blind eye of your understanding, come with the limping foot of your energy, come with the maimed hand of your faith, come just as you are, for he who is God can certainly heal you. None shall say unto the healing flood of his love, *"Thus far you shall come, but no farther."* The utmost length of human sickness can be reached by this Great Physician. Have confidence, O poor doubting heart! Have unstaggering confidence in the divine Healer.

Although our Lord Jesus healed as divine, remember that he also possessed power to heal because of his being *human*. Is it not written, *The chastening for our well-being fell upon Him, and by His scourging we are healed*? He used no other remedy in healing our sin-sickness but that of taking our sicknesses and infirmities upon himself. This is the one great cure-all. Blessed be the Son of God that the medicine, bitter as it is, is not for us to drink, but was all drained by himself. He took the terrible cup in Gethsemane, and drank it dry on our account. The sharp but healing cuts of the lancet are not made in our bodies, but he bore them in his own flesh. When the plowers made deep furrows, those furrows were not upon the sinner's shoulders, but upon the shoulders of the sinner's Substitute. Did you ever hear, O earth, of such a physician as this? who heals by suffering himself, whose pains, and sorrows, and griefs, and pangs, and torments, and anguish, and death are the only medicine by which he removes the woes of men? Blessed Son of God, if I trust you, seeing that you are divine, how I will love you! How I will cling to you, seeing you are human! With what gratitude will I look up to your cross and view you, while those blessed fountains of health are streaming crimson floods, and while your heart, the source of all spiritual sanity, is pouring forth a heavenly torrent, effectual to wash the sinner from all his sicknesses! Come to this place, all you sin-sick ones, and behold the glorious Son of God, made in the likeness of human flesh, breathing out his life upon the cross! Come to this place, you that mourn for sin, you who are paralyzed and diseased with iniquity! Here is power, power still present in the dying Savior to heal you, whatsoever your diseases may be. He healed all that had need of healing while he sojourned here, and the costly balm of his atonement has lost none of its power.

The power which dwelt in Christ to heal, coming from him as divine and human, was applicable, most eminently, to the removal of the guilt of sin. Reading this chapter through, one pauses with joy over that twenty-fourth verse: *"The Son of Man has authority on earth to forgive sins."* Here, then, is one of the Great Physician's mightiest arts: he has authority to forgive sin. While he lived here below, before the ransom had been paid, before the blood had been literally sprinkled on the mercy seat, he had authority to forgive sin. Has he not power to do it now that he has died? Brethren, what power must dwell in him who to the utmost farthing has faithfully discharged the debts of his people! He has indeed authority, seeing that he has finished transgression and made an end of sin. If you doubt it, see him rising from the dead! Behold him in ascending splendor raised to the right hand of God! Hear him pleading before the eternal Father, pointing to his wounds, urging the merit of his sacred passion! What power to forgive is here! *"When He ascended on high, . . . He gave gifts to men."* He is exalted on high to give repentance and remission of sins. At this moment, sinner, Christ has power to pardon, power to pardon you and millions such as you are. He has nothing more to do to win your pardon; all the atoning work is done. He can, in answer to your tears, forgive your sins today and make you know it. He can breathe into your soul at this very moment a peace with God which passes all understanding, which shall spring from perfect remission of your many iniquities. Do you believe that? I trust you believe it. May you experience now that the healing power of the gospel is power to forgive sin! Waste no time in appealing to the Great Physician of souls, but hasten to him with words like these:

> Jesus! Master! hear my cry;
>   Save me, heal me with a word;
> Fainting at thy feet I lie,
>   Thou my whisper'd plaint hast heard.

This is not the only form of the healing power which dwells without measure in our glorious Lord. He also heals *the sorrow of sin.* It is written, *He heals the brokenhearted and binds up their wounds.* When sin is really manifest to the conscience it is a most painful thing, and for the conscience to be effectually pacified is an unspeakable blessing. Sharper than a dagger in the heart, or an arrow piercing through the loins, is conviction of sin. He that has ever smarted under the prickings of an awakened conscience well knows that there is no pain of body that can be compared to it. When crushed under the hand of God a man may form some idea of what the miseries of hell must be. Correspondingly joyous is the relief which Immanuel brings to us when he brings better balm than that of Gilead, and ministers heaven's infallible balm specific to a soul disease. When Jesus is received by faith, he lifts all our sorrow from us in a moment. One promise applied by his Spirit, one drop of his blood brought home to the conscience, and at once there is such a peace so deep and profound that nothing can rival it. What the poet wrote concerning recovery from bodily sickness is doubly true of spiritual restoration.

> See the *Man* that long has tost
> On the thorny bed of pain,
> At length repair his vigor lost,
> And breathe and walk again:
> The meanest floweret of the vale,
> The simplest note that swells the gale,
> The common sun, the air, the skies,
> To him are opening Paradise.

God grant that to you who fear his name the Sun of Righteousness may arise with healing beneath his wings!

Jesus also heals *the power of sin.* Sin may be, in your case, dear friend, so mighty, that like a whirlwind it hurries you away at its pleasure. You feel like the dry leaves which are driven by the storm; you scarcely have power to resist your passions; you have perhaps yielded so long to certain forms of evil that now you are positively powerless in strife against them. Do not, however, despair; Christ can surely deliver you. The demoniac had such an energy of evil within him that he broke the chains and bands with which he had been bound, he cut himself with stones, and he howled all night amid the tombs. But when Jesus came near to him he was soon seen clothed and in his right mind, sitting meekly at the Great Physician's feet. And so will you, poor captive of evil. Do not think that you need to be a drunkard, or that your angry temper need always be your master. Do not conceive that you must always be a slave to lust, or led captive at the devil's will. There is hope for you, man, where Christ is; and though your disease be of as long standing as your very life, yet a word from the powerful lips of the Son of God can make even you whole. The power of the gospel is a power to heal the guilt, the sorrow, and the influence of sin; Jesus Christ came into the world to destroy the works of the devil, in all their forms.

It should not be forgotten that the Lord Jesus is able to heal us of *our relapses*. I have heard men say that a relapse is what the physician frequently fears more than the primary disease, and that there is frequently a period in the healing process when the virus of disease gathers renewed energy, and the physician feels that now, and not at the first, the true battle has to be fought. We have met with men who have professed conversion, and we trust were changed, who have gone back like the dog to his vomit, and the sow that was washed to her wallowing in the mire. We have had to mourn over those in whom the change appeared to be great, but it was superficial, and soon the power of evil returned upon them. But, my backsliding hearer, Jesus is able to heal your backslidings. What a mercy that is! *I will heal their apostasy, I will love them freely, for My anger has turned away from them.* What if you be sevenfold more a child of hell than you were before? Yet even now eternal mercy that drove out a legion of devils from one of old can drive them out of you. The healing power of my Master is such that if you have backslidden ever so far, he still says unto you, "Return! Return! Return!" There shall be more joy over you, you poor lost sheep, than over ninety-nine that went not astray. He shall be more glad to receive

> **Jesus Christ came into the world to destroy the works of the devil, in all their forms.**

you, you wandering prodigal child, than he has joy even over that righteous son who remained always in his father's house.

To sum up much in little, my Master, as a physician, works cures *very suddenly;* he touches, and the deed is done at once. He works cures *of all kinds.* Such as have been the stumbling stones of other physicians have been readily overcome by him. *He never fails.* He has not in his diary one single case that has overmatched his mighty power. He heals *effectually;* the disease never again reigns when he has once dethroned it. When he casts the devil out of the man, he shall not return. He heals with his word even those who think that they cannot be healed. There is no hospital for incurables now as to souls, for incurables there are none. The Friend of sinners *is able also to save forever those who draw near to God through Him.* Oases of disease so putrid that men say, "Put them out of sight"; vices so detestable that the very mention of them makes the cheek of modesty to blush – such as these the master-hand of Immanuel can heal. With God nothing is impossible, and with the Son of God nothing is difficult. He can save the chief of sinners and the vilest of the vile. In the highest conceivable degree the power of the gospel is power to heal. Come, poor sinner, and behold him who is able to heal you of your deadly wounds. Come look upon him now and live.

> Raise to the cross thy tearful eyes,
>   Behold, the Prince of Glory dies;
> He dies extended on the tree,
>   And sheds a sovereign balm *for thee.*

A second remark arises from the text: there are special periods when the power to heal is most manifestly displayed. The verse before us says that on a certain day the power of the Lord was present to heal, by which I understand that there were certain periods when he delighted to put forth his divine power in the way of healing to an unusual degree. The sea is never empty; it is indeed always as full at one time as at another, but yet it is not always at flood. The sun is never dim; it shines with equal force at all hours, and yet it is not always day with us, nor do we always bask in the warmth of summer. Christ is fullness itself, but that fullness does not always overflow; he is able to heal, but he is not always engaged in healing. There are times when the power to save is more than usually evident – times of refreshing, seasons of revival, days of visitation, acceptable days, days of salvation. Any student of the world's history who has read it in the light of true religion will have observed that there have been favored periods when the power of God has been peculiarly present to heal men. My solemn conviction is that we are living in such an era, that this present moment is one of the set times when God's power is peculiarly clear; I gather this from many signs, but even the text assists me in my belief.

Observe that on the occasion mentioned in the text *there was a great desire among the multitude to hear the Word.* In the opening of the chapter we read that they pressed upon our Lord by the sea. Further on we find them coming from all parts of the country in multitudes. Special mention is made of doctors of the law and Pharisees, the last people to be impressed, who nevertheless, overcome by the common enthusiasm, were found mingling with the throng. We are told that the people thronged the house at such a rate that the paralyzed man could not be brought into the congregation except by the makeshift of breaking through the roof. When God's power is moving, there will be a corresponding motion among the people; they will long to hear when God's power is with the speaker. Take it as a sign of grace when the houses dedicated to worship are full. Consider that the Lord is about to fill the net, when the fish crowd around the boat. We cannot expect the gospel to be blessed to those who do not hear it, but we may lawfully and properly expect it will be a blessing to those who have an intense anxiety to listen to it. At the present hour I see a religious awakening among the masses of London, not so great a one as we could desire, but still it is there, and we must be grateful for it. We shall not long have to put up with the wicked nonsense of Puseyism; public opinion will aid us in putting it down. It has taken a long time to wake up our nation, but it will awaken after all. I think I see the tide of popular feeling turning in the right direction. Men are just now occupied with religious thought, and whether they think rightly or wrongly, there is more attention just now paid to religious truth than there has been for many a day; and where ministers do but preach simply and lovingly the gospel of Christ at this moment, they find no lack of hearers. This is a sure sign that the power of the Lord is present to heal.

Observe next that the healing power was conspicuously present when *Christ was teaching.* Note carefully the favored hour: *One day He was teaching.* Jesus linked the healing with the teaching. It was so with the material healing, but much more with the spiritual healing, for *faith comes from hearing, and hearing by the word of Christ.* Brethren, is there not among our own brethren, of whom we can speak with the most certainty, more teaching of Christ now than there was? I am persuaded that the most of my brethren preach more faithfully and fully the simple truth of Christ Jesus than they once did. Teaching is returning to the pulpits. Now mark, dear hearer, whether you be saved or not, if you are present where Christ is fully preached, where he is lifted up, exalted, proclaimed, and commended to you, then you are in a place where he is also present to heal; for is it not written, *"I, if I am lifted up from the earth, will draw all men to Myself"*?

A further sign of present power is found most clearly in *the sick folks who were healed* by Jesus. Now we know that in this very house not a Sunday passes without souls being converted. We have before our church meetings the cases of hundreds whom God has blessed by the simple telling of the story of the cross. This, then, is proof positive that with Christ being taught, and souls being blessed, he is in a remarkable manner present to heal.

One other thing must be noted, namely, that this particular time mentioned in the text was *prefaced by a special season of prayer* on the part of the principal actor in it. Did you notice it? He withdrew himself and prayed, and then the power of the Lord was present to heal them. Is it so that even with regard to Christ himself, the Lord and Giver of Life, in whom dwells the fullness of the Godhead, and who has the Spirit without measure, yet before that Spirit is publicly manifested in any high degree there must be a special retreat for fervent prayer? How plainly does this say to us that the church must pray if she would have the healing power! But, my brethren, we have prayed. There has been such prayer put up by this congregation as I believe was never excelled, even in apostolic times; and last Monday was a day of wrestling of such a kind that the blessing could not be withheld. I have almost ceased to ask further; I wait in joyful anticipation of the heavenly visitation. I come not forth today so much as a sower as a reaper. I believe that the fish are taken in the net, and that we have only to pull it to land. God grant the net may not break by reason of the multitude of fish! For God is with us, and most certainly in this house this day. Wonders of grace are being worked. While we are yet speaking, men are being inclined to look to Christ; while we are lifting him up, tearful eyes are looking to him; and in many a heart there may be heard the cry, "I will arise and go to my Father." Now with all these signs meeting together – a desire to hear, a set time of private prayer, the teaching of the Word, and the unmistakable blessing of souls under that Word – I gather that we have arrived at this present moment at that state which is described in the text.

Passing on to a third thought, we observe that when the power of the Lord is present to heal, it may not be seen in all, but it may be shown in special cases and not in others. It is a melancholy reflection that men may be in the region of divine power, and yet not feel its operations. I have read this verse through a great many times with one object; I have tried, if I could, to make the text mean that the Pharisees and doctors of the law were present, and that the power of the Lord was present to heal *them*. But the text does not teach us so; the power of the Lord was not present to heal the doctors and Pharisees, for they were not healed. The word *them* agrees with the noun further back, according to the frequent usage of the New Testament by which the pronouns are not made to refer to the nearer noun, but to another more remote. The power of God was present to heal the sick, not to heal the doctors, nor the Pharisees; and yet how nearly they seem to have gained it, for had they but known *their* sickness, and been willing to confess *their* infirmity, there was power enough to have healed even them. But as it was, we do not find that one of them was healed – not so much as a single doctor of the law or a Pharisee felt the power which was passing so near to them that they were amazed and staggered and fell to quibbling about it. Dear friends, this very melancholy observation must be applied to some that are present now. You may be in the midst of this congregation, which is under remarkable visitations of God's grace, and yet there may be no power

> The power of God was present to heal the sick, not to heal the doctors.

present operating in your heart to heal you. You will observe that those who missed this grace were not the harlots; infamous as they were by character, they felt the power of the love of Jesus and entered into his kingdom. We do not find that this power was lacking among the publicans; we have an instance here of one of them who made a great feast in his house for Christ. Where, then, was the power lacking? Where was it unsought and unfelt? It was in the first place among *the knowing people,* the doctors of the law. These teachers knew too much to submit to be taught by the Great Rabbi. There is such a thing as knowing too much to know anything, and being too wise to be anything but a fool. The knowledge of the doctors was that which puffs up, and not the knowledge which comes from God. Ah, dear hearer, beware of head knowledge without heart knowledge; beware of being so orthodox as to set yourself up as a judge of the preacher, and to refuse to be obedient to the truth. Beware of saying, "Oh yes, yes, yes, yes, that is very applicable to So-and-so, and very well put." Do not criticize but feel. It would be better for you that you had been a common plowboy, whistling at the plow, who never heard these things until today, and have now listened to them, and have received them in all their novelty and power and beauty for the first time. This would be better for you than to have heard them till they ring in your ears like the bell which you have heard every Sabbath day, of whose monotony you are weary. Beware of going down to hell with a millstone of sound doctrine around your necks, for if you will be damned, you may as well perish knowing the truth as not knowing it. No, if you catch the formula and lay hold upon the creed, and imagine yourself to be teachers of others, it is even easier to perish in that state than it is if you came in to hear the Word untaught until this time in its glad message. These were the knowing ones who had no power to be healed.

Those, moreover, who had a good opinion of themselves were left unblessed. The Pharisees! no better people anywhere, from Dan to Beersheba, than the Pharisees, if you would take them upon their own reckoning. Observe with due respect their public character. Were they not most eminent? See the breadth of the borders of their garments! How visible were their phylacteries! How diligently did they wash their hands before they ate! How scrupulous about straining out gnats from their wine! How careful to tithe the dill, and mint, and cummin! Yet these were the people who obtained no blessing from Jesus as they only cared about outward appearances, yet were full of hypocrisy.

How many people there are of this kind! "Well," says one, "I know I never robbed anybody; I have brought up my family respectably, and conducted myself with such decorum that nobody could possibly find fault with me." Just so, and you will not have Christ because you think you are whole, and that you have no need of a physician. "Ah!" says another, "surely if we do our duty to the best of our ability it will be all right with us." If you think thus you will find that when you have done your duty to the best you can, you will have no part nor lot in a Savior, because obviously, on your own showing, you do not require one. The Lord Jesus will take your own showing, and will say, "I never knew you. How should I know you? You were never sick; you never needed me; you declared that you were whole; and you would not stoop to accept the salvation which I, the Savior, came to bring." Thus will Jesus speak to you who now proudly despise his grace.

Once again, the people who did not get the blessing were not only the knowing ones and the very good ones, but they were also *the people who stood by*. As one observes, they did not come to be preached *at*, they came for Christ to preach *before* them. That used to be the old style of sermon prefaces – "A sermon preached *before* the honorable or worshiped company of So-and-so." Now that is the worst kind of preaching anywhere, preaching before people; preaching right at people is the only preaching worth hearing and worth uttering. But they did not come for Christ to operate upon them; they were not patients, they were visitors in the hospitals. Like visitors they went around to the beds and looked at the prescriptions put over the sick, and observed each case, and when the physician came in and began to exercise his art upon the sick, they stood by and criticized his treatment, imagining all the while that they were not sick themselves. If they had been lying on the bed sick they could have been healed, but they took only a superficial interest in the healing, for they came not to partake in it. Beware, my dear friends, of going to places of worship merely to be lookers-on. There will be no lookers-on in heaven, and there will be no lookers-on in hell. Take care that you do not play the looker-on in the worship of

God here. Every truth as spoken by God's servants has a bearing upon you. If it be threatening, and you are in the gall of bitterness, it is yours, tremble under it! If it be the promise of divine love, then if you have no part in it, be afraid, be ashamed, be alarmed, and fly to Christ that you may partake in it. Those who get no blessing are those who suppose they do not particularly need it, and stand by, having merely come to see and to be seen, but not to receive a cure.

Those who felt not the healing power sneered and quibbled. They said further down in the chapter, *"Who can forgive sins, but God alone?"* When a man gets no good *out of* the ministry, he is pretty sure to think there is no good *in* the ministry; and when he himself for lack of stooping down to drink finds no water in the river, he concludes it is dry; whereas it is his own stubborn knee that will not bend, and his own willful mouth that will not open to receive the gospel. But if they quarrel, if they raise questions, if they dispute, we know their breed, we understand the race to which they belong, and we know how Jesus said to them of old, *"You brood of vipers, how will you escape the sentence of hell?"* If any shall not escape, surely they shall not whose only hearing of the gospel is to make it the object of their sarcasm and ridicule, who look derisively even at the cross itself with a dying Savior upon it, and thrust their tongue into their cheek, and make jests and merriment of the agonies of the world's Redeemer. Beware, lest you have those jests in your mouth on earth which you will have to digest in hell! Beware, lest your mockery return upon you at the last great day, when the words of Solomon shall be fulfilled: *"Because I called and you refused, I stretched out my hand and no one paid attention; . . . I also will laugh at your calamity; I will mock when your dread comes."* There were persons then to whom the present power of Christ to heal was of no service whatever, and there may be such now. Friend, are you such a one?

In the last place, I want Christian people here to observe that when the power of Christ was present, it called forth the energy of those who were his friends to work while that power was manifest.

My dear brethren, the members of this church especially, what I have to say is earnestly addressed to you. You will perceive that as soon as ever it was discovered that the power of healing was present, loving hearts desired to bring in others that they might experience it. Four persons took each a corner of the stretcher and brought in a paralyzed man who could not come of himself, and they let him down with much inconvenience through the roof. God is blessing the church now. Christian men and women, join together to pray for your friends who cannot or will not pray for themselves; and if you meet with any in deep distress, paralyzed with despair, who cannot lift the finger of faith, strive to bring them to hear the gospel, bring them to where Christ is working miracles. If one of you cannot prevail to lay the case before the Lord, let two of you unite; if two should not be enough, let four blend their petitions; if four should not suffice, tell it to the church, and ask the whole to pray; but do strive to bring dying sinners to where Christ is working spiritual miracles.

If you read further on in the chapter you will learn how to bring some persons to the Savior who would never hear of him otherwise. Levi made a great feast, for he thought to himself, "I would like Jesus to come and preach to the publicans. They are such great sinners, just such as I am; if I could but get them to hear him they might be converted. But," he thought, "if I ask them, they would say they could not afford to give up a day's work, they will not care to listen to a sermon; so (said he) I will get them this way: I will invite them to my house for a feast; they will be sure to come then, and then I will ask Jesus to come and eat with them, and I know he will not let them go without saying a good word." So you see he used a skillful plan as hunters do when they are anxious to catch their prey. Now, can you not be as watchful and thoughtful in your generation as Levi was? Can you not get the outcasts and the neglecters of the Sabbath to your own house or to anybody else's house, and use means to bring them under the sound of God's Word? Why, if you have a few flowers in your back room, if it rains in the summertime, do not you always put them out in it? All the pots you put out in the garden to let them catch the shower. Do so with your friends, your neighbors, your children, your relatives; while the rain of grace is dropping, try to get them under the influence of it, and if they will not come by one means, then try another, only do get them where the power of the Lord is present, for perhaps Jesus may look upon them and they may look to him and may be healed.

And oh! Let me say in closing, if they should not be saved, the responsibility will not then rest with you, even as the responsibility does not rest with me. We have proclaimed to you in this house many times that Christ Jesus came into the world to save sinners. We have told you that the heavenly Father is willing to receive returning sinners, that he delights in mercy, that he is free to blot out sin. We have told you that the blood of Christ can make the blackest clean, that all manner of sin and blasphemy shall be forgiven unto men. We have urged you to flee away like doves to Jesus' wounds. The power of the Spirit of God has led many of you to come to him, and you are saved; but alas! there still remains a multitude who are still unsaved. Well, if you perish, it is not because Christ has not been taught in your streets. You will go down to hell, some of you, with the light shining on your eyelids, but with your eyes willfully closed against it; you will perish with the voice of mercy ringing in your ears; and in hell you will be awful monuments to the justice of God, who will then say to you, "You sinned against light and knowledge, and against love and mercy." If they perish who despised Moses' law, how shall you escape if you neglect so great a salvation? May the Holy Spirit now with mighty energy apply the precious blood of Jesus to every hearer, and unto God shall be glory world without end. Amen.

> **If you perish, it is not because Christ has not been taught in your streets.**

> Blest Savior, at thy feet I lie,
>   Here to receive a cure or die;
> But grace forbids that painful fear,
>   Almighty grace, which triumphs here.
>
> Thou wilt withdraw the poison'd dart,
>   Bind up and heal the wounded heart;
> With blooming health my face adorn,
>   And change the gloomy night to morn.

Chapter 8

Sitting There

One day He was teaching; and there were some Pharisees and teachers of the law sitting there. (Luke 5:17)

A congregation is a strange aggregate: it is like the gatherings of a net, or the collections of a dredge. If it is a very large one, it is specially remarkable. What strange varieties of creatures meet in the Noah's ark of a crowded house of prayer! If anybody could write the histories of all gathered here, the result would be a library of singular stories.

You, my dear friends, who usually worship here, have probably no idea of the strange medley of nations, ranks, professions, conditions, and religions which are represented in one of the great congregations of this tabernacle. I am often myself greatly startled when I come across the tracks of people quite unknown to me, except by the newspapers, who have mingled in these vast assemblies. I could not have imagined that they would ever have entered a place where the gospel is preached. It is noteworthy that God always selects our congregations for us, and his arrangements are always wise. I have frequently said to myself, "I shall have a prime congregation today"; and in some instances this has been very singularly the case. Persons have come to this place who had themselves no thought of coming, till some special matter drew them; and then the word spoken has been so clearly suited to their case that it made them marvel. If they had sent notice of their coming, and the preacher had known all about them, he might not have ventured to be quite so personal; for he has unwittingly entered into minute details and secret items which knowingly he would never have revealed. The Lord who knows what is done in the closet knows how to direct his ministering servant so that he shall speak to the point, and speak to the heart.

In the present congregation we have a large company of people who have long known the Lord, and have for years rejoiced in his name. We have another company of persons who do not know the Lord savingly, but yet are well acquainted with the gospel, and are not far from the kingdom of God. They are almost persuaded; they wait in the borderland. Oh, that they would cross the frontier and become dwellers in Immanuel's land! We have also among us some who are far removed from divine life, a people about whom we have little or no hope. Yet it is from among these that we reap the richest spoils for Christ, for he has compassion on the ignorant, and on those that are out of the way. I am fond of that phrase "out of the way." The Lord save all of you who are out-of-the-way ones!

In every congregation we have a fourth class, who would decline to be classed at all: they may be said to be here and not here. They are spectators rather than hearers. Like the gentlemen mentioned in our text, they are *sitting there*. They are too respectable to be numbered with the vulgar crowd. No, no; they are only callers, *sitting there*. They would not like to have it supposed that they are regular hearers, much less converts; they are *sitting there*. They are not repenting; they are not believing; they are not entering into the truth at all, but they are just *sitting there*. They have come to look on, take notes, and make remarks. They are on the outskirts of the battle, but they are not combatants at all; they are *sitting there*, where they hope they are out of gunshot.

It is about these who are *sitting there* that I shall now speak, for I am afraid they are becoming far too comfortable in the seats which they have chosen. They are sitting as God's people sit, and yet they are not truly among them, but only *sitting there*. They are a very irritating and disappointing part of our assemblies; but, at the same time, there they are, and we would not turn them out even if we could. We are glad to have these persons to dig into; for who knows but that out of them God in infinite mercy may select individuals who will never again sit there, but who will be heart and soul with Christ and his people, and even become leaders of the host of God?

Let me freely speak to you concerning certain ones of those who sat there. They were by no means to be despised, for some of them were eminent persons. They were Pharisees, members of the separate sect, who kept themselves to themselves, and were stiff-necked about the externals of religion. Very superior indeed were these Pharisees; and you could see by their faces that they felt themselves to be persons of importance. With these were doctors of the law, the learned men who had studied the Scriptures very carefully, counted the words of each holy book, and found out the middle letter of it. These doctors of the law had come to hear the uneducated peasant from Nazareth, concerning whom they had a very strong, but by no means favorable, opinion. They had heard about him, and they condescended to give him a hearing, half blushing at their own modesty in doing so. Not, of course, that he could teach *them* anything; they were merely *sitting there,* and nothing more. We do not see many of these great folks among our crowds, and perhaps there are none such here on this occasion, but we cannot be sure. I do not much care to know whether the learned and profound are here; but they do come among us at times, though it is only to sit there. I will say no more about these remarkable people just now, for many others come into congregations merely to sit there. They have not come with any wish to learn, or understand, or feel, or be saved; they are only *sitting there.*

Let our first topic answer the question, What were these people doing? They were *sitting there.* There is a good deal in this. First, *they were indulging their curiosity.* They had come out of every town of Galilee, and Judea, and Jerusalem to know what this stir was all about. They had heard the great fame of Christ for working miracles, and this drew them into the throng which continually surrounded him. Besides this, the crowd itself drew them. Why was there such a large company? What could it be all about? They would like to know for the sake of curiosity. They would for once hear the man, so that they might be able to say that they had heard him, but they were not going to be influenced by what they heard; they would hear him as outsiders, merely *sitting there.* They were curious, but not anxious. As a rule, very little comes of this kind of attendance at places of worship; and yet I would rather have people come from this motive than not come at all. Curiosity may be the stepping-stone to something better; yet, in itself, what good is there in it? Persons on Sunday go to St. Paul's, to Westminster Abbey, to the tabernacle, to this place and to that, and they suppose that they are worshiping God, whereas they might just as well have gone to see a show; in fact, it is going to a show and nothing more as far as their motive is concerned. Do not flatter yourselves; if you go to places of worship merely to look around you or to hear music, you are not worshiping God. If you come to this great house to gratify your own fancy, you are no more worshiping God than you would be if you walked in the fields. You are only, in a very poor and groveling sense, *sitting there*.

Many come into our assemblies and sit there in this respect – that *they are altogether indifferent*. I do not suppose that these scribes and Pharisees were quite good enough to be altogether indifferent: they leaned the wrong way, and were bitterly opposed. Too many act as if they said, "I come to hear a noted preacher; but what his doctrine may be I neither know nor care." They do not ask, What is this doctrine of the fall? What is this depravity of heart? What is this work of the Spirit? What is this vicarious sacrifice? They do not care to know whether they are concerned in anything that is spoken of; nor do they ask, What is this new birth, this translation from darkness to light, this sanctification of nature? They hear a theological term and dismiss it as no concern of theirs. They do not want to know too much. This atoning sacrifice – they hear so much about it; this shedding of the precious blood of Jesus, this putting away of sin by the sacrifice of Jesus – they will not lend an ear to this saving mystery, but treat it as a matter of little or no consequence. It is nothing to them that Jesus should die. O dear sirs, it ought to be something to you! If there is anything worth questioning, it is your own state before God, your position as to eternal things, your condition at this moment in reference to sin – whether it stains you scarlet, or whether you have been washed from it in the fountain which Christ has opened. If there is anything worthy of a man's question, it is the matter which concerns his own soul for eternity. I wish to God

> If you go to places of worship merely to look around you or to hear music, you are not worshiping God.

you would no longer be found *sitting there,* but would in earnest feel, "There is something here for me. Perhaps for me there is a peace which I have never known, a joy which I have never imagined. I will see for myself. Perhaps for me there is a heaven of which I have up to this time despaired; I will make a searching inquiry, and see whether or not it is so." May that be your resolve, and may you no longer be among those who sit there in empty indifference!

The scribes and Pharisees were *sitting there* in another, and a worse, sense; for *they were there to criticize in an unfriendly spirit,* and either find faults, or invent them. I see them take out their notebooks to jot down a word the Savior said which they thought could be twisted. How they nudged one another, as he said something which sounded unusual and bold! Oh, could they but catch him! When at last he said to the sick man, *"Your sins are forgiven you,"* I think I see their eyes flash with malignant fire. "Now we have got him! Now we have got him! This man blasphemes." They hoped he had now said more than he could stand to; and they asked in triumph, *"Who can forgive sins, but God alone?"* They were *sitting there,* watching the Savior as a cat watches a mouse. How eagerly they sprang upon him!

My hearers, this was a wretched business, was it not? It is a very poor business to go to the house of God to criticize a fellow mortal who is sincerely trying to do us good. It will not, in the present case, affect the preacher much; for his skin is hardened, and he feels not the tiny strokes of ordinary rebuke. In no case can ungenerous criticisms do any good; but the pity of it is that when we earnestly desire to show to you the way of salvation, some of you would hinder us by petty observations upon a faulty mannerism, a slight blunder, a mispronunciation of a word, or an inaccurate accent. Alas, what small things put eternal truth on one side! I do not know, and I would not like to say if I did know, what petty trifles people will carry away and talk of, after we have been solemnly pleading with them about heaven, and hell, and the judgment day, and the wrath to come, and the way to escape from it. Was it Carlyle who spoke of the cricket as chirping amid the crack of doom? I am apt to think that many people are like that cricket; they go on with their idle chitchat when Christ himself is set before them on the cross. Assuredly this is poor work. I am hungry, I come to a banquet; but instead of feasting upon the delicacies, I begin to criticize the dress of the waiters, abuse the arrangements of the banqueting hall, and vilify the provisions. I shall go home as hungry as I came, and who will be blamed for it? The best criticism that you can possibly give of your friend's entertainment is to be hearty in partaking of it. The greatest honor that we can do to Christ Jesus is to feed upon him, to receive him, to trust him, and to live upon him. Merely to gripe and to question will bring no good to the most clever of you. How can it? It is a pitiful waste of time for yourself, and a trial of temper to others. Yet there are many who, like the scribes and Pharisees, are in this manner *sitting there*.

Now, I do not care to go farther into these different forms of *sitting there*, but no doubt *some kindly admire, but do not profit*. Hundreds of people are *sitting there* who are attentive hearers and warm friends, and yet have no part nor lot in the matter. They have been more or less regular attendants at this house of prayer for, perhaps twelve, fourteen, fifteen, or twenty years, and yet they are not one whit the better. Some go from public worship to the public house, and yet they would not neglect church or chapel on any account. Many are no better at home for all they have heard; their spouses are sorrowful witnesses to that fact. Why, some of you have been prayed for time out of mind, and you have been preached at as well, and still you are *sitting there*. I cannot make out why you come so constantly and yet profit so little. It would seem to all who knew you a very odd thing if you were seen loafing about a certain shop for an hour and a half one day in the week for twenty years, and yet you never bought a pennyworth of goods. Why do you hang around the gospel shop and yet purchase nothing? On your own showing you are a fool. I do not like using a hard word, still it is used in Scripture for such as you are. He who believes a thing to be so important that he spends one day in the week in hearing about it, and yet does not think it important enough to accept it as a gift, proves himself to be unsound by his own actions. How will you answer for it at the last great day when the judge shall say, "You believed enough to go and hear about salvation; why did you not believe enough to accept it? You believed enough to quarrel for it; you would stand up for the doctrine of the gospel; and yet you yourself perished in your sin." What answer will you give, you who are *sitting there*? You will have to give some answer, so what will it be? Oh, that you would use a little common sense about your souls, and would leave the seat of the foolish for the stool of the repentant, and no more be of those who are *sitting there*.

Secondly, let us ask what was happening while these persons were *sitting there*. They had entered the room where Jesus was preaching, where crowds were listening, where miracles of mercy were being worked. They were criticizing, griping, and nitpicking, but what was happening to them all the while?

Well, first, *they were incurring responsibility*. Sirs, you cannot hear the gospel and refuse it, and yet remain as you were. You are either better or worse after hearing the gospel. It is made to you either a savor of life unto life, or else of death unto death. Remember, it will be more tolerable for Sodom and Gomorrah in the day of judgment than for Bethsaida and Chorazin, who had heard the gospel. The refusal of the gospel is a crowning crime; there is no sin like it. Does not the Word of God say so? This is no gloomy talk of mine. The Lord Jesus taught that the men of Nineveh would condemn the men of Jerusalem because they took warning and Jerusalem did not. Oh, you who have heard the gospel so long, and have been *sitting there* all the while, what a mountain of guilt rests upon you! How shall you escape? What must become of you after such base ingratitude?

> You are either better or worse after hearing the gospel.

Besides that, *they were gathering hardness of heart*. Every hour that you listen to the gospel, and bar your heart against it, you are less and less likely to admit it. The bolt that is rusted is hard to move back from its place. The path that has long been trodden by daily traffic has become hard, as though it were paved with stone; hearts that have often been crossed by the gospel become like iron beneath its tread. I fear your consciences have grown hardened by the traffic of the gospel. I know that it is so with many. The Lord forgive them. If I could have a congregation that never heard the gospel before, I would feel more hopeful than I do when I speak to you who have heard it for years. What is now likely to affect you? What fresh arguments can I bring? I can tell you some new story perhaps, but what of that? You have had too many stories already. It is not so easy a matter to retain your attention now as it once was; the voice has grown familiar, and the manner is stale to you. Can I hope that I shall now reach the hearts at which I have shot so many arrows which have all missed the mark? O God, have mercy upon those who have been *sitting there* so long!

Once again, let me remind you that those who were *sitting there* were obstructing Christ all that they could. There is a something – every preacher has felt it – there is a something in a congregation itself which affects the preacher, even as he affects the congregation. I soon feel when godly men are praying for me and crying, "O Lord, help him to preach!" I cannot tell you how it is, but so it is, that some congregations freeze me, and others set me on fire. When the doctors of the law and the Pharisees are *sitting there,* they drag us down, and we cannot do many mighty works. If my eye catches the glance of one of these ice-men, if I perceive his wretched indifference and detect his half-concealed sneer, I am weakened by it. I imagine I hear such folks saying, "We care nothing for what you say. We do not belong to those whom you can influence. We are clad in armor plates against your weapons." This chills one to the marrow. Now, this is the tendency of your conduct if you are *sitting there* – you chill the preacher, and in chilling the preacher you do boundless mischief to the congregation. Don't you know that it was said even of Jesus, *He did not do many miracles there because of their unbelief*? Even he, as man, was in a measure dependent upon those who surrounded him. When he saw their faith he healed the sick of the paralysis; and at another time, when he saw their unbelief, he looked around with indignation. It is a terrible fact that certain ones of you may be so acting as to hinder the salvation of others by your indifference to the sacred message. I believe that this is eminently the case with you who are very good people in all but the one thing needful. You do not fear God, and your very goodness works for evil. The example of a foul and rotten prodigal will not influence certain minds, for they are disgusted by its grossness, and driven to seek something better. But when young men see an excellent person like you, so moral and amiable, without religion, they gather from your example that godliness is not absolutely needful, and they take license to do without it. Thus, you who are *sitting there* may be a curse where you little suspect it; you may be encouraging others in the attempt to live without the Savior.

Yet let me not finish this topic without repeating the remark that we are glad to have these people *sitting there* rather than not coming at all. Being in the way, the Lord may meet with them. If you go where shots are flying, you may be wounded one of these days. Better to come and hear the gospel from a low motive than not to come at all. Remember Hugh Latimer's quaint story when he urged all his hearers to go and hear the gospel. He even praised that sleepless woman who had been taking sleeping medicine, but found that there was no drug strong enough to make her sleep, till at last she said, "If you would take me to the parish church I know that I could go to sleep, for I have slept there every Sunday for many years." She was taken to that place of rest and was soon at peace. "Well, well," said Latimer, "she had better come for sleep than not come at all." And so I say: even if you come here to sleep, the Lord may arouse you to seek and find the Savior. Still it is a wretched business – this *sitting there.*

Next, let us ask, What was the reason these people were *sitting there*? Why did they come to hear Jesus, and yet did not become a part of the really attentive congregation, but were hovering around the skirts of it and *sitting there*? I would not needlessly offend any of those who have come to this place at this time, but let me quietly say a few things which may be applicable to them.

In the first place, in the case of the scribes it was *self-conceit* which made them sit there. They were divided from the common throng by a sense of superiority. They said, "What have we to do with hearing Jesus of Nazareth and his message concerning the pardon of sin?" "Why," they said, "we are highly educated people, and do not need to listen to so plain a preacher. His salvation we do not want, for we are not lost." Jesus himself said, *"It is not those who are well who need a physician, but those who are sick,"* thus indicating that it was their good idea of themselves which kept them back from him. That is the reason why so many sit by. In their own opinion they are quite as good as the best, and are not in need of any great change. They are most respectable people, and they believe that they are also upright and generous. A man went out of this place one evening who was spoken to by one of our friends who happened to know him in trade, and had him in good repute. "What! have you been to hear our minister today?" The good man answered, "Yes, I am sorry to say I have." "But," said our friend, "why are you sorry?" "Why," he said, "he has turned me inside out, and spoiled my idea of myself. When I went into the tabernacle I thought I was the best man in Newington, but now I feel that my righteousness is worthless." "Oh," said the friend, "that is all right; you will come again, I am sure. The Word has come home to you, and shown you the truth; you will get comfort soon." That friend did come again, and he is here today. He takes pleasure in that very truth which turned him inside out; and he comes on purpose so that the Word of the Lord may search him, and try him, and be to him as a refiner's fire. He that is most afraid to be turned inside out is the man who most needs to undergo that process. Alas! many will not let the Word search them. They say within themselves, "That is good, very good; but it is not for me." Such are those that sit there; they sit in a corner, out of the wind of the winnowing fan. Do you not see them draw themselves up, and look very solemnly at other people, as if they would say to their neighbor, "There, you take that home! That doctrine is good for you sinners, but the preacher has no reference to me."

These people were *sitting there* because there was in them *no sense of personal need,* no perception of their own nakedness which only Christ can cover, and no sense of inward hunger which only Jesus can remove. They did not want a Savior for themselves, though they were quite willing to hear him preached to others; they did not require mercy for themselves, though they were pleased that sinners should hear of it. They could see, and therefore needed not that their eyes should be opened. They had all things, and had no poverty to plead. So it always will be in the preaching of the Word; those will hear it with gladness who perceive that they want what it presents to them, but others will take no interest in it. Conscious need inclines the ear to hear; and until the Spirit of God works this in us, we shall be as deaf as posts to the voice of love, and will continue *sitting there.*

There was also about these people *a mass of prejudice.* Their conservative tendency kept them aloof. Carried a certain distance, this tendency is good, but it may turn a man into a pillar of salt, and prevent his fleeing for his life. Having drunk the old wine, these immovable people do not desire new, because they feel sure that the old is better. Yet if the old wine is sour or musty, and the new wine is sweet and good, it is a pity to prefer the bad to the good. The old intoxicating wine of salvation by human merit, or by ceremonies, is by many preferred to our Lord's own new wine of the kingdom, namely, justification by his righteousness through faith. "Believe and live" is set aside for *the man which doeth those things shall live by them* (KJV). They prefer Sinai to Calvary, their own filthy rags to the Lord's perfect robe of righteousness. They stick to the old covenant, which is taken away, and cannot endure the everlasting covenant of grace. The prejudice of proud human nature is hard to overcome; men are not willing to search the Scriptures, and see whether they are right or not; but they stick to their inherited falsehoods.

Many are *sitting there* because of *resolute unbelief and determined self-confidence*. O friends, it is born in us by nature to believe in ourselves. What is that but clear idolatry? It is not till we are born again that we come to believe in Jesus Christ, and so to trust in the living God, and receive a living hope. May the Lord deliver us from that old, good-for-nothing confidence in self, confidence in works, confidence in outward ceremonies, and confidence in the flesh! Oh, that we might pour the old and musty wine on the ground, and taste of the new wine, crushed from the cluster by the dying Son of God; the new wine of salvation by grace, through faith, unto the glory of God! I wish to God that those who are *sitting there* on account of their conceited prejudices may be brought into the marriage feast of grace, and made willing to wear the wedding garment, and honor him who has prepared it! Prejudice is the ruin of thousands. They might be made to see, if they did not think that they saw already; they might be happy in the Lord, if their groundless conceit did not make them to be *sitting there*.

> It is born in us by nature to believe in ourselves. What is that but clear idolatry?

What shall we say of these who were *sitting there*? Just a word by way of forming an estimate of them, and then I will be done with them. Oh, that the Lord himself might deal with them by his Holy Spirit! These "sitting there" ones, these people who do not go in for the truth and faith of the gospel, but hear it, and play with it, and talk about it, and then are done with it, what shall I say of them?

Why, first they seem to me to be *wonderfully out of place when you think of the Lord who was preaching.* How could they be indifferent in his presence? He was at a white heat, and they were blocks of ice. He was all energy, and they were *sitting there.* He was spending and being spent, and they were *sitting there.* He engaged all night in prayer with his divine Father, and was now coming forth clothed with divine power to heal; and they are *sitting there.* Pretending to be doctors and teachers of the people, and therefore under great responsibility, they were yet content to be *sitting there* when Jesus was pouring out his soul. O sirs, none of us ought to be indifferent in the presence of the Christ of God. He is clad with zeal as with a cloak; how can we be lukewarm? He laid down his life for the sheep; how can we live for self? He still lives for his people, and holds back not his peace, but by his incessant pleadings he proves his everlasting interest in our cause, and for us to be *sitting there* will be horrible ingratitude! Men who have received great salvation *sitting there* while the Savior dies; or even men who are in danger of sinking at once to hell carelessly *sitting there* when the gate of mercy is set open before them by the pierced hand of Jesus! Oh, it is sadly strange! Lord, teach this foolish generation wisdom! Let them not still be *sitting there*!

It was equally unsuitable also with the condition of the rest of the congregation. See, there is such a crowd around the Lord Jesus that they are wanting to bring in a man who is paralyzed, and they cannot get him near. Nobody will make way; they are all so eager to hear and to get a blessing. At last they take the paralyzed man to the top of the roof; they actually break up the tiling; they let the man down with ropes over the heads of the people, yes, right in among the learned lawyers and the proud Pharisees. The pieces of the tiles are falling everywhere; the dust is on the doctors and the religious leaders. See how eager, how earnest, how impetuous the people are! And yet these gentlemen are *sitting there* with cold indifference! See them taking out their notebooks to jot down an expression with which they may find fault! See how they coolly observe little points in what is done! They are not moved, not they! A man is about to be healed who has long been paralyzed, and they treat it as if it were an interesting case in the hospital, around which a company of medical students gather, as to a show. How can they act in this way? Are they made of stone or iron? Common humanity might affect them, one would think; but no, they will not enter into anything that Jesus says or does; they are merely *sitting there.*

It will be an awful thing for some of you to be cast away forever, and then to remember that you sat next to people who were saved; sat next them at the very time when they heard about eternal life. How will you bear to know that these people were saved by that powerful sermon which drove even you to your knees, but you shook off the impression, grew careless, and again continued in your sin? This reflection will sting you as a serpent does when you are past hope and are driven forever from the presence of God. This will be as the worm that never dies, when you say to yourself, "I was present when Jesus by his grace renewed men's hearts. I was present when my companion heard, believed, and was saved; but I willfully refused to hear, and turned away from the only Savior." What shall I say to the husband who will have to remember that she who in this world lay in his bosom, wept for him, told him that she had found a Savior, and begged him to think of his immortal soul, and turn unto the Lord? You will remember how you hardened your heart against the blessed influence, and refused the holy tears of one you loved so well. Or is it so, that your darling child came home from the Sunday school weeping on account of sin, and you, the mother who ought to have thanked God for blessing your offspring, ridiculed your child's repentance? This is *sitting there* in a most horrible way – *sitting there* to scoff and oppose. While others are saved, you are *sitting there.* Why, if I were paralyzed today, if I were lying here and I saw the Master healing you who were sick, I think I should at least cry out as best I could, *"Jesus, Master, have mercy on [me]!"* I do exhort any of you who are unconverted to take these words out of my mouth, and with your whole heart use them in prayer. Cry, "Lord, have mercy upon me! Christ, have mercy upon me!"

I had much more to add upon this point, but time admonishes me. Let me in a few sentences speak to some who should not be among those who are *sitting there.* You that feel your soul-sickness will not be of that number. You feel your guilt; you feel your need of Christ; you are broken down today; then do not for a moment just sit there. Rise, he calls you! Press through the crowd to Jesus. Believe in him and live. May his Spirit lead you to do so at once!

Before I found the Savior, I visited nearly every place of worship in the town where I lived, but I did not find full salvation at any one of them. I believe that it was through my own ignorance. In the little Primitive Methodist chapel, when I heard Christ preached, and was bidden to look only to him, I found rest for my soul; but the reason why I found him was because his grace had made me know that I needed him. I do not suppose that the sermon which was made useful to me had anything in it more remarkable than other gospel sermons. The special point was that the Lord had prepared me to receive the gospel message. They say that the water of the Nile is very sweet. We have heard some of our fellow countrymen assert that a very little of it was too much for them, and that they never wished to drink of it again. There is no use in disputing about tastes, but surely people might agree upon the quality of water. Yet some praise this Nile water to the skies, and others call it muddy stuff. The reason why the water of the Nile is so sweet to Egyptians is that their climate is dry, and the people are thirsty, and other water is scarce. Under a burning sun a drink of water is very refreshing. To the soul that is thirsty for mercy and reconciliation and eternal life, every promise of the Lord is delightful. Nothing puts such a savor and flavor into the gospel as that work of the Holy Spirit, by which we are made to feel our great need of it.

Oh, if you have not found Christ – you that are seeking him – go to every place where Christ is preached till you do find him. If you do not get the heavenly blessing in one place, go to another; do not stop where there is no blessing merely because it is your regular place of assembly. You need bread, and if one baker has not got it, go to another. Seek after the Savior as men dig for gold or search for diamonds. I have heard of a man who had long attended one of the churches in Scotland, and as he did not get any good from it, he went off to listen to certain irregular preaching, and there he found peace with God. The old minister warned him of his wickedness in being away from the church and said, in Scotch, what I must put into English, "Donald, you should not have gone to hear that man; he is not of the old church." "Well," said Donald, "but I wanted a blessing, and I felt I must go anywhere to get it." "Well," said the minister, "Donald, you should have waited at the pool, like the man in the gospels, till the water was stirred." "Well, sir," said the man, "but you see that man saw that the water was sometimes stirred, and though he did not get in himself, yet he knew that others stepped in and were healed, and that encouraged him to wait a little longer, in the hope that his turn might yet come. But I have lain at your pool these forty years, and I never saw the water stirred, neither did anybody get healed in it; and so I thought it was time for me to look somewhere else." Indeed it was. We cannot afford to be lost for the sake of churches or chapels. O my hearer, do seek the Lord with all your heart, and seek him on and on till you find him. Do not be a mere *sitting-there* one any longer; but obey the call which bids you to draw near. Be not content to sit in any pretended house of prayer where prayer is not heard and souls are never saved. Do not let down your bucket into any more dry wells. Go where Jesus is. Examine all the denominations, and do not stay at any until you can say, "I have found Jesus." If he is not preached in one place, hasten to another. Keep your ears and your heart open. *Seek the Lord while He may be found; call upon Him while He is near.* Do not fall into the habit of going to a place because you always went there, and always planned to go there. Why, some of you have almost grown into your seats, and are as wooden as that which bears you up. O mere *sitting-there* one, I implore you, do not remain in this wretched case. May your cry to the Lord be at this moment, "Give me Christ, or else I die!"

May God help you to make your hearing a reality, your sitting under the gospel a true reception of it!

You who are in great sorrow, I do not think it possible that you can be altogether sitting-there ones! You have been disappointed in love; you have met with a world of trouble, or else you have been the round of amusements, and have seen no end of merriment, but you are sick of it, and weary of the world and of yourself. You feel that you might as well try to fill your belly with wind as fill your soul with the world's amusements, and you have come here jaded and nauseated. Your heart is laboring and heavy-laden, and you yearn for rest. Come and try my Master. He invites you; he pleads with you to come. He cries to you, *"Come to Me, all who are weary and heavy-laden, and I will give you rest."* He means what he says. You have labored enough for the world, and its wages are not worth having. Come now to him whose gift is eternal life. May his Holy Spirit lead you to come at once and delay no longer! You are one of those who cannot afford to be *sitting there,* for sin curses you, death threatens you, and eternal wrath pursues you. I know how it will be with you unless grace prevents it: you will go home, and the sermon will be over, and many of you will still be sitting-there ones, for you will shake off conviction and be careless still. Remember, I have warned you. Will you despise the warning?

A poor fallen woman is here at this time, worn out with her crimes. Does she desire to know the Savior? Let her confess her sin and forsake it, then she will not be *sitting there.* There is a brokenhearted youth here who begins to reap the wild oats he has sown. Will he sit there? Does he wish to know how his heart can be changed, his sin forgiven, his soul comforted? Let him arise and go to his father, and no longer be *sitting there.*

And so I close with a full and free gospel call. Come, and welcome, you who willingly would come to Jesus. Come just now, with all your sins around you, and behold *the Lamb of God, who takes away the sin of the world.* If you want to know what it is to come to him, know that it is to *trust him.* Go to your chamber, and look up and say, "Jesus, I cannot see you, but you are wherever there is a broken heart. Behold, I seek you; reveal yourself to me. I trust you to forgive me, and to renew me." Jesus will not refuse you, for he casts out none that come to him. I said "Go home," but I will alter that word. Keep your seats, and seek him where you are and as you are. Before you leave this place, commit yourselves into that dear hand which was pierced for the guilty, and is always ready to grasp a sinner. As the pearl-fisher is happy when he finds a handful of pearls, so is Jesus happy when he lays hold on poor sinners, and takes them to be his own. Commit your souls to his keeping. Trust him wholly! Trust him only! Trust him now. Today escape for your lives, and find refuge in the Rock of Ages. Jesus cries, *"Turn to Me and be saved, all the ends of the earth."* O Lord, lead all these sinners to look to Jesus by your Holy Spirit for your mercy's sake! Amen.

Chapter 9

First Forgiveness, Then Healing

Seeing their faith, He said, "Friend, your sins are forgiven you." (Luke 5:20)

I have read to you now the narrative of the healing of the paralyzed man. I spoke last about the Pharisees and the doctors of the law who were *sitting there.* I tried to represent the position of many in our congregations who are just *sitting there.* I preached to the outsiders of the congregation on the diverse reasons which led to this *sitting there.* I must confess that I did not reckon on so large a blessing as I have already seen as the result of that sermon. When I came here on Monday afternoon, that being Pentecost Monday, when everybody is supposed to take a holiday, I was surprised, on my arrival at about three o'clock, by a friend running up to me and saying, "We are glad you have come, sir, for there is a room full already." There was quite a nice number of friends who had come forward from the congregation, and who one after another said, "We cannot be *sitting there* any longer; we feel that we cannot remain among the sitting-there ones, but that we must come in and partake of the gospel feast, and join ourselves with the disciples of our Lord and Savior Jesus Christ."

This blessed result of my sermon has set the bells of my heart ringing all week, and I have felt deeply thankful to God for it. I said to myself that as I had taken one arrow which had sped so well out of that quiver,

I would take another. Having spoken to those who are *sitting there*, I think I will now speak to those who are not just *sitting there*, but who indeed are the principal persons in the congregation, namely, those who are sick and sorry and who need the Savior. For this paralyzed man, who was let down by ropes through the ceiling, was the most remarkable person in that congregation. We may readily forget those Pharisees and learned legal gentlemen; but we can never forget this man to whom, as soon as they *let him down through the tiles with his stretcher, into the middle of the crowd, in front of Jesus,* the Savior said, *"Friend, your sins are forgiven you."* I trust that, at this time, there are some present in this audience who are not *sitting there,* but who are already praying, *"God, be merciful to me!"* and some whose prayers are rising to heaven in accents like these: *"Lord, help me!" "Lord, save me, or I perish!"* You are the principal persons in the congregation both to the preacher and to the preacher's Master. He cares more about you, and about what shall take place in you, than about any of the Pharisees or doctors of the law who may be *sitting there.* God is glorified in scattering his miracles of mercy where there is the greatest need of them. Our Lord Jesus, when the poor man was let down by his four friends through the ceiling, said to him at once, *"Friend, your sins are forgiven you."* Matthew puts our Savior's words thus: *"Take courage, son; your sins are forgiven"*; while Mark's record is, *"Son, your sins are forgiven."* Well, Jesus may have uttered all of these words, and all the different versions of the story may be correct, for it is not every man's ear that catches the whole of every sentence that is spoken, and we may be glad that there are three Gospel writers who have recorded what the Savior said. There is no real difference in the sense, and the difference in the words may only show that Jesus said all three sentences.

I am going, on this occasion, to talk a little about this man, first, *before his forgiveness;* next, a little more *about his forgiveness itself;* and then a little about what followed *after his forgiveness.*

First, then, let us think of this man before his forgiveness. We are not told much about him. If I indulge in imagination a little, you will take it for what it is worth. This man, it seems to me, first, had *faith which went out towards the Lord Jesus.* Evidently, as I read the narrative, he had been suddenly paralyzed. This affliction usually comes suddenly;

men who have been about their business, as active as usual, have been in a moment struck down with paralysis. This man appears to have been completely paralyzed, so as to have been unable to move; and, as he lay in that helpless state, he heard that Jesus of Nazareth had come to the city, and he believed that Jesus of Nazareth was able to heal even him. It does not strike me that his friends would have brought him to Christ unless at his own request; the most rational explanation of the whole proceeding seems to me to be this: he believed in Jesus as able to heal him, and he continued to cry out earnestly, and to pray that he might somehow or other be taken into Christ's presence. He could not stir hand or foot, but he had friends, and he begged those friends to take him to Jesus.

Well now, there never was a soul yet that had faith in Christ but what Christ revealed himself more fully in the way of love to that soul. If you know that you cannot save yourself, if you believe that Christ can save you, and if your one anxiety is to be laid at his feet, that he may look upon you and save you, he will assuredly accept you. *"The one who comes to Me,"* says he, *"I will certainly not cast out."* Whether he comes running, or walking, or creeping, or carried by four, so long as he comes, Christ will accept him; and if his faith be but as a grain of mustard seed, our Lord Jesus will not let it die. If there be but a smoldering faith, he will not quench the smoking flax. Do you believe this? If you do, let it cheer you and comfort you. There is something that is well with your soul already. It was better to be paralyzed and to have faith in Christ than to be walking upright like the Pharisees and lawyers who had no faith in him. The apparent wretchedness of your condition is not the real wretchedness of it; it may even turn out to be the blessedness and the hopefulness of it. If you believe in Jesus, I care not how far you have fallen, nor how great is your inability; if you believe in Jesus, you are brought into contact with omnipotence, and that omnipotence will heal you.

> It was better to be paralyzed and to have faith in Christ than to be walking upright like the Pharisees and lawyers who had no faith in him.

This man, I believe, further, thought that Christ could heal him, but *he began to feel his great sinfulness.* I am certain that he did, because Jesus never does forgive where there is no repentance. There was never yet the decree, *"Your sins are forgiven you,"* until first there was a consciousness of sin and a confession of sin. *If we confess our sins, He is faithful and righteous to forgive us our sins and to cleanse us from all unrighteousness.* This man, lying there paralyzed, wept at the thought of his past life, his omissions and his commissions, his falling short and his transgressions, and his heart was heavy within him. He seemed to say to his friends, "Get me somehow to the great Prophet; get me within sight of this wonderful Savior. Oh, get me within touch of him, that I may be restored, that I may have this great load, which presses me down so sorely, taken off my heart! Worse to me even than the paralysis is this awful sense of sin. Take me, oh, take me into the presence of this Messiah, this Son of David, that he may have mercy upon me!" That I conceive to have been his condition before the word of pardon was spoken to him.

Next, being hopeful himself, *he inspired those around him with hope.* Of course, they would not have taken him to Christ if they had not had some sort of belief that possibly he might be healed. It is wonderful what sick people can do even when they can do nothing; how, when they seem to be utterly powerless, they find a strength in feebleness. Their very helplessness seems to be a plea where there is anything of generosity left in the heart of those who are near them. So this man pleaded, "I believe Jesus will heal me, I believe he will have mercy upon me; get me to him, do get me to him."

They resolved to do it if they could, and *he was willing to be carried to Christ.* Four stout, stalwart men said, "Yes, we will get you to him somehow, though it is a difficult task, for the house is small, the room is crowded, and there is sure to be a crowd at the door." "But oh!" said the poor man, "try to do it, for it is my only hope. If I could but get where Jesus could see me, he would look on me and save me. Oh, get me to him, get me to him!" The paralyzed man would make no dispute about how it was to be done, so they carried him to the door of the house, and then they said to the people crowding around, "Make way for this poor paralyzed man," and he would say, "I pray you, friends and neighbors, make way," but they could not. Perhaps they too had their friends who wanted to be healed, or they themselves had an anxiety to hear the great Teacher, so they pushed and pressed to get as near him as they could. You see, those quibbling Pharisees and doctors of the law had got in first, and they blocked up the road. They are always in a poor sinner's way. What must be done? The poor man's bearers would have abandoned the task, I think, but he said, "No, do not give up trying to get me in; it is my only hope. Oh, get me to him! Get me near him!"

So next, the man was *willing to be lowered into the presence of Christ.* There was no other way but to go up those stairs outside the house, and to take him to the top of the roof; and he, not fearing as many would have done, said, "Alas, break it up, and let me down." These four men, belonging to a fishing town, were adept in the use of ropes, and they soon had their tackle ready, and they broke a way through the roof. As I told you in the reading, I always feel pleased at the idea of the dust and the debris of the roof coming down upon the heads of the Pharisees and doctors of the law. It always delights me to think that those gentlemen would have dust on their heads for once; since they were there, they were bound to have a little of it. Of course, when these gentlemen come to a place of worship, one feels bound to be respectful to them; but if they come at an untimely hour, when there is any rough work going on, one does not feel any particular regret. If, when souls are being saved, these gentlemen would have their corns trodden upon, we do not even ask their pardon, or make any apology. Such a work as Christ had to do could not stand still for the sake of reverence to the learned doctors of the law; so the roof was broken up, and this man, though paralyzed, was not afraid to be let down. It is probable that there were no outcries from him when they began to let him down. I think, if it had been my case, I might have been afraid that one rope would go a little faster than the other. But no, the man keeps still in his paralysis and courage mingled, till down drops the stretcher right in front of the Savior.

There he lies upon his stretcher, on the floor of the house, *right in front of the Savior's eyes,* exactly where he wanted to be. Here I address myself to some who would give all that they have if they could but be brought under the eye of Jesus. The one thought of such a sufferer is, "Oh, that I could be near him! Oh, that I could be near him! Oh, that he would look on me, and cure my helplessness, and pardon my sin!" What a wonderful picture this scene would make! The crowd is obliged to make way, or else they will have to bear the man and his bed on their heads; so he is dropped down into their midst, and there he lies. The great Preacher has been preaching, and he stops. There is an interruption which is indeed no interruption to him. His conversation is but broken off for a minute, to be illustrated with engravings that men may see in later years, that what they have heard is but the text, and that the miracle which is now to be worked shall be the engraving which shall convey the Teacher's wonderful meaning to all eyes. So the poor paralyzed man lies there before the Savior.

Is that where you desire to lie, dear friend? In your deadly sorrow and sin and weakness, do you wish to lie at the Savior's feet? That is where I want you to lie; and if you will to lie there, that is where you do lie. The Lord Jesus is in the midst of us tonight, and you can at once cast yourself down before him. Do so, tell him about your paralysis; tell him how sick you are, how sinful you are. No, you need not speak so that I can hear you; his ears will hear the whisper of your soul. Your heartbeats will be vocal to his heart, and he will note all you say or feel in your inmost soul. Just lie before Jesus; and as you lie there, what are you to do? This man did not speak a word; but, as I believe, he lay there repenting that he should never have lived as he had done, mourning that he should never have wasted his life and misspent his time. I think, too, that he lay there believing, looking at that wondrous Man, and believing that all power was in him, and that he had only to speak the word, and the sinner would be at once forgiven. So he lay there, in the presence of Jesus, hoping and expecting forgiveness and healing.

Now, in the second place, we are to consider the forgiveness itself. This poor paralyzed man had not lain there long before the blessed Master broke the silence and said to him, *"Friend, your sins are forgiven you."* I think that the four men up on the roof, looking down to see what would happen to their friend, would hardly understand what that sentence meant. They had brought him to Jesus because he was paralyzed, but he had wanted to come first of all because he was a sinner. He did desire to have his paralysis cured, but secretly in his soul there was another matter which they might not have understood if he had tried to interpret it to them. It was his sin that was his heaviest burden; and the Savior, the great Thought-reader, knew all about that sin, so he did not first say to him, *"Get up and walk,"* but he began by saying, *"Friend, your sins are forgiven you."*

Observe that *the pardon of sin came in a single sentence.* He spoke, and it was done. Jesus said, *"Friend, your sins are forgiven you,"* and they were forgiven him. Christ's voice had such almighty power about it that it needed not to utter many words. There was no long lesson for the poor man to repeat, there was no intricate problem for him to work out in his mind. The Master said all that was required in that one sentence: *"Friend, your sins are forgiven you."* The burden of a sinner does not need two ticks of the clock for it to be removed; swifter than the lightning's flash is that verdict of forgiveness which comes from the eternal lips, when the sinner lies hoping, believing, and repenting at the feet of Jesus. It was a single sentence which declared that the man was forgiven.

Next, remember that it was *a sentence from One who was authorized to absolve.* He was sent by the Father on purpose to forgive sin; and do not imagine that he has now lost his authorization to forgive, for *He is the one whom God exalted to His right hand as a Prince and a Savior, to grant repentance to Israel, and forgiveness of sins.* Jesus is appointed as High Priest on purpose that he may stand on God's behalf, and declare the remission of sin. What Jesus said was spoken with divine authority. It is vain for a priest to say to a sinner, "I absolve you." What can he do in such a case? He, or any other man who does not call himself a priest, may speak in his Master's name and say to the repentant one, "If you do sincerely repent, if you truly believe, I know you are forgiven, and I comfort you with the assurance of this forgiveness." So far, so good; but the Master alone can really give the pardon; it must come from him who has power upon earth to forgive sins.

> The burden of a sinner does not need two ticks of the clock for it to be removed.

Now, my hearer, have you never been forgiven? Are you in your pew, and yet lying at that dear Master's feet, and do you desire above all things that he should say to you, *"Your sins are forgiven you"*? And do you believe that he can say it, and will you accept it from him as being by divine authority? If so, I think he says it to you, for in his own Word he declares that they who believe in him are forgiven. He says to each one of those who are repentant, and believe in his grace, *"Your sins are forgiven you."* Take the pardon and go your way. Do as Martin Luther did in the days of his dark distress when a brother monk said to him, "Do you not believe in the Creed, and do you not say, 'I believe in the forgiveness of sins'? Now believe in the forgiveness of sins for yourself." Trust Christ's Word, and you will be believing what is absolutely true. Trust it, take the comfort of it, and go your way. It is thus that Jesus Christ, by the preaching of the gospel, and by the revealed Word of God, says authoritatively to each repentant one, *"Friend, your sins are forgiven you."*

Further observe that this sentence, although it was but one, and was so short, yet was *wonderfully comprehensive: "Friend, your sins are forgiven you."* Not one sin alone, nor many sins, but all your sins are forgiven you. When you go into particulars, you are apt to leave something out; therefore, the declaration is made all-inclusive, there are no particulars given. *"Your sins are forgiven you."* Sins against the holy God? Sins against a righteous law? Sins against the gospel? Sins against the light of nature? Sins of this kind and sins of that kind? No, there is no counting. *The blood of Jesus His Son cleanses us from all sin.* *"Friend, your sins are forgiven you."* Murder, adultery, theft, fornication, blasphemy? Yes, in a word, *"any sin and blasphemy shall be forgiven people."* *"Friend, your sins are forgiven you."* What a far-reaching pardon it is! *"Your sins are forgiven you."* At one sudden sweep of the divine wave of mercy they are all washed away. There is no such thing as a half-pardon of sin. I heard someone talking the other day about original sin being forgiven and the other sins being left. But sin is a whole, it goes or it stays altogether; it cannot be broken up into pieces, it is all there or it is not there at all, and it is not there if you believe in Jesus. This blessed and comprehensive sentence sets free from every jot and taint and stain of guilt: *"Friend, your sins are forgiven you."*

Observe, also, that *this sentence contained no conditions;* and the blessed gospel, speaking to every repenting and believing sinner, gives him absolute forgiveness. Behold, the tally is destroyed, the record of your debt is nailed to the cross; and as for your sins, they are like the Egyptians when the Red Sea swallowed them up – the depths have covered them, and there is not one of them left, however great or many they may have been. If you are now a believer in the Lord Jesus Christ, he says to you now by his Word, *"Friend, your sins are forgiven you."* I pray the blessed Master by his Holy Spirit to make his Word come home with power to many here. Oh, that those dear lips, which are as lilies dropping sweet-smelling myrrh, would themselves speak to you! Oh, that those wounds of his, which are mouths that preach pardon to sinners, might speak to you and say, *"Your sins are forgiven you"*! There is no mouth that speaks pardon like that gash in his side, out of which his very heart speaks, as he says, "I have loved you, and given myself to death for you. Your sins I have borne on the tree, and put them away once for all. *Friend, your sins are forgiven you."* Oh, that Jesus himself might thus speak effectually to many of you!

But note that *this sentence sufficed the receiver.* When the Savior afterwards raised this paralyzed man to health and strength, he did not do it to let the man himself know that his sins were forgiven. The man knew that already, and did not need any more evidence of it; but Jesus did it for another reason. To the scribes and Pharisees he said, *"But, so that you may know that the Son of Man has authority on earth to forgive sins,"—He said to the paralytic—"I say to you, get up, and pick up your stretcher and go home."* Those unbelieving men had not evidence enough that Christ could forgive, but he to whom Christ spoke wanted no further proof than the power of that voice in his own conscience; and if he shall speak to you, my hearer, you will not need any books about the evidences of Scripture, the proofs of inspiration, and so on. To you, this indisputable miracle of pardoned sin shall stand forever as a holy memorial of God's mighty grace. It shall be unto you for a sign, for an everlasting sign that shall not be cut off, that God has pardoned you and spoken peace to your soul; and this God shall be your God forever and ever. To every soul that is in a similar case to that of the poor paralyzed man lying repenting and believing at the feet of Jesus, his Word gives the comfortable assurance, "Believe, and your sins, which are many, are all forgiven you." Believe it, and go your way in peace.

Now I close by noticing, thirdly, what followed after this man's forgiveness. He was absolutely, irreversibly, eternally forgiven; for *the gifts and the calling of God are irrevocable.* He never plays fast and loose with men; he never issues a pardon from his throne and afterwards executes the pardoned sinner. His pardon covers all that may come afterwards as well as all that has gone before. But what happened to this man?

I believe that, first, there was *an inward peace that stole over his soul.* If you could have looked into the face of that paralyzed man, while still paralyzed, and lying there on that stretcher, you would have seen a wonderful transformation. Did you ever see a face transfigured? If you are a soul winner, you have often seen it. All human faces are not beautiful, some are absolutely repulsive; the countenances of some who have lived long in sin are dreadful to look upon. Yet I have noticed faces that at first I could scarcely endure, but when the persons have been gently led to the Savior, and they have perceived the love of God for them, and have at last believed, and felt within their soul the kiss of peace, why, they have looked positively beautiful! I would have liked to have had them photographed, only it was too sacred a thing. Speaking of a person's facial features, the grace of God is such an eternal beautifier that the face from which you would have turned away in disgust, and said, "There can be no good thing behind that countenance," is absolutely changed by the Lord's mighty working. I say not that a single feature may be altered; the person may be the same in feature, but oh! what a marvelous difference there is in the expression of the whole contour of the countenance when free grace and dying love have cast their magic spell over the spirit, and the Holy Spirit has made the dead to live, and the person has been born again in Christ Jesus. Well, that change took place in this man's mind; I am sure it did when Jesus said to him, *"Your sins are forgiven you."* He was in no hurry to be raised from his paralyzed state; he does not appear to have said a word, and those scribes and Pharisees looked on with their mean countenances, but they did not frighten him; he lay quite still, and was in no haste even for the Master's next blessing. It would come in due time, he knew it would, and he was of good cheer, for had not Jesus said to him, *"Take courage, son; your sins are forgiven"*?

But next followed *the man's immediate cure.* The Master said to him, *"Get up, and pick up your stretcher and go home."* Our blessed Master was accustomed to preaching the gospel in a way which I have heard some friends greatly question. They tell us that we ought not to bid men to believe and repent, because they cannot. There are two parties on opposite sides of this question. One says, "If you tell a man to believe and repent, that proves that he can," which I do not believe; and others say, "If they cannot repent, you ought not to exhort them to do so," which also I do not believe. Though I know them to be as helpless as that poor paralyzed man, unable to lift hand or foot, yet in the Master's name we do say, as the Master was accustomed to saying, *"Get up, and pick up your stretcher and go home."* "Oh!" says one, "I could not say that to an unregenerate man." Do not do it, brother, if you cannot do it; go home, and go to bed, for what is the use of you for such work? The man who can speak miracles is the one who is needed, and the man who can speak as his Master has bidden him to speak. Surely, the faith does not lie in believing that the man can himself do what he is bidden to do; the faith lies in believing that Christ can do it, and therefore, speaking in Christ's name, we say to the sinner just as the Lord Jesus did to the man with the withered hand, *"Stretch out your hand,"* and he does so. Look at Ezekiel speaking to the dry bones in the valley. "Ezekiel, do you believe that these dry bones can live?" "Not I," says he. "I know that they are dead." The Lord says to him, "Ezekiel, *prophesy over these bones!*" How can he do it? It would be inconsistent with what he said just now. "I have nothing to do with that," says he. "I was sent by the Lord to do it, and I do it in the name of God." That which may seem perfectly inconsistent with your reason is quite consistent when faith brings in the supernatural element with which God moves those to whom he gives the commission to preach the gospel in his name.

> The faith does not lie in believing that the man can himself do what he is bidden to do; the faith lies in believing that Christ can do it.

The Savior said to this man, *"Get up, and pick up your stretcher and go home."* Now observe *his precise obedience. Immediately he got up before them.* The tendency of a paralyzed person is to be paralyzed in will. There are some persons, no doubt, who have ailments that can easily be cured if they believe they can be cured, because there is not much the matter with them after all; but this man was completely paralyzed, yet he so fully believed in Christ that he *got up* and stood before the Master. Then Jesus said, *"Pick up your stretcher."* I think I see him undo those four ropes, and quickly he shoulders his stretcher. "Walk," says the Master, and he walks. *"Go home,"* says the Master. He might have stopped and said, "No, Lord. Do let me stay and hear the sermon out"; but no, not a word did he say about it, but off he went to his home.

Oh, that all were as obedient to Christ as this man was, that having the simplicity of faith, they would render the fullest obedience! But thus it often is that the very chief of sinners, when pardon is given to them, have given to them at the same time a tender conscience, a willing mind, and a yielding spirit. *"Whatever He says to you, do it,"* said Jesus' mother to the servants at Cana of Galilee; and that is good advice for you. If Christ has healed you, obey him, obey him at once, obey him exactly, and obey him in everything, be it little or be it great. If some say it is nonessential, remember that what is not essential to salvation may be essential to obedience. Do it if Jesus commanded it. Do it whether it appears to you to be essential or not. That is not a question for you to ask, that is a heartless, loveless question. He has healed you, do what he bids you, as he bids you, when he bids you, and raise no question about it. Take up your stretcher and go to your home, if so he bids you. Or, if he puts it to you, *"He who has believed and has been baptized shall be saved,"* then believe and be baptized. Be obedient unto him who deserves to be obeyed.

Now, lastly, this man, it is said, *immediately he got up before them, and picked up what he had been lying on, and went home glorifying God.* I think I hear what he said. "Glory!" he cried. "Glory be to God!" He felt so glad, so happy, that he took up his stretcher before them all, and as he walked along he glorified God; and would not you have done the same if you had been paralyzed and had been restored as he had been? And will you not do so? If you have been sin-bound, and Christ has set you free, surely you will take the earliest opportunity of telling others what Jesus has done for you, and you will seek to glorify his name. I did not wonder when a brother lately said to me, "I have been spending all the morning in the workshop telling the men that I have found the Savior," and one, last Sunday, turned to his wife in this tabernacle and said, "I am saved!" She said to him, "Don't disturb the worship," but I almost wish he had done so. What a mercy it is to be saved! Salvation puts a new sun in our sky, and a new joy in our hearts. Believe on Jesus, and this salvation is yours. God grant that it may be, for his dear Son's sake! Amen.

Chapter 10

May I?

"If I may" (Matthew 9:21 KJV)

The woman in the narrative was fully persuaded that if she did but touch our Lord's garment she would be made whole. What she had heard and seen concerning Jesus made her sure of his superabundant power to heal the sick. A touch would do it, yes, even a touch of his clothes. Her one and only question was, Might she touch him? Could she touch him? She would surely be healed if she could touch him, but was this allowable? Was this possible? I know that multitudes of sin-sick men and women are vexed with this same question. Oh, that I could help them over the difficulty! May the Holy Spirit, the Comforter, aid me!

This poor diseased woman did not utter this *"if"* of hers with her lips. Perhaps if she had, it might not have troubled her so much; for a silent doubt usually eats right into the heart. You have heard of the Spartan boy who had hidden a fox in his bosom, and allowed it to eat into his vitals before he would admit to it. Beware of having a doubt hidden away in your heart, gnawing and tearing. If you are even now suffering from "If I may, if I may," reveal the trouble to some tender Christian friend and you may soon escape from it.

But the sufferer now before us had the courage to put the question to a practical issue; she tested herself as to whether she might or not. She had the good sense, the grace-given wisdom, not to wait until she had solved that question in her mind, but she went and solved it, as a matter of fact, whether she might or not. She went and actually touched the hem of the garment of the Savior, and she was made perfectly whole. Oh, that those I am now addressing would have the bravery and the earnestness to do the same! Oh, that they would put the disturbing question to a practical test at once! There can be but one result; for as many as touched him were made perfectly whole. Now, I know that souls are going to be saved tonight. Who they are I cannot tell; but some are certain to come to the Savior and this night to be made perfectly whole. I know it because we prayed an hour ago for it downstairs, many of us, and we felt the assurance that we were heard. My dear son, in praying just now, I am sure felt a very remarkable liberty at the mercy seat, and the witness of the Spirit within that he was heard. The Lord has heard the petitions which we have presented in the name of Jesus. You are going to be saved. I wish to God that every unconverted person here would lean forward and say, "May it be *I*. God grant that salvation may come to *me*." I am going, therefore, in the simplest way possible, without any attempt at a sermon, to try to talk so as to meet this burning question which lies within, festering and irritating many an earnest heart – this doubtful inquiry: *"If I may."*

You know, many of you, who Jesus is, and you believe him to be the Son of God, the Savior of men. You are sure that *He is able also to save forever those who draw near to God through Him.* You have no doubt about those eternal truths which surround his Godhead, his birth, his life, his death, his resurrection, and his second coming. The doubt is concerning yourself personally – "If I may be a partaker of this salvation." You feel quite certain that faith in Jesus Christ will save anyone – will save you if you exercise it. You have no doubt about the doctrine of justification by faith. You have learned it, and you have received it as a matter beyond all dispute, that he who believes in him has everlasting life; and you know that he who comes to him he *will certainly not cast out.* You know the remedy, and believe in its effectualness; but then comes the doubt – may I be healed by it? At the back of your belief in faith hides the gloomy thought, "May I believe? May I trust? I see the door is open and many are entering. May I? I see that there is washing from the worst of sins in the sacred fountain. Many are being cleansed.

May I wash and be clean?" Without formulating a doubt so as to express it, it comes up in all sorts of ways, and robs you of all comfort and, indeed, of all hope. When a sermon is preached it is like when one sets a table out with all manner of dainties, and you look at it, but do not feel that you have any right to sit down and partake. This is a wretched delusion. Its result will be deadly unless you are delivered from it. Like a leech it preys upon you, croaking evermore. When you see the brooks flowing with their sparkling streams, and you are thirsty, does there arise the thought in your heart that you are not permitted to drink? If so, you are out of your mind; you talk and think like one bereft of reason. Yet many are in this state spiritually. This doubting your liberty to come to Jesus is a very wretched business; it mars and spoils your reading and your hearing and your attempts to pray; and you will never get any comfort until this question has been answered in your heart once for all: "May I?"

> **This doubting your liberty to come to Jesus is a very wretched business.**

Our Authorized Version may not be exactly correct in this passage; but I do not care whether it is or not, so far as my address is concerned, for it does not depend upon the accuracy of a text. I am quite satisfied to preach from it tonight; but there is another translation in the Authorized King James Version, which I dare say is more accurate. I will preach from that when I am done with the first. This shall be our subject – *"If I may"*; or first, *"if I may be allowed"*; secondly, *"if I may be enabled"*; thirdly, *"if I do."* This last is the Revised Version: *If I do but touch his garment, I shall be whole.*

First, take it as we have got it here: "If I may be allowed, or permitted, to touch the hem of his garment, I shall be made whole." That is your difficulty, is it not? – whether you have liberty and warrant to come and trust Christ – whether you, such a sinner as you are, are permitted to rest your soul upon his great atonement and his finished work. Let me reason with you a little.

In the first place, you are quite sure of this – that *there is nothing to forbid your coming and resting your guilty soul upon Christ.* I shall defy you, if you will read all the Old and New Testaments through, to put your finger upon a single verse in which God has said that you may not come and put your trust in Christ. Perhaps you will reply that you do not expect to read it in the Bible, but God may have said it somewhere where it is not recorded. Well, I answer you there; for he says, *I have not spoken in secret, in a dark place of the earth: I said not unto the seed of Jacob, Seek ye me in vain* (KJV). Now, he has bidden you over and over again to seek his face, but he has never said that you shall seek his face in vain. Dismiss that thought. Again I return to what I have said: there is nothing in the Scripture that refuses you permission to come and rest your soul once for all upon Christ. It is written, "*Let the one who wishes take the water of life without cost.*" Does that exclude you? It is written, "*Everyone who calls on the name of the Lord will be saved.*" Does that shut you out? No; it includes you, it invites you, it encourages you. And I come again to what I have said – that nowhere in the Word of God is it written that you will be cast out if you come, or that Jesus Christ will not remove your burden of sin if you come and lay it at his feet.

Ah, no; a thousand passages of Scripture welcome you, but not one stands with a drawn sword to keep you back from the tree of life. Our heavenly Father sets his angels at the gates of his house to welcome all comers; but there are no dogs to bark at poor beggars, nor so much as a notice that trespassers must beware. Come, and welcome. There is none to say to you, "No."

Further, do you not think that *the very nature of the Lord Jesus Christ should forbid your raising a doubt about your being permitted to come and touch his garment's hem*? Surely, if anyone were to paint the Lord Jesus Christ as an ascetic, repelling with lofty pride the humbler folk who had never reached his dignity of consecration – if any were to paint him as a Pharisee driving off publicans and sinners, or as an iceberg of righteousness chilling the sinful, it would be a foul slander upon his divine character. If anyone were to say that Jesus Christ is exacting – that he will not receive to himself the guilty just as they are, but requires a great deal of them, and will only welcome to himself those who are, like himself, good, and true, and excellent, that would not be truth but the direct opposite of it; for, "*This man receives sinners and eats with them*" was thrown in his face when he lived here below; and what the prophet said of him was most certainly true, if anything was ever true: "*A bruised reed He will not break and a dimly burning wick He will not extinguish.*" Little children are wonderful judges of character;

they know intuitively who is kind. And so are loving women. They do not go through the processes of reasoning, but they come to a conclusion very soon as to a man's personal character. Now, the children came and climbed onto our Redeemer's knee, and the mothers brought their infants for his blessing. How can you dream that he will repel *you*? The women wept and bemoaned him; whoever might refuse him they pitied him, and therefore I am sure that he is not hard to move. Therefore I want you to feel sure of this – that there is nothing in the Savior's character which can for a moment lead him to discard you and drive you from his presence. Those who know him best will say that it is impossible for him ever to refuse the poor and needy. Not a blind man could cry to him without receiving sight, nor a hungry man look to him without being fed. He was touched with a feeling of our infirmities – the most gentle, and loving, and tender of all that ever dwelt upon this earth. I pray you, then, take it for granted that you may come boldly to him without fear of a rebuff. If he has power to heal you when you touch him, rest assured that you may touch him. You may believe, there is no question; for Jesus is too loving to refuse you. It will give the Lord Jesus joy to receive you. It is not possible that he should say no to you; it is not in his nature to reject you from his presence.

> It is not possible that he should say no to you; it is not in his nature to reject you from his presence.

Will you think, yet again, of *the fullness of Christ's power to save,* and make a little argument for it? Well now, you often judge a man's willingness to help by the power that he has. When a person has little to give he is bound to be economical in his giving. He must look at every penny before he gives it, if he has so few pence to spare. But when a nobleman has no limit to his estate you feel sure that he will freely give if his heart is generous and tender. The blessed Lord is so full of healing power that he cannot need to stop himself as to the miracles of healing he shall work; and he must be, according to the goodness of his nature, delighted to overflow, glad to communicate to those who come. You know if a city is distressed by lack of water, the corporation will send out an order that only so much may be used, and there is a stoppage of public baths and factories, because there is a scarcity of the precious fluid. But if you go along the Thames when we have had a rainy season, you laugh at the notion of a short supply and economical rules. If a dog wants to drink from a river, nobody ever questions his right to do so. He comes down to the water and he laps, and, what is more, he runs right into it, regardless of those who may have to drink after him. Look at the cattle, how they stand knee-deep in the stream and drink, and drink again; and nobody ever says, as he goes up the Thames, that those poor London people will run short of water because the dogs and the cattle are drinking it up before it gets down to London. No, it never enters our head to petition the conservators to restrain the dogs and the cows, for there is so much water that there must be full liberty for everyone to drink to the full. Your question is, "May I? May I?" I answer that question by this: there is nothing to forbid you; there is everything in the nature of Christ to encourage you; and there is such a fullness of mercy in him that you cannot think that he can have the slightest motive for withholding his infinite grace.

Moreover, suppose you come to Christ as this woman came, and touch the hem of his garment – *you will not injure him*. You ought to hesitate in getting good for yourself if you would injure the person through whom you obtain that good. But you will not injure the Lord Jesus Christ. He perceived that virtue had gone out of him, but he did not perceive it by any pain he felt; rather do I believe that he perceived it by the pleasure which it caused him. Something gave him unusual joy. A faith-touch had reached him through his clothes, and he rejoiced to respond by imparting healing virtue from himself. You will not defile my Lord, O sinner, if you bring him all your sin. He will not have to die again to put away your fresh burden of transgression. He will not have to shed one drop of blood to make atonement for your multiplied sin; the one sacrifice on Calvary anticipated all possible guiltiness. If you will come just as you are, he will not have to leave heaven again, and be born again on earth, and live another sorrowful life in order to save you. He will not need to wear another crown of thorns, or bear another wound in his hands, or feet, or side. He has done all his atoning work; do you not remember his victorious cry – *"It is finished"*? You cannot injure him though all your injurious thoughts, and words, and speeches be laid upon him. You will not be robbing him of anything though your faith-touch should convey a life into yourself. He has such a fullness about him that if all you poor sinners will come at once, when you have taken away all merit that you need, there will be as much merit left as there was before. When you deal with the infinite you may divide and subtract, but you cannot diminish. If the whole race were washed in the infinite fountain of Jesus' merit, the infinite would still remain.

Let me tell you that if you come to Jesus and just trust him tonight – only trust him – *you shall rather benefit him than injure him*, for it is his heart's joy to forgive sinners. He longs and thirsts to heal wounded consciences. My Lord is hungering, even now that he is in heaven, to bring poor sinners to his Father's feet, and reconcile them unto him, so that you will bless him, you will increase his joy if you will return to the great Father whose house you have left. You will delight his heart as again he finds the lost piece of money, carries back the lost sheep, and welcomes home the returning prodigal. I think you need not keep on saying, *"If I may"*; for these cheering reasons ought to convince you that you are fully warranted to trust in him whom God has set forth to be a prince and a Savior, to give repentance unto Israel, and remission of sins.

Might not this also help you? *Others just like you have ventured to him, and there has not been a case in which they have been refused.* I thought, like you, when I was a child, that the gospel was a very wonderful thing, and free to everybody but myself. I would not have wondered at all if my brother and sisters as well as my father and mother had been saved; but, somehow, I could not get a hold of it myself. It was a precious thing, quite as much out of my reach as the queen's diamonds. So I thought. To many the gospel is like a streetcar in motion, and they cannot jump upon it. I thought surely everybody would be saved, but I should not have thought thus; and yet, soon after I began to cry for mercy I found it. My expectations of difficulty were all sweetly disappointed. I believed and found immediate rest unto my soul. When I once understood that there was life in a look at the Crucified One, I gave that look, and I found eternal life. Up to this time I have never met with anybody who did give that look and was refused; but they all say,

> I came to Jesus as I was,
>   Weary and worn and sad;
> I found in him a resting-place,
>   And he has made me glad.

Nobody ever bears a contrary witness. I challenge the universe to produce a man who was chased from Christ's door, or forbidden to find in him a Savior. I pray you, therefore, observe that since others have come this way to life and peace, God has appointed it to be the common thoroughfare of grace. Poor guilty sinners, there is a mark set up: "This way for sinners. This way for the guilty. This way for the hungry. This way for the thirsty. This way for the lost. *'Come to Me, all who are weary and heavy-laden, and I will give you rest.'"* Why surely, you need not say, *"If I may."*

And why do you think – and this is one more question I would put to you – *why do you think that the Lord Jesus Christ in his mercy has led you here today?* "Oh, I always come," says one. Then what has induced you always to come where Christ is talked about so much, and where he saves so many? Surely the Lord means to accept you if you will believe on Jesus! "But I do not come here usually," says one; "I only stepped in here today, I am afraid, out of curiosity." Yes, curiosity moved you, but may it not be that compassion moved God to guide you here? I like to hear a wife say, "My husband is not a member of the church, sir, but he comes to hear the gospel, and therefore I have hope for him." Ay, yes; if we get them into the battle, a shot will come their way one of these days. I love to see yonder hungry sparrows round about the window; they will get courage enough to pick up a crumb of mercy one of these days. I hope so. And why should it not be *now*? If the trouble is *"If I may,"* I will ask you whether it does not help to remove that trouble to reflect that you are still on praying ground and pleading terms with God. You might long before this have been cast into despair. Should not the Lord's long-suffering lead you to repentance and induce you to come to Christ?

Now listen, friend: there is no room to say, *"If I may,"* for, first of all, *you are invited* to come and accept Christ as your Savior – invited over and over again in the Word of God. *The Spirit and the bride say, "Come." And let the one who hears say, "Come." And let the one who is thirsty come; let the one who wishes take the water of life without cost."* *"Ho! Every one who thirsts, come to the waters; and you who have no money come, buy and eat. Come, buy wine and milk without money and without cost."* Jesus Christ invites all those that labor and are heavy-laden to come unto him, and he will give them rest. God is honest in his invitations. Be you sure of that. If God invites you, he desires you to come and accept the invitation. After reading the many invitations of the Word of God to such as you are, you may not say, *"If I may."* It will be a wicked questioning of the sincerity of God.

In addition to being invited, *you are pleaded with.* Many passages of Scripture go far beyond a mere invitation. God persuades and pleads with you to come to him. He seems to cry as one that weeps, *"As I live!" declares the Lord God, "I take no pleasure in the death of the wicked, but rather that the wicked turn from his way and live. Turn back, turn back from your evil ways! Why then will you die, O house of Israel?"* Our Lord and Master, when he made the feast and they that were bidden did not come, sent out his servants to compel them to come in. He used more than a bare invitation, he put forth a divine compulsion. I would beg, persuade, exhort all of you who have not believed in Jesus to do so now. In the name of Jesus, I implore you to seek the Lord. I do not merely put it to you, "Will you or will you not?" but I would lay my whole heart by the side of the request and say to you, "Come to Jesus. Come and rest your guilty souls on him." Do you not understand the gospel message? Do you know what it asks and what it gives? You shall receive perfect pardon in a moment if you believe in Jesus. You shall receive a life that will never die – receive it now, quick as a lightning flash, if you do but trust in the Son of God. Whoever you may be, and whatever you may have done, if you will with your heart believe in him whom God has raised from the dead, and obey him henceforth as your Lord and Savior, all manner of sin and iniquity shall be forgiven you. God will blot out your iniquities like a cloud. He will make you begin *de novo* – afresh, anew. A new creature in Christ Jesus will he make you. Old things shall pass away and all things become new.

But there is the point – believing in Jesus; and you look me in the face and cry, "But may I?" May you? Why, you are exhorted, invited, implored so to do. Nor is this all. *You are even commanded to do it.* This is the commandment – that you believe on Jesus, whom he has sent. This is the gospel: *"He who has believed and has been baptized shall be saved; but he who has disbelieved shall be condemned."* There is a command, with a threatening for disobedience. Shall anybody say, "May I" after that? If I read, *"You shall love the Lord your God with all your heart,"* do I say, "May I love God?" If I read, *"Honor your father and your mother,"* do I say, "May I honor my father and my mother?" No. A command is a permit and something more. It gives full allowance and much more. As you will be damned if you believe not, you have herein given yourself a right to believe – not only a permission, but a warrant of the most practical kind. Oh, can you not see it? Will you not cry unto God, "Lord, if you will damn me if I do not believe, you have in this given me a full gospel liberty to believe. Therefore I come and put my trust in Jesus."

"If I may" – why, I think that this questioning ought to come to an end now. Will you not give it up? May the Holy Spirit show you, poor sinner, that you may now lay your burden down at Jesus' feet, and be at once saved. You may believe. You have full permission now to confess your sin and to receive immediate pardon; see if it be not so. Cast your guilty soul on him, and rise forgiven and renewed, from this point on to live in fervent gratitude, a miracle of love.

That is the first meaning of the text: "If I may be permitted to touch the hem of his garment, I shall be made whole."

But then there arises in other hearts this equally bitter question: "But can I? I know that I may if I can, but I cannot." This woman, seeing the pressing of the crowd, might have said, "If I can touch the hem of his garment, I shall be made whole; but can I get at him? Can a feeble person like myself force my way through the throng and touch him?"

Now, that is the question I am going to answer. The will to believe in Christ is as much a work of grace as faith itself, and where the will is given and there is a strong desire, then a measure of grace is already received, and with it the power to believe. Do you not know that the will to commit adultery is, according to Scripture, reckoned as adultery? *"Everyone who looks at a woman with lust for her has already committed adultery with her in his heart."* Now, if the very thought of uncleanness and the will towards it is the thing itself, then a desire or will to believe contains within itself the major part of faith. I say not that it is all, but I do say this – that if the power of God has made a man will to believe, the greater work has been done, and his actually believing will follow in due course. That entire willingness to believe is nine-tenths of believing. Inasmuch as to will is present with you, the power which you find not as yet will certainly come to you. The man is dead, and the hardest thing is to make him live; but in the case before us the reviving is accomplished, for the man lives so far as to will: he wills to believe, he yearns to believe, he longs to believe; how much has been done for him! Rising from the dead is a greater thing than the performance of an act of life. Already I see some breathings of life in you who are longing and yearning to lay hold on Christ. You shall yet lay hold on him, and live in his presence. I would have said to that woman, had I been there and known then what I know now, "Oh, woman, that faith of yours, that if you can but touch the hem of his garment you will be made whole, is a greater thing than the actual touch can be. It is not at present so operative, but it is a more singular product of grace. You have within you already the greater work of grace, and the less will follow. A thousand persons could press through the crowd and touch the hem of the Savior's robe, but you are the only person in whom God has worked the faith that a touch will make you whole. I might say of such a faith as that, *'Flesh and blood did not reveal this to you'*; and if you are in that condition, there is a very great work done in you already, and you need not doubt the possibility of your touching the sacred clothes."

> Faith in Christ is the simplest action that anybody ever performs.

But mark this: faith in Christ is the simplest action that anybody ever performs. It is the action of a child; indeed, it is the action of a newborn babe in grace. A newborn babe never performs an action that is very complicated. We say, "Oh, it is such a babyish thing," meaning thereby that it is so small. Now, faith comes at the moment that the child is born into God's family; it is simultaneous with the new birth. One of the first signs and tokens of being born again is faith; therefore, it must be a very, very simple thing. I venture to put it very plainly when I say that faith in Christ differs in no respect from faith in anybody else, except as to the person upon whom that faith is set. You believe in your mother; you may in the same manner believe in Jesus Christ, the Son of God. You believe in your friend; it is the same act that you have to do toward your higher and better Friend. You believe the news that is commonly reported and printed in the daily journals; it is the same act which believes the Scripture and the promise of God.

The reason why faith in the Lord Jesus is a superior act to faith in anyone else lies in this fact – that it is a superior person whom you believe in, and superior news that you do believe; and your natural heart is more averse to believing in Jesus than to believing in anyone else. The Holy Spirit must teach your faith to grasp the high things of Christ Jesus; but that grasp is by the hand of a simple childlike faith. But it is the same faith, mark you that. It is the gift of God insofar as this – that God gives you the understanding and the judgment to exercise it upon his Son, and to receive him. The faith of a child in his father is almost always a wonderful faith; it is just the faith that we would ask for our Lord Jesus. Many children believe that there is no other man in the world so great and good, and right and kind and rich, and everything else as their father is; and if anybody were to say that their father was not as wonderful a man as Mr. Gladstone, or some other great statesman, they would become quite grieved; for if their father is not king, it is a mistake that he is not. Children think so of their parents, and that is the kind of faith we would have you exercise towards the Lord Jesus Christ, who deserves such confidence, and much more. We should give to Jesus a faith by which we do him honor and magnify him exceedingly. As the child never thinks about where the bread and butter is to come from tomorrow morning, and it never enters its little head to fret about where it will get new socks when the present ones are worn out, so must you trust in Jesus Christ for everything you want between here and heaven – trust him without asking questions. He can and will provide. Just give yourself up to him entirely, as a child gives itself up to a parent's care, and feels itself to be at ease. Oh, what a simple act it is – this act of faith! I am sure that it must be a very simple act, and cannot require wisdom, and so forth, because I notice that it is the wise people who cannot do it; it is the strong people who cannot do it; it is the people who are righteous in themselves who cannot reach it. Faith is a kind of act which is performed by those who are childlike in heart, whom the world calls fools, and ridicules and persecutes for their folly. *For consider your calling, brethren, that there were not many wise according to the flesh, not many mighty, not many noble; but God has chosen the foolish things of the world to shame the wise, and God has chosen the weak things of the world to shame the things which are strong, and the base things of the world and the despised God has chosen.*

There are persons with no education whatever, who just know their Bibles truly, and have an abundant faith; they are poor in this world, but rich in faith. Happy people! Alas, for those wise people whose wisdom prevents faith in Jesus! They have been to more than one university, and have earned all the degrees that carnal wisdom can bestow upon them, and yet they cannot believe in Jesus Christ, the Son of God. Oh, friend, do not think that faith is some difficult and puzzling thing, for then these senior wranglers and doctors of divinity would have it. It is the simplest act that the mind can perform. Just as I lean now with all my weight on this rail, and if it breaks I fall; so lean you your full weight on Jesus Christ, and that is faith. Just as a babe lies in its mother's bosom, unconscious of the thunderstorm, or of the rocking of the ship, quite safe and happy because it rests in the bosom of love, with all fear and care laid aside because of that true heart which beats beneath – even so do you just cast yourself altogether upon Christ, and that is all that you have to do – just, in fact, to leave off doing.

> Cast thy deadly doing down,
>   Down at Jesus' feet.
> Stand in him, in him alone,
>   Gloriously complete.

"But shall I not have to do many good works?" says one. You shall do as much as ever you like when you are once saved; but in this matter of your salvation you must fling all self-righteousness away as so much devilry that will ruin and injure you, and come simply to Christ, and Christ alone, and trust in him.

"Oh," says one, "I think I see a little light. If I am enabled, if I do but get power enough to trust in Jesus, I shall be made whole." I will ask you another question. Do you not know that *you are bound to believe in Christ* – that it is because of Christ that he is believed in? I would not make extensive claims upon your faith for myself. Often have I said to friends who have told me that they could not believe in Christ, "Could you believe in *me*? If I were to tell you that I would do such and such things, would you believe it?" "Oh yes, sir." "If anyone were to say that he did not believe what I said, how would you feel?" "I would feel very indignant, for I feel that I can trust you; indeed I cannot help trusting you." When I receive such confidence from one of my fellow creatures, I feel that it is cruelly wrong for the same person to say, "I cannot trust Christ." Oh beloved, not believe Jesus? When did he lie? "Oh, but I cannot trust him." Not trust him? What madness is this! And did he die in very truth? Did he seal his life's witness with his heart's blood, and can you not believe him? My own conviction is that a great many of you can, and that already, to a large extent, you do; only you are looking for signs and wonders which will never come. Why not exert that power a little farther? The Spirit of God has given to you a measure of faith; oh, believe more fully, more unreservedly. Why, I know that you shivered just now at the very thought of doubting Christ. You felt how unjust and wrong it was; there is dormant in you already a faith in him. *The one who does not believe God has made Him a liar.* Would you make Christ a liar? Dear hearts, I know that you would not. Although you say that you dare not trust him, yet you know that he is no liar, and you know that he is able to save you. What a strange state your mind has reached. How bewildered and confused you are, for already I think, as a looker-on, I can see that there is within your soul a real faith in Jesus Christ, and yet what doubts distract you. Why not bring faith to the front and say, "I do believe, I will believe, that the Christ who is the Son of the Highest, and who died for the guilt of men, is able to save those that trust him, and therefore I trust him to save me. Sink or swim I trust him. Lost or saved I will trust him. Just as I am, with no other plea but that I am sure that he is able and willing to save, I cast my guilty soul on him." You have the power to trust Jesus when you have already yielded to the conviction that he is worthy to be trusted. You have but to push to its practical conclusion what God the Holy Spirit has already worked in many of you, and you will at once find peace.

Still, if you think that there is something that prevents your having faith in Christ, though you know that if you had it you would be saved, I do earnestly implore you not to stay contentedly for a single hour without a full, complete, and saving faith in Christ; for if you die as unbelievers you are lost, and lost forever. Your only safety lies in believing in the Lord Jesus Christ with all your heart, and obeying his commandments. Therefore use what common sense would suggest to you as the means for obtaining faith. If I were told in the church vestry after the service something by a true friend whose word I could not doubt, and yet if what he said seemed incredible, I would express to him a wish to believe it. I would not wish to imply for a moment that *he* was not truthful, but somehow I find it difficult to believe the remarkable statement that he made. What should I do in this case? If it was pressing that I should believe this statement, I would ask him, "How did you come by the information? Where did you hear or read it? What are the precise facts?" Perhaps the moment that he mentioned where he got it from I would conclude at once that the wonderful statement was unquestionably correct. Or if he said, "Well, I give it to you on my own authority, but if you want any further information, you can get it by reading such and such a document; here is the document," why, I should read it directly. I should read with a good deal of happy prejudice in favor of my faithful friend. Anyhow, I should read it to see whether I could fully believe what he said, because I should be sure that he would not intentionally deceive me. Now, if there be anything in the teaching of the Lord Jesus Christ, or anything about him that you question, let me invite you to read over the four Gospels again, especially the story of his crucifixion. That cross of his is a very wonderful thing, for not only does it save those who have faith in it, but it also breeds faith in those who look at it.

> When I see him wounded, bleeding,
>   Dying on the accursed tree,
> Then I feel my heart believing
>   That he suffered thus for me.

There is life in a look at Christ, because in the very considering of Christ there is the breeding of a living faith. We listen to the Word, and faith comes by hearing. We read the Word, and picture the whole thing before our eyes, and we say, "Yes, I do believe it. I never saw it quite in this fashion before, but I now believe it, and I will risk my soul on it."

Now, dear hearts, if any of you who have never trusted Christ will trust him today, if you perish I will perish with you! For, though I have known my Lord these thirty-five years, I have no other hope of salvation than I had when I first came to him. I had no merits of my own then, and I have none now. I have preached many sermons, offered many prayers, given much charity, and brought many souls to Christ; but I place all that ever I have done under my feet, and desire, as far as it is good, to give to God the glory of it; but as far as it comes of myself, I would sink it in the sea. I am saved in Christ, by faith in him; but confidence in myself is detestable to me. I dare believe in Jesus Christ as my all in all, but I am less than nothing before him.

Come; we start fair, you see. If we start today, you and I will start on a level with the same confidence in the same Savior, the same blood to cleanse us, and the same power to save us, and we will meet in heaven. As surely as we meet at the cross, we will meet where the Savior wears the crown. Oh, that you would trust him now, and believe him. "I have no good works," says one. Then for certain you cannot trust in them. You will be forced to trust in Jesus only. "Oh, but I have no good feelings." I am glad to hear you say so. Then you are not tempted to trust in feelings, but will be drawn to trust wholly on your Lord. "Oh, but I feel so unfit." Very well then; you cannot trust in your fitness, but must trust in him alone. It is a blessing when spiritual poverty forces a man into the way of life.

> I am saved in Christ, by faith in him; but confidence in myself is detestable to me.

Here I close with these words. This woman said in her heart, "If I do touch the hem of his garment, I shall" – what? "I shall be made whole." It is not "If I may but touch I *may* be made whole." No; she had gotten over the *may bes* in the first struggle. It is "If I may I *shall.*" If you trust Christ you shall be made whole. If you do today actually rest yourself in Christ, as the Lord lives, you must live and be saved. Unless this Bible is all a lie, unless Jesus was a rank impostor, unless the eternal God can change, you who come and trust yourself with Jesus must and shall be saved in the last great day of account. "Bold shall I stand in that great day," for I shall tell the Lord of his own promise, and how he bid me to trust him; and if I am not saved, then his word is broken, and that can never be. He *is* true. Oh, it is this that some of you want to be done with – thinking, and talking, and considering, and hoping. You need now to come and trust, resting yourself fully and wholly on what Christ has done. He loved, and lived, and died so that sinners might not die. He brought about a complete work, of which he said as he expired, *"It is finished."* There is nothing for you to add to it, nothing for you to bring with you to make that work complete; but you yourself, stripped naked of every hope, black, foul, guilty, abominable, the worst of the worst, have only to come and look up to those five wounds, and to that bleeding, thorn-crowned head, and say, *"Into Your hands I commit My spirit,"* and you shall be saved. It is done. *"[Your] sins, which are many, have been forgiven." "Go, and sin no more."* You are his child. Go and live to the glory of your Father; and may the peace of God that passes all understanding be with you forever and ever. Amen.

Chapter 11

The Great Physician Successful

A woman who had had a hemorrhage for twelve years, and had endured much at the hands of many physicians, and had spent all that she had and was not helped at all, but rather had grown worse—after hearing about Jesus, she came up in the crowd behind Him and touched His cloak. For she thought, "If I just touch His garments, I will get well." (Mark 5:25-28)

Briefly consider this poor woman's case. She was afflicted with a disease of exceedingly long standing, which not only wasted her strength and threatened to bring her speedily to the grave, but also rendered her according to the Jewish ceremonial law unclean, and therefore unable to mix in company; thus she was doomed to be a poor, suffering, desponding, desolate woman. The physicians of those days were bold enough to attempt impossible cures, but their skill was not at all commensurate with their courage. They tormented their patients, but seldom relieved them of anything but their money.

Even a few hundred years ago many of the articles which were given to patients as medicines, and praised publicly as drugs of sovereign effectualness, were so unutterably disgusting that I should not like to repeat their names; and the processes of surgery then common among practitioners would have been exceedingly satisfactory if they had been intended to kill, but were both absurd and inhuman if proposed as beneficial operations. The science of medicine, indeed, did not then exist; and in the age of our Lord, surgery and natural science were a mass of quackery and daring claims, perhaps without much skill or knowledge to support their claims. This poor woman had, however, in her anxious desire to be restored to society and to health, gone first to one and then to another, and yet another, although all caused her suffering by acrid medicines or by severe operations; and after the end of twelve years she found herself penniless as well as worse in health.

Just then, her physical state being still the highest thought in her mind, she heard that there was a prophet who healed diseases. Having listened to one or two of the stories of the cures worked by him, and having perhaps seen some of those who had been happy enough to be the subjects of his miracles, she said to herself, "That man is doubtless sent of God. He professes to be the Messiah, the Son of David, the Son of God. I believe he is so; and if he be such a one, then he is so full of sacred force that if I may but get near enough to touch the hem of his garment, I shall be restored." Happy day it was for her when she soaked in that idea. Happier still when she put it into practice, when tremblingly she put forth her finger, touched the hem of the Savior's garment, and was at that moment restored.

I shall not need to say more concerning the narrative itself. It commends the Savior to you, shows you his great power in the physical world, and so proves his deity, and endears him to you for his mercy and compassion. But this woman has many parallels in the spiritual world. Multitudes like her are diseased with a wasting despondency, an unceasing tendency to despair, and they have been trying all the miserable comforters with which this world abounds; and after wasting their substance and their strength, they are now brought to utter spiritual destitution, and they feel they can do nothing; they are ready to perish. I hope today, if never before, they will hear of Jesus who is able to heal the most desperate cases, and that they will be resolved to appeal to him, that by a sincere – even if a feeble – faith, they may be brought into contact with his healing energy, and may today be delivered from all evil by the great Restorer's touch. God grant it, for the Redeemer's sake, by the power of the Holy Spirit, and he shall have all the praise.

I intend, first of all, *to expose the physicians upon whom poor sin-sick souls often trust.* When I have done so, then secondly, I will *show you why all these physicians, without exception, fail.* Thirdly, I shall *describe the plight of the patient after the failure of these trusted physicians;* and lastly, *show how a cure can be worked even in those.*

Let me expose the physicians who delude so many by their vain claims. Among the herd of deceivers, I single out one of the vilest first, an old-established doctor who has had a wide practice among sin-sick souls – a wicked old poisoner he is, but for all that exceedingly popular, named Dr. Sadducee. He adopts usually the homoeopathic principle, namely, to cure like by its like. He gives one form of sin as a cure for another. For instance, as soon as he sees someone melancholy with unbelief, he prescribes licentiousness. He says, "You are getting dull; you must cheer up; you ought to mix with society. A young person like you ought not to be disturbed with these serious thoughts; those are mere fanatics who alarm you; pray be calm. I would recommend you attend the theater or the music hall, for these will drive dull care away." He feels the patient's pulse, tells him it is much too low; he must really take a little stimulant and see what merriment will do.

Alas! this old but damning prescription is frequently written out and pressed upon awakened souls as if it were wisdom itself, whereas it is a piece of satanic craft and falsehood. It never did work a cure, and it never can. It bids the man to escape from drowning by plunging deeper beneath the waves. It tells him to quench the flame which is burning in his heart by adding fuel to it. It pretends to heal the leper by thrusting him into the inner recesses of the hospital for lepers, where disease runs not the most miserably. By making bad worse, the lover of pleasure hopes to recover from the qualms of conscience.

As a notable instance of Dr. Sadducee's practice, in its mildest form, I would quote the case of George Fox, the celebrated founder of the Quakers. When perplexed about his salvation, he went to diverse friends and ministers for advice. One said he thought it would do him much good to smoke tobacco; another recommended him to get married as speedily as possible; another thought if he joined the volunteers, that would certainly remove his melancholy thoughts. "Alas!" he says, "I found them as empty as a hollow drum." Such physicians minister no medicine to a diseased mind. A story is told of Carlini, the Italian actor, who being the subject of heavy depression of spirit, appealed to a French physician, and was recommended to attend the Italian theater, and, said the physician, "If Carlini does not dispel your gloomy complaint, your case must be desperate indeed." The physician was not a little surprised when his patient replied, "Alas! sir, I am Carlini; and while I divert all Paris with mirth, and make them almost die with laughter, I myself am dying with melancholy." How empty and insufficient are the amusements of the world! Even in their laughter their heart rejoices not.

Miserable comforters are all those who would drown seriousness in wine and merriment. When the heart is breaking, it is vain to offer music and the dance, or to fill high the flowing bowl. When the arrows of God stick fast in a man's soul, the world's vain songs suit not with the hour; they jar on the ear, and increase the misery which they would remove. When God awakens a sinner, he cannot be so readily deceived as when he was in his dreams. The Holy Spirit has made him feel the bitterness of sin, and bruised him with the rod of conviction; and now his broken bones demand a real and true physician, and he cannot endure the simpering deceiver who tells him that there is no resurrection, neither angel, nor spirit. It is too late to say to such a man, "Let us eat and drink, for tomorrow we die"; he dreads death, and trembles lest death should come upon him unawares.

> When the heart is breaking, it is vain to offer music and the dance, or to fill high the flowing bowl.

A much more respectable firm of physicians has been established from time immemorial in the region of Mount Sinai, near the abode of Hagar, who was known as the maid. The business is now carried on by Dr. Legality and his pupil, Mr. Civility. You will remember that, in John Bunyan's time, they were in large practice. Mr. Worldly Wiseman was their patron, and he sent the pilgrim around that way, telling him that the old doctor had much skill in delivering men of their burdens, and that if the old gentleman himself was not at home, his young man, Mr. Civility, would do almost as well.

This firm was trading, in our Savior's day, under the name of scribe and Pharisee. It was the same deceptive system, and under different names it will always be the same act of deception until the crack of doom. The theory of practice is this: "Be careful in diet and regimen, be very observant of certain laws and regulations, and then your issue of blood, or whatever it may be, shall be healed." Go all over England, and the great doctor for men's souls, the most popular physicians now living, is this Dr. Legality. The one great prescription is "Do this and do that; abstain from this, and give up the other; keep the commandments, and pray at certain hours, and these things will save you." Dressed out in different fashions, but always the same thing, this great falsehood of salvation by the works of the law is still holding men under its iron effect and deluding them to their destruction.

There may be some now present who are unhappy enough not to know the truth which Paul tells us so plainly: *By the works of the Law no flesh will be justified in His sight; for through the Law comes the knowledge of sin.* I was myself for many a day treated by this Dr. Legality, and many a black dose have I swallowed under his orders. I tried to keep the law of God, and thought that my repentance and tears must be an atonement for the past. But who can keep the law? What man can keep whole what he has broken? We have each of us already sinned, and therefore the hope of salvation by our own goodness is a vain one. The law pronounces a curse upon the man that sins but once; how can the man, then, having already sinned ten thousand times, hope by any future obedience to escape from the curse which hangs thick and heavy over his head, soon to burst in eternal storm?

Yet this is the fond delusion of humanity; Sinai is still the chosen route to heaven for the crippled sons of a father who found the task too much for him. Some of you imagine that if you do your best – if you are kind to everybody, if you are generous to the poor, if you owe no man anything, if you conduct yourselves respectably – this is enough to save you; but it is not so. He that believes not on Jesus Christ shall be damned as well in his morality as in his debauchery; he that casts not himself upon the mercy of God as revealed in the crucified Savior has shut against himself the one door to heaven, and shall never be able to enter into life.

There is another physician whom I greatly despise, but am compelled to mention him because he has entrapped many: one Dr. Ceremonial.

He is the vilest of quacks, an absolute fake, a transparent deceiver. His drugs are worthless trash, and his modes of operation are rather the tricks of one who clowns publicly, or the antics of a dancing master, than the sober teachings of thought and judgment. This Dr. Ceremonial has patented a lotion for producing regeneration in little children by the application of a few drops to their foreheads. He puts his hands on the heads of boys and girls, and by what he calls occult influence, confirms them in grace. He professes to be able to make a piece of a loaf and a cup of wine to be actually divine, and in themselves a channel of grace to the souls of men. The substances are material – a mouse may nibble at the one, a bottle will hold the other; you can touch them, taste them, and smell them, and yet fools adore them as divine, and imagine that material substances can be food for souls. Surely this Dr. Ceremonial flourishes all the more because of the monstrous absurdity of his teachings; his pills are huge, but men have wide swallows, and can receive anything.

Why, think for a minute, and then wonder for an hour: men are to be sanctified by gazing at those on bended knee, women's hats, and candles! The east is said to be a more gracious quarter of the heavens than the west, and creeds repeated with the head in that direction possess a peculiar effectualness. It appears that in spiritual operation certain colors are peculiarly effective, prayers said or sung in white are far more prevalent than in black, and according to the age of the year and the condition of the moon, dark red, violet, scarlet, and blue are more acceptable to God. I have no patience with these things, it is hardly good enough sport for laughter; but so long as fools abound, scoundrels will flourish, and this Dr. Ceremonial will get men to spend their substance in abundance, and will laugh in his sleeve to think that rational beings should be his silly fools.

I trust there are none such here. I hope none of you are so deluded. What can there be in crossings, bowings, and uttering over and over the same words? What is any worship unless the reason and heart enter into it? What can there be in one material substance to give it sanctity? Is it not as absurd as the fetishism of the Bushman, to believe that bricks and mortar, and shingles and boards, can make a holy place? That indeed, any one place can be a jot holier than another; that any plot of ground can be holier than common ground; or that any man, because certain words have been said over his godless, graceless head, can be made a dispenser of the grace of God, and a pardoner of sins? We are not so deluded, but still this quack drives a good trade, and is held in very high repute.

Here I may name one Dr. Ascetic, who has taken a house close to the abode of Dr. Ceremonial. His business, however, does not flourish quite so much now as formerly, for his methods are a little too rigorous for the times. Under his treatment men are taught that pain and virtue are much alike; that starvation is a means of grace, dirt is devotion, and horsehair next to the skin is a sanctifying irritant. Few persons like this heroic treatment, but certain brotherhoods and sisterhoods amuse themselves with the treatment in a modified form. The more heroic doses of wormwood and gall are out of fashion, but still men like something bitter in moderate quantities. In the olden times this Dr. Ascetic flourished much. Then men wore hair shirts, flogged their poor shoulders, went on mad pilgrimages, and in other ways afflicted themselves, believing that great self-denials were patent medicines by which deliverance could be obtained from spiritual diseases. This system of soul-cure had such victims as hermits in caverns, and the followers of Simon Stylites elevated upon columns, with other imbeciles which time would fail us to mention.

Even in these days we read of the nuns of St. Ann, who always sleep in their coffins upright, and become unable to sleep in any other posture. The Fakeers in Hindostan do but carry out to perfection the regulations which some in this Christian land would impose upon our respect. But all this is the mere invention of man, and he who follows it shall find that he torments himself in vain.

I shall now mention a physician who practices among Dissenters as well as elsewhere, and I am persuaded has some of you for his patients. His name is Dr. Orthodoxy. His treatment consists of this: that you are to believe certain doctrines most firmly and bigotedly, and then you shall be saved. Are there not some today whose great difficulty about salvation is that they cannot quite comprehend the mystery of predestination? If you talk to them about the precious blood of Jesus, and speak of the soul-saving effectualness of a simple trust in him, they reply, "But I cannot quite understand the doctrine of election!" and then they mention some passage of Scripture upon that subject – their notion being that if they could understand mysteries they would then be saved; if they could hold the orthodox faith in every point they would be delivered from their sins. But it is not so.

I have known scores of persons who have been held in horrible bondage by exclusively thinking upon one part of orthodoxy to the exclusion of the rest. They have grown more wretched, more distracted, and more hopeless than they were before, because having heard the doctrine of election and predestination propounded, they must forever be harping upon it. It is a blessed doctrine, and I believe it and hold it firmly, that God has a chosen people; but for all that, before men have come to Christ they often make that doctrine to be a stone of stumbling and a rock of offense. Even if you would be infallible and believe every truth as it is taught in Scripture in the most correct manner, your belief would not save you. True religion is something more than correct opinions. A man may as well descend to hell being orthodox as heterodox. There is a correct road to destruction as well as an incorrect one – I mean a way in which a man may carry truth in his right hand, as well as another road in which the pilgrim hides a lie in his left.

> **True religion is something more than correct opinions.**

One more physician I will mention, and that is Dr. Preparation. He holds and teaches that the way to be saved is to prepare yourselves for Christ, and if you prepare and make yourselves fit for Jesus Christ, then you will obtain peace. The modes of preparation are very much these: "You must deeply wound yourself; you must doubt God's power to save you, and dishonor Jesus by your fears; you must endure terrors of conscience, and be the subject of alarms." It is not said so in that Book, but still this is the current teaching of many, and is so much believed that men will not trust in Jesus Christ because they have not felt this nor experienced the other. Do I not every week meet with persons who tell me, "You invite those to come to Christ who feel their need; I do not feel any need as I ought, and therefore I may not come"? I cannot understand why such people do not open their ears, for times out of mind I say that Jesus Christ did not come into this world to save sensible sinners only, but to save sinners from their insensibility; that Jesus Christ bids sinners, as sinners, to believe in him, and does not limit the command to those who repent.

Men are not only to come *with* broken hearts, but *for* broken hearts; and if they cannot feel their need, they should come to Jesus to be helped to feel their need; for this he gives them: "'Tis his Spirit's rising beam." My Lord and Master wants nothing of you, O lost and bankrupt sinners. He bids you to come simply trusting in him, being nothing at all in yourself, and having all in him. I believe that those who think they do not feel their need often feel their need the most. If anyone should say, "I have a sense of need," then he claims to have something good; but those who confess that they have no good feelings or emotions, that they are poor bankrupts, broken down, so that their last penny is gone, to them is the gospel sent. Trust Jesus, believe that he can do what you cannot do, and in the absence of any good in yourselves, believe that all the good you want is treasured up in him, and cast yourselves empty, naked, soul-diseased as you are, flat upon the perfect work of Jesus, and you shall be saved.

I have just gone through a list of those physicians with which I believe many of you have long been acquainted.

What is the reason for their failure? Why is it that none of the prescriptions of these learned and popular gentlemen have ever been able to work a single cure? Is it not, first of all, because *none of them understand the disease*?

If the disease of human nature were only a matter of outward iniquity, or only skin-deep, through intellectual error, ceremonies perhaps might have some effect, and legal exhortations might be of some use. But since the inmost heart of man is depraved, and the sin of our nature lies in the very core of our humanity and is inherited from our birth, of what help is consecrated water, or sacraments, or good works, or anything external which cannot change the nature and turn the bias of the mind?

The will is obstinate, the affections are depraved, the understanding is darkened, the desires are polluted, and the conscience is dulled; but legal physicians make clean the outside of the cup and platter, they do not touch these inward evils. They do not really know that man is dead in sin; they treat the patient as if he had wounded himself a little, and could be salved, and bound up, and made complete again. They know not the deep pollution of sin, but imagine that man has stained himself a little, and only a little, so a sponge of reformation, and a little hot water of repentance will soon remove all unpleasant marks. But it is not so. The fountain of our being is polluted; the foundation of our nature is rotten, and not until we come to Christ do we find the physician who comes to the point and who touches the disease at its source.

Moreover, *these physicians often prescribe remedies which are impossible for their patients.* They tell the man, "You must feel so much." "Feel!" says the man, "why, my heart is like granite. If I could feel, I could do all the rest; but I can no more make myself feel than I can make myself an angel. You bid me to do what is far beyond my power." Then they bid him to work, crying, "You must press forward, be in earnest, agonize, labor!" "But" says he, "I do try; I have tried for years, but my endeavors are not such as God accepts, and I may continue trying till I perish. I want to be told a sure way to salvation at once; I long for immediate peace, and light, and liberty." These physicians prescribe walking to those who have broken their legs, and sight as a remedy for those whose eyes are gone; bidding men to do what they cannot, and never pointing them to what Jesus has done on their behalf. When the gospel bids the sinner to cease from his toiling and trust alone in Jesus, having nothing and being nothing in himself, but taking Jesus to be his all in all; and when it adds that even this is the gift of God's Spirit, then it puts before him an available method for the weakest, guiltiest, and most distressed.

Many of the medicines prescribed by these physicians do not touch the case at all. As I have already shown you, outward ceremonies cannot by any possibility affect the inward nature; and the mere performance of good works, and the utterance of excellent prayers can have no effect in quieting the conscience. Conscience cries, "I have offended God; how may I be reconciled to him? My past sins clamor for vengeance; God is not just if he does not punish me. Oh! where shall I find peace for my soul?" where but in the bosom of the Mediator?

Only at Calvary is the medicine for a wounded conscience to be found. From those five wounds of our blessed Lord healing fountains are streaming still; he that looks to him shall find peace and comfort and full salvation. But the doing and the feeling, and the performing of this and that, and ten thousand things besides, are all a mockery, a delusion, and a snare; they touch not the case. *The disease of fallen humanity is wholly incurable except by the hand of Omnipotence.* It is as easy for us to create a world as to create a new heart; and a man might as well hope to abolish cold and snow as hope to eradicate sin from his nature by his own power; he might as well say to this round earth, "I have emancipated you from the curse of labor," as say to himself, "I will set myself free from the enslavement of sin." The Lord alone can save, it is his prerogative, and they who tell me that they are to have a finger in it, that they and their deceivers, the priests, can assist a little in salvation, that their tears, their groans, their cries, their repentances and their humblings can do at least something, these I say fly in the face of God, rob him of his dearest prerogative, assault his Word, rob him of his glory, and provoke him to jealousy. God is a sovereign and will be treated as such. Woe unto the man who contends with him!

> It is as easy for us to create a world as to create a new heart.

Brethren and sisters, let me say plainly this one word, and then leave this point. Rest assured that wherever in salvation you see a trace of the creature's power or merit, you see a work that is spoiled and polluted. If there be in the fountain one drop of anything but Jesus' blood, it will not cleanse; if there be in the robe one single thread of anything but what Christ worked out for us while here below, the whole robe is polluted, and will not serve as a wedding garment. For a needy soul the work must be Christ's from top to bottom, all of him, and all of grace; but if there be anything of human merit, or anything else that comes from man, the work is marred upon the wheel, and God will not accept it. These are some of the reasons why these physicians fail to bring health and cure.

I shall describe the plight of the patient who has tried these deceivers, and now at last finds himself brought into distress.

For five years I was in that plight, seeking by every way that I knew of to find peace with God. At the end of that period my condition was much like that of this poor woman. Now, there were four pieces of mischief done in her case. First, the woman had *lost all her time.* Twelve years! Who knows the value of a day? Who can calculate the costliness of a year? Twelve years, all gone! And what a pity that these poor people who are seeking to be saved by the works of the law should be losing all that precious time!

What a pity that you, dear friends, who are not yet saved, should be getting gray, and so many years should be running to waste! They ought to be spent for the Lord. I hope they may be yet, what remains of them, but think and be humbled. You have been all this time outside the banquet door, all this time unwashed when the fountain is full, all this time unhealed when the restoring hand can save you in a minute; all this time in jeopardy, in danger of your soul, while the gate of the city of refuge has been open. It is a solemn loss of time that these delusions bring on men, and yet we cannot tear them away from them; for if we prove the folly of one, they take to another; and if we prove the folly of all, yet still will they go back to them like a dog to his vomit. They will have anything sooner than go to Christ, for Christ himself has said, *"You are unwilling to come to Me so that you may have life"*; anywhere else men will cheerfully go, but not to him.

The second mischief in the case was that *she was no better*. If she had felt a little better she would have had some encouragement. It would have been satisfactory to have some pain mitigated, some measure of the disease stopped; and so in your case, you are no better than you were when you first entered this house five years ago. You have reformed perhaps, which is good; you have given up some evil things which were once very dear to you – that is well; but still you are not one grain happier; you could not die today with any greater comfort than you could have died five years ago – you have no better hope of immortality now than you had then. No, sometimes you have imagined the darkness thickening, and the prospect of hope becoming less and less apparent. A sad thing, is it not, that after doing so much it should come to so little! You have put your money into a bag that is full of holes; you have spent it on that which is not bread, and you labor for that which does not satisfy.

The third evil in the woman's case was that *she rather grew worse*, and in addition to that, *she had suffered many things* from the physicians. She had gained a loss. The doctors had blistered here, and lanced there, and given this acrid poison and that nauseous drug, and had been skillful in nothing but in causing needless pain. So, while to effect your salvation you have been looking away from Christ to someone else, you have been needlessly troubled and tortured. Despair has hovered around your path, despondency has hung its sense of gloom above you, and you have much more gloom and shadows of death yet to endure, unless you give up all that comes of self, and cast yourself on Christ. I would take a chance on it, if I were you, for you cannot lose by it; you are as bad as you can be.

Better even if Jesus were angry to run into his arms than to remain apart from him. Jesus Christ the appointed Savior of men is able to save to the uttermost, but while you look to others it is not possible for you to be saved; they will either bolster you up with self-righteousness, which will harden your heart, or else cast you down by putting before you impossible duties, to attempt which will be to increase your despair.

> None but Jesus, none but Jesus
> Can do helpless sinners good.

Yet helpless sinners pierce themselves through with many sorrows as they fly to earthly physicians for relief. One more matter. The woman *had now spent all that she had.* Her poverty was a new ill of which the only good was that now that she had no more to spend on the physicians, she was driven to Christ. So it is a most blessed though painful experience when a man has spent all, when he discovers that he has nothing left, no, not so much as an atom of merit, or hope of ever having any. It is well when the man cries, "I have always thought that perhaps there might be an escape for me, but I have no hope left now.

As for power, I am as destitute of it as I am of merit. I feel that I would but cannot pray; I would but cannot repent; I want to believe, but I can no more believe than I can fly – it must all come from God." At such a time it will come from God, for man's extremity is always God's opportunity. When you are empty; when your stock is all gone, even to the last rag and crumb, and you are left a helpless, hopeless, undeserving, hell-deserving sinner, and can truly feel that unless God stretches out his hand to save you, you are as lost as the lost in hell are, it is then that Jesus Christ reveals himself, and the soul cries, "My Lord, the glorious Son of God, there is no hope except in you; you can save me. I cast myself upon you, whether I sink or swim; for I am persuaded that nothing else can rescue me, and while I can but perish if I do rely upon you, yet I will rely upon you. If I am cast into hell, as I feel I deserve to be, yet still I will believe that you can save me."

Ah! then you cannot perish, neither shall any pluck you out of his hands. If God gives you power to believe Christ, and trust yourself to him, you are as surely saved as God is in heaven, and Christ there pleading at his right hand.

Fourthly, now to those who have spent their all on the false physicians, I have a word to show how a cure can be worked.

This woman said to herself, "The way of cure is for me to get near to Jesus; I can see that doctors are of no good. I cannot help myself, neither can all the world besides assist me. I must press to get near to *him*. If I cannot put my arms around him, yet a little of him is enough. If I cannot press to him so as to lay hold of him with my hand, yet as much as I can touch with my finger will be enough. I know if I cannot touch him, if I can but get near the ravelings of his garment and touch one of them, it will do." It is a sweet truth, that the least bit of Christ will save.

The best of men, the whole of men, cannot benefit you an ounce, but the least drop of Christ, the least touch of Christ will save. If your faith is such a poor trembling thing that it is hardly fit to be called faith, yet if it does connect you with Christ, you shall have the virtue that goes out from him. For remember it was not this woman's finger that saved her, it was Christ whom she touched. True, the healing came by the act of faith, but the act of faith is not the healing – the healing all lies in the person, so that you are not to be looking to your faith, but to Jesus the Lord. Has your faith a good object? Do you rest in Jesus, God's Son, God's appointed propitiation? If so, your faith will bring you to heaven – it is good enough. The strongest faith a man ever had, if it did not rest on Christ, damned him; the weakest faith ever man or woman had, if it did but terminate in the precious person and all-sufficient work of Jesus, would certainly save.

The fact is, sinner, if you would be saved, you must from this moment have nothing more to do with yourself, with your goodness or your badness. "I cannot feel," says the sinner – that is yourself again. Away with that feeling; you are to be saved by what Christ felt, not by what you feel. "I cannot." What do I care about what you cannot do? Your salvation does not lie in what you can do, but in what Jesus can do, and he can do everything. Will you trust him now? Let me help your faith with two or three words as the Holy Spirit may bless them. Christ is God: has he not power to save you? Christ, the bleeding Son of God, has bowed his head to the accursed death of the cross, bearing his Father's anger that those who trust him may not bear it. Cannot the bloodstained Christ pardon sin? Christ is his Father's darling, trust in him. Will not God grant mercy when you plead for Jesus' sake? Jesus lives today – he is no dead Christ that you are bidden to trust in. He lives, and this is his occupation; he is pleading before the throne of God, and this is his plea: "Father, forgive them for my sake." Seeing he died to save, cannot he now that he lives save to the uttermost? At his last dying moment he said to the thief, *"Today you shall be with Me in Paradise."* Can he not say as much now that he wears the crown of glory? Yes, you may have come in here today without a good thought, never having spoken a holy word in your life; but he can save you as quickly as he did the thief. Alas, and though when that clock struck twelve you were a graceless wretch, yet at this moment you may be already a saved soul. Alas, and before the clock ticks again, another may be called by grace. Christ works not according to time; he is not limited by minutes. If you can turn your eye to his cross and say, "Lord, remember me," he can give as his reply, "You shall be with me before long in paradise." With God incarnate, with the God-man who bled on the cross, with the Son of God ascended, clothed with majesty, reigning in splendor, with him whose promise we this day proclaim to you, there can be neither difficulty nor debate. The promise runs thus: *"He who believes in Him is not judged"; "Believe in the Lord Jesus, and you will be saved"; "He who has believed and has been baptized shall be saved; but he who has disbelieved shall be condemned."* Will you believe in him? It is to come to him, to trust him, to lean upon him, to hang upon him, to make him your sole and only ground of dependence. Will you do this? Has God enabled you now to do it? If so, go in peace; your

> Christ works not according to time; he is not limited by minutes.

faith has made you whole, your sins are forgiven you. Go and live to his praise, who bought you with his blood. Go, young man, and serve him earnestly who has served you so well. Go now, and till life's latest hour be his servant who has been so much your friend. The Lord bless us for his name's sake. Amen.

Chapter 12

The Touch

For she thought, "If I just touch His garments, I will get well." (Mark 5:28)

The miracle of the healing of this woman occurred while our Savior was on the road to the house of Jairus to raise his daughter, and I have not much doubt that although, in itself, it was a very remarkable miracle, it was not meant to stand quite alone, but was related to the Lord's dealings with Jairus. If I read the narrative rightly, the ruler of the synagogue was about to have his faith severely tested. He had come to the Savior saying that his daughter was lying at the point of death, and begging him to come and heal her; but before he had reached the house other messengers came to say, *"Your daughter has died; why trouble the Teacher anymore?"* Now, in order that the faith of Jairus might be prepared for that shock, our Lord had afforded him the sight of a special miracle worked upon this woman. Our Lord had said to him, *"Do not be afraid any longer; only believe, and she will be made well,"* and as old Bishop Hall says, "To make this good, by the touch of the verge of his garment he revived a woman from the verge of death." It is singular that the case of his little daughter, twelve years of age, was here placed within the region of hope by our Lord's healing a woman who had been exactly at the same time subject to a grievous and incurable sickness. A woman who led a living death is healed that Jairus may believe that his dead daughter may be raised to life. Brethren, we never know when God blesses us how much blessing he is incidentally bestowing upon others. It may be that even our conversion had a far-reaching but very distinct connection with the conversion of others. Grace smiles upon its personal subject, but its object reaches beyond the private benefit of the individual. The Lord is strengthening the faith of another of his children, or it may be he is actually working faith in a convinced soul, when he is accepting and honoring our faith and saving us. We speak of killing two birds with one stone; but our Savior knows how to bless two souls, no, two thousand souls, with one single touch of his hand.

I will not, however, detain you in the throng of thoughts with which I might preface my discussion upon this interesting narrative, for I long to bring you near to the glorious person of the great Healer of men. Our Lord worked this miracle while moving on to work another; like the sun, he shines while he pursues his course, and every beam is full of grace. Not only what he does with full purpose is glorious, but he is also so full of power and grace that even what he does incidentally by the way is marvelous! The main course and design of his life must ever engross our most earnest thoughts; but even the minor episodes of his life poem are rich beyond expression, nor is there even a point of detail which is without instruction. We cannot exhaust the subject, but must be satisfied to leave out many interesting matters and come at once to the heart of the story.

First, I invite you to look at this woman as *a patient;* secondly, to observe *the great difficulties with which her faith was surrounded;* thirdly, we will come to *the vanishing point,* and see how all her difficulties fled like the mists of the morning when she thought of Christ; and lastly, we will dwell upon *her grand success.* It may be the Lord will help us to attain to some greater blessing by enabling us to follow her example. Come, Holy Spirit, and aid our faith, that it may bring us into closer and still closer contact with our divine Lord.

First, then, look at the patient. She was a woman who had suffered from a very grievous sickness which had drained away her life. Her constitution had been sapped and undermined, and her very existence had become one of constant suffering and weakness; and yet *what courage and spirit she displayed.* She was ready to go through fire and through water to obtain health. She must have had a wonderful amount of vitality in her, for where others would have been lying upon the bed of sickness, and long ago despairing, she still for twelve years continued to seek after a cure from one physician or another. Nothing dampened or daunted her; she would not give up so long as breath remained. When at last she had found the true physician she plunged into the thick of the crowd to touch him by some means or other. She asked nobody to intercede for her, but with a dauntless courage worthy to be associated with her deep humility, she forced her way through the crowd to reach the healing Christ. She displayed intense energy and unconquerable spirit in pursuit of health. O that men were a tenth as much alive to the salvation of their souls.

Note also *her resolute determination.* She would die hard, if die she must. She would not resign herself to the inevitable till she had used every effort to preserve life and to regain health. For twelve years it appears she had persevered, in different ways and in the teeth of terrible agonies. We are told that she had suffered many things from many physicians. It is bad enough to suffer many things from one surgeon, but she had suffered many things from many practitioners. The physicians of those days were a great deal more to be dreaded than the worst diseases. If I were now to read to you even a brief account of the surgery practiced in olden times, you would shudder and beg me to close the book. Any reasonable person might prefer to suffer from any form of natural disorder rather than submit himself to the hands of the doctors of those days. As for their prescriptions, they were horrible. Even those of a couple of hundred years ago, to be found in such books as *Culpeper's Complete Herbal,* are such a mess and mass of all manner of abominations that it would surely be better to die than to be drenched with such detestable concoctions. What with cupping, leeching and cutting, cauterizing, blistering, and incision, strapping, puncturing, and putting in setons, patients were made to undergo all manner of unimaginable tortures. The physicians of her day were worthy to have been familiars of the Inquisition, for they had reached perfection in the arts of torment. Yet the heroic woman before us endured every process which was supposed to have virtue in it. I know not how many operations she had endured, nor how many gallons of nauseous drugs she had swallowed, but they had certainly caused her a vast amount of suffering and bitter disappointment. Meanwhile her money had been paid away freely till she had nothing left to procure her comforts when she most needed them. As long as her money lasted she never stinted a single penny of it. The resolution of the woman is well worthy of being observed. She is determined that, if beneath the sky there is a cure, that cure she will have, and as long as there is life left in her, that life shall be spent in somehow or other seeking to baffle death of his immediate prey. I am glad when I see such resolution in an awakened soul, but how seldom is it to be seen. I am happy when a man, however ignorant of the way of salvation, nevertheless resolves, "I will be saved if salvation be obtainable. Whatever is to be suffered, whatever is to be given up, whatever is to be done, if there be any way of salvation procurable by any means, I will have it. The whole world shall not be reckoned too great an expense; self-denial of the most arduous kind shall be a trifle to me, if I may but be saved." Surely, brethren, the salvation of our immortal soul is worthy of all the intensity of zeal, constancy of purpose, and resoluteness of determination of which we are capable. Who shall count its worth? Against what shall we weigh the soul? Fine gold of the merchants is as dross compared with our undying spirit; the diamond and the costly crystal are not to be named in comparison with it. Job said, *"Skin for skin! Yes, all that a man has he will give for his life"*; and truly the ransom of the soul is precious. It is a hopeful sign, a gracious token, when there is a determination worked in men that, if saved they can be, saved they will be.

I admire also this woman's *marvelous hopefulness*. She still believes that she can be cured. She ought to have given up the idea long ago according to the ordinary processes of reasoning; for generally we put several instances together, and from these several instances we deduce a certain inference. Now she might have put the many physicians together, and their many failures, and have rationally inferred that her case was beyond hope. She might have said, "My disease is incurable. I must ask for patience to bear it till I die, but no longer dream of a cure." But no, bright-eyed woman as I have no doubt she was, she saw hope where others would have despaired. Something within her buoyed her up, and she still had hopes of better days, and so, when she heard of Jesus, her heart leaped within her. Her hope said, "The blessing has come at last. I have long waited for it, and now God has sent it to me. Here it is, and I will seize it at once. Now has the Sun of Righteousness arisen upon me with healing beneath his wings, and I will bathe in his sunlight. Now I have escaped from mere pretenders, and I have found one who has real power to heal." You see, then, the patient – a woman of spirit, of resolution, and of hopefulness. Such persons make grand workers when they are converted. May God grant that I may have many such men and women before me, and may the Master come today by his Spirit and do his healing work upon them.

But now, secondly, I beg you to join with me in considering the difficulties of this woman's faith. They must be weighed in order to show its strength. The difficulties of her faith must have been as follows.

First, she could hardly forget *that the disease was in itself incurable, and that she had long suffered from it.* Taken early, many sicknesses may be greatly alleviated, if not altogether removed; but it was now very late in the day with this poor sufferer. Twelve years – it is a long, long portion of human life during which to have been continually drained of the very sustenance of that life. To languish and bleed for twelve years is enough to render one hopeless. Can a cure be possible? Can the disease which has taken root in the body for twelve years be eradicated? Can the incurable be healed after all? Her heart would naturally ask, How can this thing be? Do you wonder that after being so long weakened by her complaint, and rendered more and more infirm by its long continuance, it looked to her to be an utter impossibility that she should be healed? Yet observe her conduct and admire it; she staggered not, but believed in Jesus.

And then again *she had endured frequent disappointments,* and all these must have supplied her with terrible reasons for doubting. "Yes," she might have said, "I remember the first physician I appealed to, how he told me it was a very small matter, and that if I would purchase a bottle of the large size of his Egyptian elixir, which he had imported from the tombs of the Pharaohs at enormous expense, I would speedily be well. Alas, he only relieved me of my gold. Then another famous professor assured me that his pills would do the work if I took them some three hundred times, and was careful to purchase them only from himself, as he alone possessed the secret, and no one else could prepare the genuine article. He had no doubt that I would be greatly improved after the three-hundredth box; but, alas, after tedious delay, I was no better." She recollected how, under each new treatment, she interpreted every little change in herself into a hopeful sign, but soon found herself rudely shaken out of her dream by an increase of the evil. Her adventures were many, but all alike were sad in their end. She remembered the grave old physician to whom she went some years ago, who shook his learned head and assured her that he had scarcely ever met with a more terrible case. It was a great mercy for her that she had come to him, for there was not another man in Palestine who understood the disease. He believed that he could certainly stop the issue by the daily use of his Balm of Lebanon, prepared from the best gums of the cedar, and the richest juices of odorous herbs, mixed in an extraordinary manner, in accordance with the suggestions of the ancients and the observations of many years of practice. It was a mercy indeed that he had a little left of this matchless balm, which she could have at a very moderate price considering how much expense it was to him. She had taken it, but it had made her feel a new pain, and had brought on a fresh disease. She had paid heavily to endure two sicknesses instead of one.

She had changed her doctor, and this time engaged a Greek physician, who heartily condemned all his predecessors as fools, and taught a system so profound that the poor woman could not understand him at all, but believed in him nonetheless for that, for she set it down to her own ignorance and his deep learning. He failed, however, and she then tried a Roman doctor, a plain, blunt, practical man, who talked no Greek, but was greatly skilled in the rough and ready treatment of wounded soldiers. After trying medicines for a very considerable time, he informed her that hers was a very suitable case for a famous operation which he had himself first practiced – a beautiful operation indeed. He had tried it on many patients, and although none had recovered, he believed that his treatment was the best known. She had declined that heroic operation, but she had endured another, and another, until she moved about painfully, with the scars in her flesh of wounds which she had received in the house of her medical friends.

When we consider the long story of which I have thus tried to make a rough draft, it would not have been at all extraordinary if she had said, "I cannot trust anybody else. Now I give it up. I would sooner die than be tortured anymore. Better to let nature alone than that I should put myself into the hands of any more of these infallible deceivers." Yet she was not dismayed; her faith rose superior to her bitter experience, and she believed in the Lord. It is more easy for me to tell this to you than it is for any of us to realize what her difficulty really must have been. If you too have tried by good works, by ceremonies, by prayers and tears, to obtain salvation, and have been defeated at all points, it is not extraordinary that you should be slow to believe that you can ever be saved. May your faith also, like hers, swim over the crests of the billows of disappointment, and may you hope in the almighty Savior.

There was also another difficulty in her way, and that was *her vivid sense of her own unworthiness*. When she thought of Jesus, she viewed him as a person who was holy as well as powerful; she reverenced as well as trusted him. I am sure she did, for though she summoned courage enough to touch him, her modesty led her to go behind him, as unworthy to be seen. She was evidently afraid to face him, lest he, knowing her unworthiness as she knew it, should refuse her and forbid her approach. She was an unclean woman, according to the ceremonial law, and the shame of her disease prevented her from venturing upon any verbal request or open petition. She had great confidence in his power and mercy, but she had equal awe of his purity, and therefore feared that he would be angry if she touched him. This must have very much hampered her. "How shall I venture to draw near to him? The other physicians I could approach, for I knew them to be very like myself; but concerning him I find that he is a prophet mighty in word and deed – a man of God, and something more. How shall I dare to approach him?" The thought that she would go behind shows her ignorance of the Lord's divinity or her forgetfulness of the attribute of omniscience, but still

> If you have tried by works, to obtain salvation, and have been defeated, it is not extraordinary that you should be slow to believe that you can ever be saved.

it proves that she labored under a sense of unworthiness, and yet she believed. Ah, when you are bowed down with a sense of your own sin and folly, may the Holy Spirit lead you still to believe that Jesus Christ is able to make you whole.

I do not know whether the other difficulty did occur to her at all, but it would to me, namely, that *she had now no money*. She had spent all her living, we are told – all her living. The physicians whom she had previously consulted had all been great in the matter of fees; they could diminish her wealth if they could not establish her health. She had carefully approached them with promises of large reward, assuring them that anything she could give would be freely rendered if she could but be cured; but now she can offer nothing. Her disease remains, but her estate is gone. She is reduced to poverty by her efforts to pursue health; how shall she come before the Great Physician of whom she has heard so much? I should not wonder but what the thought of his greatheartedness and the many cures which he had worked gratuitously helped her to get over that difficulty, but still it occurs to many to dream of purchasing salvation, and to this day many need to be reminded that Jesus gives his grace to those who have no money nor any other price to offer him. His terms are *without money and without cost,* but many awakened consciences forget this.

Perhaps the worst difficulty of all *was her extreme sickness* at that time. We read that she *was not helped at all, but rather had grown worse*. She had been bad enough before, but they had aggravated the disease with their strong acrid medicines, and sharp incisions, and fierce blisters. They had made her worse than nature would have left her if the disease had been let alone. She had reached a frightful stage of the disease and was confessedly beyond all human help. She was as bad as she could be to crawl about at all. Usually such a sickness depresses the spirits, unnerves the mind, and makes the sufferer feel a lack of energy, so that, resolute woman as she was, we should little have marveled if she had said, "No, I can do no more, I must yield; there is nothing now but to lay me down and die, for I am in such a condition that all attempts to gain health are futile." What a grand faith was hers which made her rise above her weakness, overcome her depression of spirit, throw aside the lethargy which was creeping over her, and believe that everything was altered now, for she had no longer to deal with a pretender who would fail her, but with one sent of God and clothed with infinite power who could meet her case – even hers.

So now we come to our third point, which is the vanishing point of all her difficulties. We read of her first that *she had heard of Jesus*. It is Mark who tells us that, *When she had heard of Jesus. Faith comes from hearing.* What had she heard of him? Is it not more than probable that she had been told of that scene which is pictured in Luke's Gospel, in the sixth chapter and the nineteenth verse, when *all the people were trying to touch Him, for power was coming from Him and healing them all*? On one special day great multitudes followed our Lord and pressed upon him to touch him, for whosoever touched him was healed of whatsoever disease he had. What a wonderful scene that must have been when men were so eager to be blessed that they thronged the Great Physician! Not that our Lord was more able to save on one day than on another, but that still there were certain days in which the power seemed to emanate from his person more mightily than at other times, always, as I judge, in proportion to the faith of the people who surrounded him. On that occasion, being followed by a great company who believed in his healing power, they saw such wonders worked that they made a general rush at his blessed person, and all who touched him obtained healing. Some conceive that even the healthy touched him and gained greater vigor from the touch. I should not wonder; at least, in spiritual things it is so. The woman had heard of all the wondrous cures he had worked, and she said to herself, "Then I will touch him, and be healed; for if these reports are true, then if I may but touch him I too shall be made whole." She seems to have believed Christ to be charged with marvelous power, somewhat like a Leyden jar charged with electricity, which gives forth its power most freely. She was not a woman of any very great wisdom, her chief quality was energy. She made a great blunder about our Lord and his garments, but it did not touch the vital point; she so thought of him as to glorify his power, and it sufficed. She truly believed *in him,* and if you believe in Christ, though you are in the dark about a thousand things, your faith will save you. If you do but really believe in Jesus, all your mistakes about him will not really destroy his power to bless you, nor set his heart against you, nor destroy the value of your faith. *"If I just touch His garments,"* says she, "he is so full of power that he will heal me."

The point to notice most distinctly is this: the poor woman believed that the faintest contact with Christ would heal her. Notice the words of my text: *"If I just touch His garments."* The emphasis is not on touching though. No, the point does not lie in the touch, it lies in what was touched: *"If I just touch <u>His</u> garments.* If I cannot get near enough to him to touch his flesh, if I may touch but his garments, or clothes. I am sure if I touch but that fringe, if I cannot do anything more, there will be a connection between him and me, and I shall be healed." Splendid faith! It was not more than Christ deserved, but yet it was remarkable. It was a kind of faith which I desire to possess abundantly. The slenderest contact with Christ healed the body, and will heal the soul; alas, the faintest communication will do so. Do but become united to Jesus, and the blessed work is done. Effect the connection, and the virtue comes to you. *"If I just touch His garments, I will get well."*

I want you carefully to observe that the woman did not seem to think anything about herself. You could not lay the stress upon the pronoun: *"If **I** just touch His garments, **I** will get well"*; it would not be in accordance with the context. No, it is *"If I just touch **His** garments."* It does not matter who I may be, what my uncleanness may be, what my character may be, or what my state of mind may be. If I touch but his clothes, contact being established, I shall be healed. Every person who comes into contact with Jesus by the touch of faith will partake of his healing power. She knew this, and she shut her eyes to all other considerations. She lays no stress upon any mode of touching; no – *"If I just touch His garments"* – not embrace him, nor grasp him, hold him, wrestle with him – no, she believes that any sort of contact will answer the purpose. Now it is always a blessed thing when a man is taught of God to forget himself, and even to forget his faith, and only think upon the Lord Jesus who is the object of our trust. I admire this woman's single eye: she sees nothing but Jesus. Dear heart, she felt that the virtue to heal was all *in him,* and not in her, nor in her touch. She knew that, whatever she might be, his power could master

> Every person who comes into contact with Jesus by the touch of faith will partake of his healing power.

every difficulty of her case, and that the result did not depend upon the mode of her touch, nor the length during which it lasted, but on him alone. It was from him that the virtue was to come, and come it would, however meager the contact. This faith is worth cultivating. To forget everything else, and only to consider the Lord Jesus and his power to bless – this is wisdom. Here am I, a poor lost sinner, but if I can only get to Jesus I shall be forgiven and saved. Here am I, vexed with unruly passions, diseased with this sin and that, but if I may only touch him, he is so full of healing power that, mass of spiritual disease though I may be, the moment I touch him, his virtue will battle with my disease and vanquish it forever. Behold this woman. Again fix your eye upon her till you have become like her. All her thoughts have gone towards the Lord Jesus. She has forgotten herself, forgotten the rampant fury of her disease, forgotten her being behind and out of sight, and even her own touch of him she has put into a secondary place. Everything she looks for must come out of him. She knows that connected with him she will obtain the blessing, but apart from him she will abide in her misery. *"If I just touch His garments,"* – not because his garments are in themselves powerful, but because they are *"**His** garments"* (emphasis added) – the garments which he is wearing, and which consequently will be a medium of communication with himself. There is the vanishing point then, that she has come to think of Jesus and of the certainty of cure through contact with him. If you, seeking sinners, would but think more of Christ, all would be well. You who cannot believe, if you would relinquish your perpetual thoughts about your faith and even about your sin, and begin to think of him – the Son of God, exalted to be a priest and a Savior, the Christ whose finished work is all for sinners, the Christ of the resurrection, Jesus the ever living, Jesus in whom all power dwells – I think you would soon obtain eternal salvation. When your whole heart sets itself upon him and no more upon itself, you will enter into peace, and enjoy rest for your souls.

Fourthly, let us speak of her grand success. Let me remind you again, however, of how she gained her end. She gave to the Lord Jesus an intentional and voluntary touch. Upon the intentional character of it I must insist for a minute. She pressed into the crowd, she was hustled about I do not doubt, and in her weak state she was ready to faint, or even to die. In the midst of those rough men who pressed around the Savior, she found no sympathy. But she is desperately resolute, and bound by hook or by crook to touch his clothes. She presses in behind, for she cares not where she touches him, but touch him she must. In the throng, the garments of Christ became entangled, and at some little distance from him she perceives just a bit of the blue fringe hanging out behind. Now is her time; she has only got to touch, that so strong is her faith, that even the hem of his garment suffices her, for it will make a connection between her and the Savior, and that is all she needs. Her finger is put out, and the deed is done. Yet note that she was not healed by a contact with the Lord or with his garment against her will. She was not pushed against him accidentally, but the touch was active, and not merely passive. *"You see,"* said one of the apostles, *"the crowd pressing in on You."* There was nothing remarkable or effectual about such unavoidable and involuntary touches. Her touch was her own distinct, intentional, voluntary act, and it was done under the persuasion that it would bring her a cure. Such is the faith which brings salvation. It is not every contact with Christ that saves men; it is the arousing of yourself to come near to him, the determinate, the personal, resolute, believing touch of Jesus Christ which saves. We must believe for ourselves. The Spirit helps us, but we ourselves believe. Some of you sit still and hope that the Lord will visit you, and you wait by the pool till an angel comes and stirs the water, and all that kind of thing; but that is not according to the tenor of the gospel command. The gospel does not come to you and say, "Whosoever waits for impressions shall be saved"; but it says, "Believe in the Lord Jesus Christ: for *he who has believed and has been baptized shall be saved.*" Exercise the personal, voluntary, intentional act of faith and you shall be saved.

Oh, I wish to God that some sinner here, deeply conscious of his guilt, might be aroused to perform that act today. However little your knowledge, believe in Jesus as far as you know him. Though you can only come into contact with that part of Christ which you have learned from the Scriptures, that little part of Christ is a part of himself, and you will have touched *him.* You may not be acquainted with the deep things of God, nor with the high doctrines which honor our adorable Lord, but what you do know will suffice for faith. If you say, "I will trust the Lamb of God," and really do so, then you have come into contact with him, and you are saved. Alas, though it be but a believing prayer, a believing sigh, or a believing tear, you have really reached him, and you are made whole; but the touch of faith must be your own act and deed. Nobody is saved in his sleep, nobody may claim to have been transformed into a living soul unless he can prove it by the living act of trust. There must be this appropriating faith, and this the woman had.

And now see her grand success; she no sooner touched than she was healed. In a moment, swift as electricity, the touch was given, the contact was made, the fountain of her blood was dried up, and health beamed in her face immediately. Immediate salvation! I heard a person say the other day that he had heard of immediate conversion, but he did not know what to make of it. Now, herein is a marvelous thing, for such cases are common enough among us. In every case spiritual reviving must be instantaneous. However long the preparatory process may be, there must be a time in which the dead soul begins to live. There must be a time in which the babe is not born, and a moment in which it is born. We are pardoned, or else condemned; there must be a moment in which the man is not pardoned, and another in which he is, and that must be an indistinguishable period of time. I grant you that many workings of conscience, and so on, may go before and melt into the actual reception of life, so as to make it appear a gradual work; but the actual birth, the divine hastening by which the man is made to live in Christ, must of necessity be instantaneous in every case. A man is brought by degrees to a deep sense of sin, to the renunciation of self, and so on; but there is no period in which a man lies between death and life; he either is alive unto God or he is dead in sin. If he is dead he is dead, and if he is alive he is alive, but there is no state between the two. A man is either regenerate or unregenerate; there is no borderland or neutral territory between the two conditions. This woman was healed in a moment, and God can save you, in an instant. May he do it now! If now you believe, it is done.

There may be cases in which a blessing comes to a man and he is scarcely aware of it, but this woman knew that she was saved; she felt in herself that she was made whole from her plague. I do not say that I would like to have undergone her twelve years of suffering for the sake of that moment's joy, but I am sure she was quite content to have done so. The joy of the first hour in which you know you are saved! It is almost too much to live with. It is well that it does not continue in all its vehemence and ecstasy. That flash of light, brighter than the sun! That flush, that flood, that torrent of unutterable bliss, which bears all before it; when at last we can say, "My sins are assuredly removed from me – I am saved, and know it within myself!" That joy, I say, is beyond all description. Blessed be God if we have known that bliss! Blessed be God, I say, and I would repeat the thanks a thousand times. Oh, touch the Savior, poor sinner. The Lord deliver you from anything of your own, and bring you now to look for all to Jesus, and you shall know in yourself that you are made whole from your plague.

She had next the assurance from Christ himself that it was so, but she did not obtain that assurance till she had made an open confession. She felt in herself that she was whole, but there was more comfort in reserve for her. The Lord Jesus Christ would have those who follow him come forward and no longer hide in the crowd. Those who believe ought to be baptized on confession of their faith. He who in his heart believes should with his mouth make confession of him. So Christ turned around and said, *"Who touched my garments?"* At the hearing of that question the newly kindled flame of her joy began to dampen under the fear of losing what she had stolen. Down went her spirits below zero. Then the meddling disciples said, *"You see the crowd pressing in on You, and You say, 'Who touched Me?'"* but Jesus said, as he looked around again, *"Someone did touch Me."* For not his clothes alone, but himself, had been touched by someone. That poor *someone* wanted to sink into the earth; I know she did. She trembled as Jesus looked for her. Those blessed eyes looked around, and by and by they lighted upon her, and as she gazed upon them she did not feel so much alarmed as before; but, still afraid and trembling, she came and fell down before him, and told him all the truth. Then he gently raised her up, and said, *"Daughter, your faith has made you well; go in peace and be healed of your affliction."* Now she knew her cure from Christ's lips as well as from her own consciousness. She had now the divine witness bearing witness with her spirit that she was indeed a healed one. Mark then, that those of you who desire to obtain the witness of the Spirit should come forward and confess your faith and tell what the Lord has done for you; then shall you receive the sealing witness of the Spirit with your spirit that you are indeed born of God. God help you trembling ones who have at last touched my Master's hem to acknowledge it bravely before all and especially before himself.

Brethren, the wine which comes out of these grapes is this: the slightest connection with Jesus will bless us. I desire to send you away with this one truth upon your minds. Whether you are a child of God or not a child of God, hear this weighty doctrine. This woman believed the matchless truth, that the least touch of Christ will cure. *"If I just touch His garments, I will get well."* Believe this, I pray you, each one for himself.

If you, dear child of God, feel very depressed – coldhearted, dead, sluggish – if you but touch his clothes you shall become warmhearted again. You shall get all your life and vigor and enthusiasm back again if you only draw near to your Lord. Do I hear you say, "I seem so full of doubts, so depressed in spirits, so unhappy. I trust I am converted, but I cannot rejoice." Then, brother, get a fresh hold of your Lord, for if you just touch his clothes you shall be made whole of the plague of doubting. Only draw near to Jesus, your risen Lord, by a prayer, or a believing thought, and it is done. Be it ever so slight a touch you shall be made whole. Perhaps you say, "I feel so discouraged in my Christian work, and even feel as if I must give it up. I have seen no conversions lately, and therefore I cannot go about my work with the spirit I once had." Brother, you are falling into a spiritual lethargy, but if you do but touch your Lord again you shall be made whole. Did not the Lord Jesus heal you at the first? He can heal you still. He loses no virtue when he gives forth his power. If a master takes a scholar and fills him full of wisdom, the master is just as wise afterwards as he was at first, and when our Lord grants us a fullness of grace, he remains as full of grace as he was originally. Come to him, then, you downcast saints. Come now. Come always. If any of you have backslidden; if you have

> If a master takes a scholar and fills him full of wisdom, the master is just as wise afterwards as he was at first.

become altogether wrong and out of sorts; if your spiritual digestion is bad; if your spiritual eyes are dim, so that you cannot see afar off; if your knees are weak and if your hands hang down; if your whole head is sick and your heart faint, yet still if you but touch your Lord's garments you shall be made whole. This wonderful medicine has boundless power to restore from relapses as well as to heal the first disease. I cannot help reminding you of the church at Laodicea, which was in so horrible a state that our Lord himself said he must spit it out of his mouth, and yet he added, *"Behold, I stand at the door and knock; if anyone hears My voice and opens the door, I will come in to him and will dine with him, and he with Me."* Communion is the cure for lukewarmness. When you have fallen so low that even Christ himself is sick of you – and it must be a very bad case when he becomes sick of a church – yet even then if you but dine with him and he with you, all will be well. Only get into communion with him who has life in himself and your own life shall become full of vigor. Oh, dear children of God, if you have fallen into an unhappy state, put in practice the example of the woman, and see whether Jesus is not still the same. A touch is a very simple matter, but do not, therefore, doubt its value.

As for you who fear that you are not his children, behold, I set before you an open door, and I pray God that you may be enabled to enter into it. If you just touch the Redeemer's clothes you shall be made whole. Whatever the transgression, the iniquity, or the sin of which you have been guilty, come into contact with the bleeding Lamb and you shall be forgiven. You need not even so much as touch, for there is life in *a look*. A look will set up sufficient contact to bring salvation. *"Turn to Me and be saved, all the ends of the earth."* They *looked to Him and were radiant, and their faces will never be ashamed.* Do but look, do but get out of yourself to him somehow or other, and it is done. Though a glance will not carry a thread as thin as a spider's cobweb, yet it will establish a connection. The ray of light which comes from Jesus' wounds to your eye will be link enough and along it eternal salvation will come to you. Get to Christ, sinner, get to Christ at once. Have you come to him? Then you are saved. Confess your faith, and give Jesus honor. Love him with all your heart; and while angels are rejoicing over you, do be glad also. Christ has saved you, praise him forever and ever. May the Lord add his blessing for Jesus' sake. Amen.

Chapter 13

Sincere Faith

Mark 5:21-43

Verses 21-22 – When Jesus had crossed over again in the boat to the other side, a large crowd gathered around Him; and so He stayed by the seashore. One of the synagogue officials named Jairus came up, and on seeing Him, fell at His feet.

Jarius paid our Lord respect and deference, as was his due. See here an instructive sight: the law at the feet of the gospel. This is the place for the law; the best work the law can do is to bring us to the feet of Jesus. The official had an earnest request to make, and therefore he put himself into a lowly, pleading position. We too shall succeed in prayer when we plead with all humility, bowing in the dust before the Lord.

Verses 23-24 – And implored Him earnestly, saying, "My little daughter is at the point of death; please come and lay Your hands on her, so that she will get well and live. And He went off with him; and a large crowd was following Him and pressing in on Him.

We are told elsewhere that this was his only daughter, and that she was twelve years of age. All the father's heart was set upon her; his life was wrapped up in the child's life. She was now *in extremis*. She will die unless the great Teacher comes and raises her up to health again. There was faith in this official, and therefore we read, *And He went off with him.* Faith ensures the aid of Jesus without delay, and if you and I can trust him he will go with us. Friend, can you rely on Jesus? Then shall it be written of you also, *And He went off with him.*

> Verse 25 – *A woman who had had a hemorrhage for twelve years.*

In this passage of our Lord's life he blesses two women – the daughter sick unto death, and the woman sorely diseased. A large portion of the cures that Jesus worked were upon men, but those worked upon women are nearly all especially noteworthy. Surely of miracles of a spiritual kind the women have a double share. This poor woman had been a sufferer for twelve years, that is to say, just as long as the daughter had lived. How many only live to suffer, their existence being little better than a prolonged wasting away.

> Verses 26-27 – *And had endured much at the hands of many physicians, and had spent all that she had and was not helped at all, but rather had grown worse—after hearing about Jesus, she came up in the crowd behind Him and touched His cloak.*

After hearing about Jesus. Faith comes from hearing. Whatever you do not hear, take care that you hear much of Jesus. Some preach the church; it would be better by far if they preached the church's Head. Some preach up a creed; it would be wiser to proclaim him who is the essence of the creed. Attend those places where most is said of Christ, for it is by hearing of him that you will be blessed as this poor woman was. That which she heard brought her to Jesus, and coming to Jesus is the great thing to be desired. When she had heard of Jesus

> **Attend those places where most is said of Christ, for it is by hearing of him that you will be blessed.**

she determined to obtain for herself the healing which he was able to bestow. Have you no such resolve?

> Verse 28 – *For she thought, "If I just touch His garments, I will get well."*

Not "If I *may* just touch his garments," as if she meant to lay stress on the mere touch. The woman believed that everywhere Jesus was full of healing energy even to his garments, and therefore she felt, "If I just touch his clothes, I shall thus come into contact with him, and I shall be whole." Nor did she rest content with theory; she carried it out into act: she pressed through the crowd and *touched the fringe of His cloak*, as Luke informs us. O that all good intentions were as promptly turned into actions!

> Verse 29 – *Immediately the flow of her blood was dried up; and she felt in her body that she was healed of her affliction.*

Immediately. Mark is very fond of that word *immediately;* and truly the instantaneous action of our Lord at the call of faith is so remarkable that we do not wonder that the Gospel writer should record it. Are there not sick souls here who would gladly obtain an immediate salvation? A touch of Jesus will win it.

> Verses 30-31 – *Immediately Jesus, perceiving in Himself that the power proceeding from Him had gone forth, turned around in the crowd and said, "Who touched My garments?" And His disciples said to Him, "You see the crowd pressing in on You, and You say, 'Who touched Me?'"*

Peter led the way in this remark, acting as the spokesman for the rest. Jesus is always right, even when to the eye of sense he appears to be wrong. We ought never to suspect him of making a mistake; indeed, for us to question him would be great presumption.

> Verse 32 – *And He looked around to see the woman who had done this.*

He knew who it was, but evidently he looked for *the woman*. He looked around, not to make a discovery of what was unknown, but to look on one whom he would gently bring out of her hiding place. Taking a long and steady gaze around the multitude, he at last singled her out.

> Verse 33 – *But the woman fearing and trembling, aware of what had happened to her, came and fell down before Him and told Him the whole truth.*

Here is another instructive sight. Just as we saw the law at Christ's feet, here we have a needy sufferer at Christ's feet. What a picture! If the ruler of the synagogue had a right to be at Jesus' feet, much more did this poor healed one who owed everything to him. Oh, you who have been saved by Jesus, worship him; fall at his feet with reverence, sit there with attention, and abide there in obedience.

> Verses 34-35 – *And He said to her, "Daughter, your faith has made you well; go in peace and be healed of your affliction." While He was still speaking, they came from the house of the synagogue official, saying, "Your daughter has died; why trouble the Teacher anymore?"*

The word for "trouble" is a very strong one, as if they judged it to be exacting on the ruler's part to take the Savior to his house. Surely it implies that there were such signs of weariness upon our Lord that friendly minds judged it to be troubling him to induce him to struggle through the crowd to the house. Sometimes these sidelights reveal more of the condition of the Man of Sorrows than the narrative actually records. Ah, there is no fear of troubling Jesus now; it is his joy to visit where he is prayed to come.

> Verse 36 – *But Jesus, overhearing what was being spoken,*

said to the synagogue official, "Do not be afraid any longer, only believe."

This was as much as to say, "That is all you can do, and all you need to do. Just trust me. Be not staggered if death itself be there. I am greater than death." Would our Lord have spoken thus if he had not been conscious of infinite power, conscious indeed of his deity? How say some among you that he is not the Son of God? Assuredly he speaks the language of omnipotence. These are not the words of a mere man; hear them and practice them – *"Do not be afraid any longer, only believe."*

> Verses 37-38 – *And He allowed no one to accompany Him, except Peter and James and John the brother of James. They came to the house of the synagogue official; and He saw a commotion, and people loudly weeping and wailing.*

That is to say, they saw the hired mourners who came there to mimic sorrow. Everything false and hired must go out when Jesus enters to work his wonders.

> Verse 39 – *And entering in, He said to them, "Why make a commotion and weep? The child has not died, but is asleep."*

She was not dead once and for all. He knew that she was dead for the time, but he spoke broadly, looking at the future, and in his sense she was not dead, since in a few moments she would be among them alive. Her brief death was in effect no death, but a mysterious sleep.

> Verse 40 – *They began laughing at Him.*

How this sentence ought to encourage any who, in doing right, meet with condemning words and reproach. *They began laughing at Him.* Will you ever think it hard that you should be ridiculed when the Lord, the Prince of Glory, is laughed at? No, my brethren, say in your hearts,

> If on my face for thy dear name
> > Shame and reproaches be,
> All hail reproach, and welcome shame,
> > If thou remember me.

> Verse 40 – *But putting them all out.*

And here is another flash of deity. Did you ever notice how the Lord Jesus frequently does things which are perfectly unexplainable if performed by a mere man, as when he went into the temple and cleared out the buyers and sellers with a scourge of small cords, and when in Gethsemane he only said, *"I am He,"* and they fell backward? Here, again, he put out of the room all the minstrels and hired mourners. Does it not show that occasionally a majesty flashed from the human person of Christ which overwhelmed everybody, and was perfectly irresistible? Yes, in his deepest humiliation our Lord had a glory about him which revealed the indwelling God.

> Verse 40 – *He took along the child's father and mother and His own companions, and entered the room where the child was.*

Christ and death together in one room: this is a grand picture! Look at the pale, dead child and the life-giving Lord. We know what the issue will be when our Lord enters the arena with the last enemy.

> Verse 41 – *Taking the child by the hand.*

That chill, motionless hand! See how the little girl lies before him like a dew-laden lily damp with the depression of death.

> Verse 41 – *He said to her, "Talitha kum!" (which translated means, "Little girl, I say to you, get up!").*

He spoke to her in her own dear mother tongue. How sweet to be recalled to life by sounds which were so familiar. There is something simple about all the calls of heavenly love.

> Verses 42-43 – *Immediately the girl got up and began to walk, for she was twelve years old. And immediately they were completely astounded. And He gave them strict orders that no one should know about this.*

He did not wish to have this miracle published. There were reasons why, just then, there should not be much noise made about his miracles. Besides, our blessed Savior was ever gentle and modest, as it is written, *"He will not quarrel, nor cry out; nor will anyone hear His voice in the streets."* He did not seek the honor of men. Let us do nothing with the view of its being blazoned abroad.

> Verse 43 – *And He said that something should be given her to eat.*

This command is natural enough, but how oddly that it follows a miracle. Could not he who gave her back to life have satisfied her appetite without food? Yes; but Jesus is ever careful with his miracles, and this is the mark of the true Christ. Look at antichrist, and see her lavish marvels at Lourdes, and a thousand shrines – shovelfuls of them. Paul speaks of these signs and lying wonders as the trademark of the mystery of iniquity. But the Christ works no needless miracle; he pauses where the need of the supernatural ceases. He also teaches us this lesson, that when he gives spiritual life it is our duty to furnish it with suitable nutrients of divine truth. We should teach and console those who are newly born into the household of faith; especially is this the duty of parents and those who are our fathers in the church. Let us not fail to obey our Lord's precept, and may God thus bless the reading of his Word to us.

> **The Christ works no needless miracle; he pauses where the need of the supernatural ceases.**

> *Immediately Jesus, perceiving in Himself that the power*

> *proceeding from Him had gone forth, turned around in the crowd and said, "Who touched My garments?" And His disciples said to Him, "You see the crowd pressing in on You, and You say, 'Who touched Me?'"* (Mark 5:30-31)

We just now read the story of this woman who was immediately healed. Spiritual persons know that the miracles recorded by the Gospel writer are true, because they have seen them reproduced. That is to say, we have not seen an issue of blood stopped by the touch of Christ's garments, but we have seen the spiritual counterpart of it. We have seen men and women healed of all kinds of spiritual and moral diseases by coming into contact with our Lord Jesus. They have touched Jesus, and they have been made whole; for Jesus lives still, and his healing work is not ended, but has only entered into another phase. Jesus has said, *"Lo, I am with you always, even to the end of the age";* and, being with us, he is not here inactively or ineffectually, but he is here, the same yesterday, today, and forever, to work the same miracles, only not on men's bodies, but also on their souls. Jesus is present to heal leprosies of the mind, and to open the eyes of the understanding. Yes, he is still among us to raise those who are dead in trespasses and sins. Though we live in a great hospital for lepers, yet are we comforted because we see that Jesus walks the hospitals, and still heals on the right hand and on the left all those who come in contact with him. At the sight of his wonders of grace we cry out as they did in the days of his flesh, *"He has done all things well."*

As the miracles of our Lord Jesus Christ are pictures of his wondrous works in the spiritual kingdom, so are they also instructive, because they set forth most vividly much impressive and precious truth. I have but one desire now, and that is to lead some poor sin-sick soul to Jesus, and I shall not be satisfied unless very many shall for the first time break through this crowd and press forward to touch the hem of Christ's robe and find immediate healing thereby.

I shall speak upon three things. First, I will speak upon *this wonderful person,* who, if he is but touched, gives out a healing virtue. Secondly, I will speak upon *that very remarkable touch,* which is evidently a distinct thing from the touch and pressure of the eager, curious crowd.

And then I will ask you to answer *the singular personal question* which the Savior puts to this assembly: *"Who touched Me?"* Perhaps some are here today who shall be able to say with trembling assurance, "I touched him, and he has made me whole." May the Holy Spirit cause it to be so.

First, then, I have the blessed work, far beyond my power, but, oh! how sweet to my soul, of speaking upon this wonderful person.

The Lord Jesus Christ, as he stood in the midst of the crowd, was charged with *power.* An effective healing force was in him. Sometimes he emitted it by words, frequently by the touch of his hand, and, in this case, it seemed to stream even from his garments when he was but rightly and properly touched. He was charged with omnipotent blessing, and those who came into contact with him were made whole. Do not think, dear friends, that he is less full of benedictions for the sons of men today. No, if I may venture to say as much, he is fuller still of healing power, for he has bowed his head to death and worn the thorn-crown, and he has risen from the tomb and gone up into glory leading captivity captive. In our midst at this moment he is, if it be possible, more charged with energy to bless than even when he walked the fields of Palestine, and healed the feeble men and women of his time.

Observe that Christ's power to bless lay mainly in *the fact of his deity.* That humble, weary, wayworn man was the Son of the Highest. Because he was still very God of very God, his will was omnipotent. He did but speak to fever or leprosy, and they left at his bidding. Even as the centurion put it – *"For I also am a man under authority, with soldiers under me; and I say to this one, 'Go!' and he goes, and to another, 'Come!' and he comes, and to my slave, 'Do this!' and he does it"* – even so the divine Christ did but will it, and diseases fled at his bidding. He is not less divine today. At this hour he cries, *"Turn to Me and be saved, all the ends of the earth; for I am God, and there is no other."*

But his power to bless us lies also in *the fact that he had become man* for our sake. I speak with lowly reverence, but *"it is written, that the Christ would suffer."* He found it needful to be surrounded by infirmities that he might save us from our infirmities. He was able to heal not only because he was God, but also because he was *Immanuel, "God with us."* Oh, the blessed mystery of the incarnation! What a fountain of mercy it is to us miserable sinners! He that spanned the heavens stooped to be wrapped in swaddling clothes and laid in a manger. He that bears up the pillars of the universe was himself weary here below, and by his weakness gave us strength. Because he took our sicknesses, therefore is he able to deliver us from spiritual sickness and make us every bit whole. Oh see, my brethren, God incarnate present among us, *able also to save forever those who draw near to God through Him.*

In addition to this, it is never to be forgotten that our blessed Master, being both divine and human, was also *endowed with the Holy Spirit without measure.* Often are we told in Scripture that he was able to do these mighty signs and wonders because the Holy Spirit was with him. Even now that same Holy Spirit is with him in abundance of power. Jesus, whom I preach to you, the man of Nazareth, the mighty God, has the residue of the Spirit, by whose power he can remove from us all the guilt and power of sin, and can make us perfectly whole, that is, holy.

Is not this a thing to be delighted in – that there should be such a Savior, and such a Savior accessible today? Every sort of spiritual sickness the blessed physician of souls can heal. I am able to say that I have seen him heal such sicknesses. I think I have been witness to the cure of every sort of sin. At any rate, he is healing me of my own sicknesses, and I am under his tender care, persuaded that he will make even me perfectly whole before he is done with me. I have seen the proud man, who could not else have been cured of his haughtiness, come and sit at Jesus' feet and learn of him, until he has been made meek and lowly. I have seen the obstinate man come to Jesus and gladly take Christ's yoke upon him, and become willingly and joyfully obedient to the supreme will of him who bought him with his blood. Often have I seen the unclean and the profane enticed to Jesus by his gentleness, and they have been made pure. Now, often have these eyes seen the despairing ones who have been on the verge of madness cheered and comforted till they have sung for joy of heart. How frequently have I seen the coward made brave, the miserable made gentle, the revengeful made forgiving by coming into contact with Jesus! You cannot love my Lord and love sin. You cannot trust my Lord and yet delight yourselves in iniquity. Only get near to him, and he will begin a cure upon your character, and, before long, will

> **You cannot trust my Lord and yet delight yourselves in iniquity.**

perfect it. If your sickness should be a delight in the pleasures and the pursuits of the world, he will teach you not to love the world, nor the things of it. Do you suffer from selfishness? He shall teach you to deny yourself. His lance and nails and cross shall crucify you with himself till self-seeking shall die. Are you afflicted with a laziness that will not let you be active? My Master's zeal shall fire your soul till, like him, you shall be consumed with energy. I do not mind what your fault is, my brother or my sister; but this I know, that there is power in my divine Lord and Master to redeem you from that fault. He can destroy evil and create good. Behold, he makes all things new!

Ah, now, if I were addressing myself to a number of persons that were blind, or deaf, or sick, and I told them that Christ was here to heal them of their bodily infirmities, what a rush there would be. Set Jesus up in Trafalgar Square to be touched by all manner of sick folks, and I warrant you the crowd would press one another to death in their eagerness to get at him. But, surely, spiritual sicknesses are worse. It is worse to have a blind spiritual eye than a blind bodily eye. But men do not think so, and consequently they are not anxious for spiritual health. I may praise up my Master, as I willingly would, even to the skies, and yet men will care nothing for him, for they would just as soon be morally and spiritually sick as not; and some of them are even proud of their sicknesses. Well, what shall become of you? In that day when God shuts out the spiritually sick folks – the diseased, the disturbed, the putrid, the corrupt – when he casts them into Topheth because they cannot be permitted to stand among his saints in his holy house in heaven, whose fault shall it be that you were not healed? Who shall bear the blame that you died in your sins? Not the Lord Jesus Christ, but yourselves, because you chose your own delusions, and would have none of him.

Thus have I feebly tried to set him forth; and oh, how I wish that you desired him and longed for him, for he is here, and a touch of him will save you! Poor souls, must he pass you by?

And now, secondly, I want to say a little, by God's help, about the remarkable touch of this woman.

Such a touch as hers may be given to Jesus at this good hour. We cannot by our finger literally touch his garments; but there is a spiritual touch that can still be given to Christ, which will draw virtue out of him, so that all our spiritual diseases shall immediately be healed. This contact is not always described in Scripture as a touch; sometimes it is represented as hearing. *"Incline your ear and come to Me. Listen, that you may live."* There is a link between you and me today in the fact that I speak and you hear. Well, a spiritual connection, of which this is the analogy, if it be set up between Christ and you, will cure you of your sin. Sometimes this contact is described as being formed by a look. This is the favorite symbol. *"Turn to Me and be saved, all the ends of the earth."* It is apparently a very meager connection which is set up by a glance; and yet if you have such a contact between you and Christ as the eye made between the dying Israelite and the brazen serpent, it will save you. Here in this narrative the contact is symbolized by a touch. The patient by her touch was linked with Jesus, and felt in her body that she was healed of her plague.

Now, do you not wish to touch Jesus and be made whole, that is, holy? If you do, remember that the touch must be a voluntary one. If any of you were brought into a supposed connection with Christ when you were children, without consciousness of what was done, I charge you, do not put any confidence in the ceremony. Religion performed for you, when you were unconscious and gave no consent to it, cannot possibly save you. Whatever there might be in it, there is nothing saving in it. You must come into a voluntary union with Jesus if you would be made whole. It must be an intentional contact. Some were pressed against the Savior as they pushed against each other, and as the crowd surged to and fro; but this woman was not driven against Christ without her consent. Oh no, she was eager to get at him. She pushed; she strove; and at last she reached the fringe of his garments, and a contact was established intentionally by her finger. She wished to be made whole, and she touched Christ with that view. You too must come to Jesus with the view of being delivered from the guilt, penalty, and power of sin; and you must get into contact with Christ with the intent that he should be your Savior. I entreat you to see to this, and may the Holy Spirit lead you to do it at once.

"Oh," say you, "but I do not know how to get into contact with the Savior." The best way, the only way, is by believing in him. If you, today, say in your heart, "I trust Christ to save me," there is immediately a contact between you and Christ of the right kind: you are the trusting one, and he is the person trusted in. There is a point of union between you and Christ, and this will save you; for there never was one yet that did wholly trust the blood and righteousness of Jesus without finding himself fully justified in so trusting. The rule of the kingdom is – *"It shall be done to you according to your faith."* If your faith be only as a grain of mustard seed, if it is genuine faith, it shall work in you the cure of your soul's disease, and you shall live unto righteousness. The point of contact is a main consideration, and I pray you look to it. Do you not see that when the woman's finger touched Christ's garment there was established at once a connection between the two, along which the divine virtue flashed? I will not illustrate this by electricity, for such an illustration will suggest itself to you all; but the fact is that faith sets up a contact between the sinner and Christ, and through this the healing virtue comes to us.

Faith on our part is an act of reception. We agree to receive Christ as what God has made him to be: a propitiation for sin. We accept him as our Savior, Teacher, Leader, Ruler, and in all these senses he is ours. Whatever God the Father says that Jesus is, we agree that he is that, and we take him to ourselves to be all that to us. Especially since he has come to save his people we accept him as our Savior. I have sometimes quoted to you the words of Luther, who often put a truth so broadly that he overshadowed other truths, and uttered language which would not bear to be closely looked into, though most fit to set forth his immediate meaning. Luther says, "I will have nothing to do with saving myself. Jesus Christ is a Savior: I leave my soul wholly in his hands." That puts it very broadly, but it is what I mean within a little; that is to say, you must just go and say, "I cannot deliver myself from the power of sin, but I know that Jesus can deliver me, and I put myself into his hands that he may do it." When faith thus unites us to Jesus, the healing virtue will flow from him to us.

> **When faith thus unites us to Jesus, the healing virtue will flow from him to us.**

"Oh, well," says one, "I have often heard you preach about being saved from sinning by Christ, but I do not feel that I can do anything." Just so. That is why I want you to get Christ to work in you and for you. "Oh, but I am nobody." That is the very sort of person I delight to discover, that Jesus Christ may make you into somebody and say, "Somebody has touched me." A nobody is made into somebody when he once touches Jesus Christ. "Oh, but I am . . . ." There will be no end to these objections, and therefore let me say plainly, Never mind what you are. The question is, What is the Lord Jesus Christ? If he is able to save you, then trust him, rely upon him, rest your soul with him. Did I hear someone reply, "I do not see how that will make me better"? My speedy answer is that faith, simple as it seems, is the one thing which, by God's grace, shall make you a new man. Here is the philosophy of it – If you trust Jesus, you will love him; if you love him, you will serve him. Believing that Jesus has saved you, gratitude springs up in your heart and becomes the motive power by which a new life is begun and continued. I pray you try it. I do remember years ago when I tried the power of faith in Jesus. It was a poor, feeble trembling touch that I gave to Christ, but by it from sadness and despair I rose to gladness and hope. I had something to live for, and I had the expectation of being able to accomplish it, too, when I had touched him. And at this hour, when I am sick and sad and sorry and sinful, I go to him, and I am blessed. If I want washing, he must wash me; if I want clothing, he must clothe me; if I want strength, he must invigorate me. He is all in all to my soul; and so I do but tell you what I know myself, and persuade you by my own experience to trust him.

Lastly, the poor woman, having touched the hem of Christ's garment, and being made whole, was about to slink away, when the Master asked the remarkable question which brought her to the front, so that she was obliged to confess what Christ had done for her.

I wish to God that all of you who have felt the power of Christ would bear testimony to the fact. As a rule, those who have been converted in this place have not been backward to confess Christ, but still some among you who love my Lord have never yet affirmed your attachment to him. You are on Christ's side, but you do not wear his uniform and acknowledge his cause. You do not confess him, though he has promised that those who do so he will confess at the last day. We are all too fond of ease, and so it happens in this world of ours that much of the force of goodness remains unused because men are inactive and reserved. Who covets the front of the battle? Only a bold, brave man whose heart God has touched. He comes to the front, and remains the object of opposition when caution might dictate that he should shelter himself from the conflict. Oh, my dear friend, if you love Jesus Christ, my Master, I ask you never to be ashamed to be on his side, and on the side of the right and the true, the just, and the kind. Take your place like a man, and declare yourself a soldier of the cross. Too many are like the timid woman of our text: they receive benefits from Jesus, and then try to lose themselves in the crowd. I will tell you a little about that.

The touch that brings virtue out of Christ is one that cannot be perceived by our fellow men. That young man over yonder touched Christ today, but he who sits close to him is not aware of it. The saving act is done in secret, and sometimes it is almost a secret to the person himself: he hardly dares to think that he has been so bold. This poor woman shrank into herself; she knew that she was cured, but she was afraid to think of what she had done to get the cure. I have known many poor souls who have come to believe in Christ and yet feel as if it was presumption to do so. It appears to a truly humbled conscience to be so great a mercy to be forgiven that it feels hardly justified in daring to think that Jesus could have put away its sin.

Listen to me you who are trembling. Let not your fears rob your Lord of his honor. You must confess your faith, for Jesus loves that those whom he heals should acknowledge it. That is why he turned around and said, *"Who touched my garments?"* He delights in that tender declaration, wet with many tears. If you have done good to one of your neighbors, you think it hard if no word of thanks is spoken. I have known benevolence almost shriveled up for lack of gratitude. My Master is not of such a temper, but still he welcomes words of humble acknowledgment. He loves to hear the bleating of the sheep which his shoulders have brought back to the fold. He loves that much love which comes of having much forgiven. Do not, then, hold your tongue. If Jesus has indeed healed you, tell him of it, and tell his people of it to his praise. Such grace ought to be known. Is there anything to be ashamed of? For my part, I glory in being saved by Christ. If he that is a Christian is a fool, write me down among the fools. Say you not so, poor working brother? When you go into the workshop and they say, "These Christian people are a set of hypocritical Presbyterians," will you not answer, "Then put me down among them." If your Lord and Master did not grudge to stand in the courtyard for you till they did spit in his face, what a coward you must be if you ever draw back from professing your faith in him out of a fear of ridicule. If he acknowledged your cause even unto death, never blush to be regarded as his follower. Let every cowardly thought be banished from your spirit. If Jesus saved you from going down into the pit and made you a new creature, never be ashamed in any company to say, "Christ has made me whole, and henceforth I am his."

From that day, the healed woman and Jesus had instituted a friendship that never ended; they had conversed together, and their lives were openly linked together. Would you not wish the same thing to happen to you?

To this woman Christ said, *"Go in peace."* What a blessing she gained by being fetched out of her hiding place; for had she gone away without an open confession, she might often have been disturbed in mind by the fear that a stolen cure would not be permanent. The Master said, *"Go in peace,"* and a profound calm fell upon her spirit, as when the seabirds sit on the waves and all the winds have fallen into a deep sleep. She was a happy woman from that day on, for Jesus had said, *"Go in peace,"* and what could trouble her anymore?

> **If he acknowledged your cause even unto death, never blush to be regarded as his follower.**

Now, it may be that some of you who love Christ will go to heaven safely enough, but you will miss a vast amount of comfort on the road because you have never openly confessed that you belong to Christ. Perhaps certain ones of you will never get peace till you declare your discipleship, and link your whole life with Jesus. When you do that, and take up his cross with all its shame, and are known to be a Christian in every society into which you enter, then shall your peace be like a river.

I am almost done, only I would put to the whole congregation the question, "Who has touched Christ today?" O that some would answer in their hearts, "I have touched him today by faith." Why should you not all trust the appointed Savior? Do you tell me that you do not understand what faith is? It is trusting – trusting wholly upon the person, work, merit, and power of the Son of God. Some think this trusting to be a strange business, but indeed it is the simplest thing that can possibly be. To some of us, truths which were once hard to believe are now matters of fact which we should find it hard to doubt. If one of our grandfathers were to rise from the dead, and come into the present state of things, what a deal of trusting he would have to do. He would say tomorrow morning, "Where are the flint and steel? I want a light"; and we should give him a little box with tiny pieces of wood in it, and tell him to strike one of them on the box. He would have to trust a good deal before he would believe that fire would thus be produced. We should next say to him, "Now that you have a light, turn that tap and light the gas." He sees nothing, but is annoyed with an offensive smell. How can he believe that light will come from that invisible vapor? And yet it does. "Now come with us, grandfather. Sit in that chair. Look at that box in front of you. You shall see your likeness directly." "No, child," he would say, "that is ridiculous. The sun take my portrait? I cannot believe it." "Yes, and you shall ride fifty miles in an hour without horses." "I do not believe it," says he. "What is more, you shall speak to your son in New York, and he shall answer you in a few minutes." Would we not astonish the old gentleman? Would he not need all his faith to believe this? And yet these things are believed by us without effort, because experience has made us familiar with them. Faith is greatly needed by you who are strangers to spiritual things; you seem lost while we are talking about them, and our very words puzzle you. But oh, how simple it is to us who have the new life and have communion with spiritual realities. We have a Father to whom we speak and he hears us, and a blessed Savior who hears our heart's longings, and helps us in our struggles against sin. It is all plain to him who understands. May the Spirit of God bring every one of you to understand it! What a joy it would be if we all touched the Savior, would all be healed of sin, and all be admitted to stand at his right hand forever. Then, whoever we may be, and however much we may differ in rank and talent, we shall all heartily join to sing the new song, "Worthy is the Lamb that was slain to receive honor and glory forever and ever. Amen."

Chapter 14

Tell It All

But the woman fearing and trembling, aware of what had happened to her, came and fell down before Him and told Him the whole truth. (Mark 5:33)

Jesus was pressing through the throng to the house of Jairus to raise the ruler's dead daughter; but he is so profuse in goodness that he works another miracle while upon the road. While yet this rod of Aaron bears the blossom of an unaccomplished wonder, it yields the ripe almonds of a perfect work of mercy. It is enough for us, if we have some single purpose, to go immediately and accomplish it; it would be imprudent to expend our energies by the way. Hastening to the rescue of a drowning friend, we cannot afford to exhaust our strength upon another in like danger. It is enough for a tree to yield one sort of fruit, and for a man to fulfill his own peculiar calling. But our Master knows no limit of power or boundary of mission. He is so prolific in grace, that like the sun which shines as it fulfills its course, his path is radiant with loving-kindness. He is a fiery arrow of love which not only reaches its ordained target, but also perfumes the air through which it flies. Virtue is always going out of Jesus, as sweet odors exhale from the flowers; and it always will be emanating from him, as light from the central orb. What delightful encouragement this truth affords us. If our Lord is so ready to heal the sick and bless the needy, then, my soul, be not slow to put yourself in his way, that he may smile on you! Be not slack in asking, if he be so abundant in bestowing! I will give earnest heed to his word today, for it may be, though the sermon should be mainly intended to bless another, yet incidentally, and by the way, Jesus may speak through it to my soul. Men speak of killing two birds with one stone, but my Lord heals many souls on one journey. May he not heal me? Thou Son of David turn your eye and look upon my distress, and let me be made whole this day!

The afflicted woman in the narrative came behind Jesus in the press and won a cure from him – all unobserved by the multitude. Ah, how many there may be in the crowd who are really healed by Jesus Christ, but concerning whom little or nothing is known! It is delightful to *see* conversion-work, to trace the good hand of the Lord, and to rejoice therein; but, beyond a doubt, when the secrets of all hearts shall be revealed, we shall find that Jesus Christ has worked ten times more wonders than eye has seen or ear heard. We must not dream that we know all that our infinite God is doing. The works of the Lord are great, and are sought out by all them that have pleasure therein, but even these seekers see not all.

> Full many a gem of purest ray serene
> The dark unfathomed caves of ocean bear;
> Full many a flower is born to blush unseen,
> And waste its sweetness on the desert air.

Let each timid hearer now say, "If it be so that there are many who receive God's grace, who through much trembling hide themselves from the eyes of men, may it not be so with me – may I not venture secretly to touch the Lord, and since the virtue streams abundantly from him, may I not hope that he will bless me, even me, unknown, unnoticed though I be."

I commence with these two or three notes of encouragement, just to tune my harp, for I desire to sing a song to the Lord's well-beloved, of which the burden shall be – *"Comfort, O comfort My people."* The story of this trembling woman, from first to last, though it is but a piece of byplay, as I have said before, is one of the most touching and teaching of the Savior's miracles. The woman was very ignorant. She fondly imagined that virtue came out of Christ by a law of necessity, without his knowledge or direct will. She supposed that the holiness and divinity of his nature had communicated a mysterious effectualness to his garments. Just as the bones of Elisha had restored a dead man to life, so she conceived that the garments worn upon the living body of the Savior might remove her sickness. She had true faith, but there was, to say the least, a tinge of superstition in it. Moreover, she was a total stranger to the generosity of Jesus' character, or else she would not have gone behind to steal the cure which he was so ready to bestow. Misery should always place itself right in the face of mercy. Had she known the love of Jesus' heart she would have said, "I have but to put myself where he can see me; his omniscience will teach him my case, and his love at once will work my cure." We admire her faith, but we marvel at her strange ignorance; for how could she imagine that she would be hidden from one whose garment could stop her issue of blood? He who could cure her secret malady could certainly perceive her secret touch. After she had obtained the cure she rejoices with trembling; glad was she that the divine virtue had worked a marvel in her, but she feared lest Christ should retract the blessing and put a negative upon the grant of his grace. How sad that she should have such unworthy ideas of our gracious Master; little did she comprehend the fullness of his love.

You and I have not so clear a view of him as we could wish; we know not the heights and depths and lengths and breadths of his love, but we know him better than she did – at least we know for sure that he is too good to withdraw from a trembling soul the gift which it has been able to obtain. But here is the marvel of it: little as was her knowledge, great as was her unbelief, and astounding as was her misconception of our Lord, yet her faith, because it was real faith, saved her. If we have faith as a grain of mustard seed, there is life in that grain, and die it cannot. A ray of faith ensures complete deliverance from the blackness of darkness forever. If in the list of the Lord's children you and I are written as the feeblest of the family, yet being children, and heirs through faith, no power, human or devilish, can reverse our adoption. If we cannot clasp the Lord in our hands with Simeon, if we dare not lean our heads upon his bosom with John, yet if we can venture in the press behind him, and touch the hem of his garment, we are made whole. Take courage, you that are so timid that you seldom read your titles clear to mansions in the skies, for the title is nonetheless sure because you cannot read it. I wish to God your faith were stronger, but God forbid that I should wound your sensitive spirits and discourage your growing hopes. My Master did not put out the smoldering wick, he did not break off the battered reed, and neither must the servant do so. I would rather see you, with all your timidity, exercising a real faith in Jesus, than to mourn over you, as lifted up with rash presumptuous confidence, without a solid ground for your boldness. Better to go limping to heaven than running to hell. Better to enter into life lame or maimed, than having two hands and two feet to be cast into hellfire. Take courage, I say, you trembling one. To cry, "Abba," with tears and groans, is better than to shout with loud boastings, "Peace, peace," where there is no peace. Happier far to be in the fold with the tender lambs than to be driven away with the strong and lusty goats.

Now let us turn aside to hear what this woman says. She has a word for two classes. First, *to the repentant,* urging him to a full confession. She *told Him the whole truth* – the repentant do the same. Next, *to the true convert,* an exhortation to an open profession; for she declared before them all how she had been made whole. Secret disciple – *"Go and do the same."*

This timid woman shall be an example to all who are repentant to make a full profession of their state and condition. She *told Him the whole truth.* There need be no difficulty about the matter of prayer with a soul that needs help from Christ. Never question your power to pray acceptably if God has given you a sense of need. Say not, "I have no eloquence; I cannot arrange my words; I cannot fashion a suitable form of extemporaneous address." Remember that none of these things are necessary. All that is wanted for acceptable prayer is, that in the name of Jesus, you will tell the Lord the whole truth. You require no argument more moving than your misery; you need no description more glowing than your sad case itself affords you. Though you know not how to plead your cause as an advocate in a court of law, plead it as the publican in the court of mercy. The simple statement of your wants, and the sincere expression of your desire that those wants should be supplied, for Jesus' sake, is all the prayer that God asks of you.

We should, dear friends, if we would come before the Lord acceptably, tell him the whole truth about *our disease.* This woman did so. Her malady was such that her modesty had prompted her to conceal it from the throng, but she must not hide it from Jesus. Her disease had rendered her unclean, so that she had no right to mingle with the crowd, since her touch defiled all who touched her. All this defilement she must own in the presence of the Healing One, nor must she – now that her Lord demands it – hide it from the multitude who are round about her. Not to gloat over sin, but to show how sensible we are of it, we ought to make a full declaration of our disease to Jesus, and when he wills it, we must conceal from no one what sinners we were until grace reclaimed us. Sin is our disease. Sinner, acknowledge it. Go, show yourself, in all your foulness, to the Great High Priest. Confess the depravity of your nature; tell him that your whole head is sick and your whole heart is faint. Do not draw the picture flatteringly when you are in prayer. Confess that your thoughts are foul, your imaginations filthy, your heart corrupt, and your judgment perverted. Tell him that your memory will treasure up foolishness, but that it drops the words of wisdom from its feeble hand. Tell him you are altogether as an unclean thing, and that all your righteousnesses are as filthy rags. Make a clean breast of your overt acts. Tell him, when you are alone in your closet, precisely what you have done. Do not disguise your crimes, nor mince matters by using dainty terms. If you have been a thief, tell him so; if you have been a drunkard, confess it not thus – "Lord, I have sometimes indulged the flesh"; but say, "Lord, I have been drunk." Put it plainly. Acknowledge it in your privacy before God by its own proper name. It is a great temptation of Satan, with convinced souls, to induce them to apply grand titles to their sins. I pray you do not do so. Acknowledge, sinner, just what you have been, and wear the sackcloth and ashes which suit your state. Call a spade a spade, and do not go about trimming your way. This is not the time for your Agags to go delicately; they must be hewed in pieces before the Lord your God. Confess the aggravations of your sin; conceal not from God that you sinned against light and knowledge, against many warnings, and the strivings of an awakened conscience. Do not hesitate to acknowledge that you have wiped away the tear which the gospel forced from you, and have gone once again into the world's sin, and lost every good impression. It is well for us, if we are seeking the mercy of God, to state the worst of our case and not the best. It is a sure sign that mercy will soon come when we are ready to confess to the full our misery. O sinner, where are you? Have you been before my God in prayer? Go again, and be more full and clear in your confession; you cannot describe your case in terms too black. It is not possible for you to exaggerate either your natural or acquired guilt. You are a wretch undone without his sovereign grace; tell him so; and if you can find no words, let the groans and sighs and sobs of confession pour forth from you, for it is the heart and soul of true and sincere prayer to lay yourself in the dust at Jesus' feet, and tell him the whole truth.

The woman next told the Lord of *her sufferings*. The peculiar disease with which she had been afflicted drained away her strength. She must have presented a most emaciated appearance; there was no flush of health upon her hollow cheek, and her gait was that of utter weakness. The toil which her poverty compelled her to endure to earn a livelihood must have been very painful to her, for strength she had none. Her purse was drained by physicians, and her heart by the flood of blood. Poor creature! we can little tell of the days of languishing and the nights of pain she endured, and the seasons of despondency and despair which would come upon her spirit in consequence of the weakness of the flesh. But she told him the whole truth; she told him briefly, but yet completely, all she had endured. Tested soul! You with whom God's Spirit is at work, tell the Lord, if you would pray right, all your sufferings. Tell him how your heart has been broken, how your conscience has been alarmed. Tell him how your very sleep is scarred with dreams, how your days are made as black as though they were nights by a lack of hope. Tell him that sin has become a torment to you, that the places in which you could once find pleasure have now become howling wildernesses to you. Tell him the harp has lost its music, the cup its enticements, the table its charms, and society its delights, for you are full of your own ways, and your sins have become a burden to you. Let your sorrows flow in salty floods before the Lord of Hosts, for though no stranger can meddle with your sorrow, yet your God understands it. Tell him, then, tell him, troubled sinner; tell him the whole truth.

Next, I am persuaded that this woman did not hesitate to tell him of *her futile attempts* to find a cure. She had been to other physicians, and she had suffered many things by them; that is to say, some of them had put her under various operations of the most painful character, and others had compelled her to drink medicine nauseous in the mouth and mischievous in the bowels. These ancient professors of physics had given her sleepless nights and days of intense anguish, all of which she might have borne with patience if she had been one iota the better; but she rather grew worse. Her doctors, it seems, were her worst disease; they added to the issue of her blood a waste of her money; they gave her consumption in her purse and vexed her with the plagues of fees. Her substance might have yielded her many little comforts, and some extra nourishment to sustain her under the fearful drain upon her system; but the doctors sucked like vampires, and made an issue in her pocket more rapid than that in her person. She tells the Lord, although that confession was as good as saying, "Lord, I have been everywhere else, or else I would never have come to you. I have tried everyone, and it is only because all others have failed that I present myself before you." You would think such a confession as that would make him angry, but it was not so. I would not have you keep back this part of the tale from your Lord and Master.

Tell him you have been to other physicians; remind him of how you went to Moses, how he took you to the foot of Sinai, and made you exceedingly fearful and quaking, but never stopped your wounds. Tell him how you rested upon Mr. Civility, and his father, Mr. Legality, who said they had skill to take the burden from your back, and who directed you to do this and do that most irksomely, but never ministered one atom to your cure. Tell him of your many prayers, and how you have trusted in them. Tell him of your good works, and how you used to rest your confidence in them. You may spread before him the story of your infant sprinkling, your confirmation, your churchgoing, your chapel-going. Tell him how you were always up for early prayers, and kept the saints' days; how you tried to mortify the body, and deny yourself many comforts. Tell him how you did everything sooner than come *to him;* and say that even now, if you had not been forced to do it, you would not have come, for you are so vile by nature, and so great an enemy to the cross of Christ, that you would not have come to him if you could have found a shadow of hope elsewhere. "Well," says one, "would that be praying?" Yes, dear brother, yes, dear sister, that is the soul of prayer, to tell him the whole truth. We cannot expect that he will give us pardon till we make our confession fully and without any reserve. If you will cover any sin in your heart, your sin shall condemn you; if there be one secret corner of your soul in which you hide away any of your corruptions or follies, there shall a cancer spring up which shall eat into your very soul. Tell him the whole truth and hide nothing from him, even this your wicked, willful pride in going after your own righteousness, and not submitting yourself to the righteousness of Christ; tell him the whole truth.

This poor woman told him *all her hopes.* She said with many a tear, "Lord Jesus, when I had spent my all, and could no longer run after the various physicians of different countries, I heard of you. It was one evening as I lay on my couch, too faint to sit upright. A neighbor came and told me that a son of hers who had been born blind had received his sight; and she said that the same man, named Jesus of Galilee, a mighty prophet, had also restored one who was dead – a widow woman's son at the gates of Nain. Then I said in my heart, perhaps he will heal me; and my soul that had been given up to despair enjoyed for a moment a beam of hope, for my soul said, 'If it be possible for him to raise the dead, then he can stop my issue of blood; and if he did open the blind eyes, then he can restore me.' I thought, if the journey be never so long I will take it; if the way be never so rough, if I may but creep into his presence I will be among the company, and perhaps, when he is stretching out his hand to bless, he will bless me, even me; and perhaps the man is so full of healing virtue that if he will not look on me, yet if I get near enough to look on him I shall be made whole." So she would tell him of that hope; the many disappointments that she met with when she was pressing through the throng; how the strong men jostled her and the rough men pushed her back; how the thoughtless many told her to be gone; and how the zealous few were jealous of her place, and struggled to get before her. She would tell him how at last she did come near enough to touch the fray of his garments, and how she ventured to touch in the hope that she would be made whole. Then she would plead that as she already felt a change for the better, she humbly hoped that he would not take away this omen of love, but that he would carry out the cure and send her away perfectly restored.

If you desire to pray right, pour out your hopes before the Lord. I remember when I sought the Lord, I said to him, "Lord, I have read in Scripture that you heard Saul of Tarsus, and that you saved Manasseh. I am a sinner it is true, great as they are; but surely you can save me, and my soul hopes that yet you will turn an eye of pity and say unto me, 'Your sins are forgiven.'" Sometimes that hope grew so strong that I felt as if I should be saved; I knew I should. Then, again, that hope went down so low that it seemed impossible that he could have pity on me; and I remember I asked him how it was he could have buoyed me up with that fond hope, and put the Scriptures in such a way that they looked as if they were meant for me, and were sent to beckon me to Christ, and yet I could find no comfort in them. Now, you must do the same. Spread those disappointed hopes of yours before your God, and tell him the whole truth.

But be sure you tell him also *your fears*. I dare say the woman said to him, "Oh, thou Son of David, I thought at one time it was foolish of me to come to you, for I know, O Jesus of Nazareth, that you are very careful concerning the law. Now the law says that a woman with an issue of blood is unclean, and I thought I had no right to come near to you – that you would say to me, 'Woman, woman, how dare you mix with the throng and make all these people legally unclean? And what is this your brashness that you should think of touching me? You whose touch is a defiling one, how could you venture to come near to me?' Lord, I thought of going back scores of times, but it was my necessity that made me bold. I felt I had no right to come, but come I must. When I did get the cure from you, I touched you secretly without any invitation, without daring to do it before your face, and now I am afraid you will curse me and say, 'Get you gone,' and add another disease to me, and so break the back that is already bent with a crushing load." How soon her fears were removed when she had told them.

Now, poor sinner, tell all your fears, whatever they may be. You think your sins are too great. Tell him so. You fear you are not one of his chosen. Tell him so. You think that he has never called you. Tell him so. You believe that if you did come to him he would refuse you. Tell him so, if you dare; but I think you would hardly utter so flat a contradiction to his own words, *"The one who comes to Me I will certainly not cast out."* Do you feel your heart is so hard? Tell him it is like a lower millstone, that the stone might melt before your heart would yield. Do you feel as if you could not tell him? Tell him that you feel as if you could not tell him. Whatever it is, let all the truth come out.

No, no! you need not look into the prayer book, for you will not find much there that suits a convinced sinner. You need not buy a book of family devotions; your own poor cries are better than the best written forms. "Oh, my prayer will be so broken!" Well then, it will be all the more suitable for a broken heart. But then you say, "It is such an unworthy prayer." Yes, but then you are an unworthy soul; the prayer is fitting for the person. If the great God should hear you, you will know that it was not because of your prayer, but because of Jesus; for all you did was to tell him the truth, and if that prevails with him, then his heart of love, and the sufferings of the Savior must have moved him to have pity on you.

> Secret sins are all committed in the face of God.

I pray God the Holy Spirit guide these words which are meant to encourage you who have been seeking Jesus. Let me urge you to tell the whole of the story for these reasons. *The Lord knows it all beforehand;* you cannot hide it. Whatever your sin may have been, though it was perpetrated at night, though it was under the shadow of the thickest darkness, he saw it all. Secret sins are all committed in the face of God. Was it a theft which no one has yet discovered? Or was it only a thought, a black thought that no ear, not even your own, ever heard? God saw it; God heard it. In his book everything which you have done is recorded against you. Be not foolish, then, and deny not that which is published on the housetops of glory. The judge will publish it at last. If you hide it all your lifetime, it will come out then. Go then, tell it – tell it now. *To tell this to God will be a very great service to you.* It will tend to make you feel your need more. I believe that often when the repentant one begins his confession, he is not half so conscious of guilt as at the close of his prayer. If you will bring your soul to look at your sin, to study its foulness, to meditate upon its heinous ingratitude, while you are considering the subject, the Spirit of God will work upon you, and your heart, like the rock in the desert, struck by this rod, shall gush with streams of repentance.

If your heart be very grieved, do, I pray you, remember that confession is one of the most rapid ways of getting relief. While the banks hold good, the lake swells; let them break, and the water is drained off. Let a vent be found for the swollen lake up yonder on the mountains, and the mass of water which might otherwise inundate the valleys will flow in fertilizing streams. When you have a festering wound, the surgeon puts in the lancet and gives you ease. So confession brings peace. I wish to God without any delay that you who need a Savior would go to him and confess your sin very plainly. Jesus is no hard-hearted foe, no cruel judge. He loves you. Awakened sinner, he will love to hear that story of yours; and before you have finished it, he will give you the kiss of love and say, *"I have wiped out your transgressions like a thick cloud and your sins like a heavy mist."* Trust the immense generosity of Jesus' infinitely tender heart to give you your soul's desire, the complete and perfect forgiveness of your sin.

We now change the subject for a very short time, to address those who are converted, but who, like this woman, have not yet acknowledged their faith in the presence of others.

Our Savior will do nothing by halves. The woman may be content with having her body healed, but Jesus is not satisfied till her soul is recovered too. She has gained the cure, but she would probably go slinking away with the retiring multitude to hide herself from all observation. This will not be for her good, nor for the Master's honor; therefore, he takes the means to get a plain confession from her. Turning around, he says, *"Who touched My garments?"* At first, there is no answer. He puts it again: *"Who touched My garments?"* They all deny. Peter, moreover, takes upon himself to rebuke the Savior for asking so absurd a question: *"Master, the people are crowding and pressing in on You,"* says he, *"and*

You say, 'Who touched Me?'" But he looked around, and probably fixing his eyes at last upon the woman herself, he said, *"Someone did touch Me, for I was aware that power had gone out of Me."* That *"someone"* came out of the crowd, and falling flat on her face, she declared before them all, so Luke says, what had been done in her.

Now, in the great work of salvation, as we have remarked formerly, there are many who are saved who through timidity do not come forward and confess what Jesus Christ has done for them. I believe that our Lord often uses singular means to make his secret ones come out and acknowledge him, and the words I may speak just now may be a part of his plan by which he will make yonder *"someone,"* whoever that may be – this sister someone, this brother someone, who has touched him – come out and declare before all what the Lord has done.

His reasons for constraining her to make an open confession were doubtless three. First, *it was for his glory.*

> "Why should the wonders he hath wrought
> Be hid in darkness and forgot?"

When I look abroad upon nature, it is true I do not see nature fussily trying to make itself tidy for a visitor, as some professors do, who, the moment they think they are going to be looked at, trim up their godliness to make it look smart. But on the other hand, nature is never bashful. She never tries to hide her beauties from the gazer's eye. You walk the valley; the sun is shining and a few raindrops are falling; yonder is the rainbow, and a thousand eyes gaze at it. Does it fold up all its lovely colors and retire? Oh no! it shrinks not from the eye of man. In yonder garden all the flowers are opening their bejeweled cups, the birds are singing, and the insects are humming amid the leaves. It is a place so beautiful that God himself might walk therein in the evening, as he did in Eden. I look without alarming the bashful beauties of the garden. Do all these insects fold their wings and hide beneath the leaves? Do the flowers hang their heads down? Does the sun draw a veil over his modest face? Does nature blush until the leaves of the trees are scarlet? Oh no! Nature cares not for gazers, and when any come to look upon her, she does not hasten to wrap a mantle over her fair form, or throw a curtain before her grandeur. So the Christian is not to be always wishing to expose what is in him; that would make himself a Pharisee. Yet, on the other hand, if God has put anything that is lovely and beautiful and of good repute in you, anything that may glorify the cross of Christ, and make the angels happy before the eternal throne, who are you that you should cover it? Who are you that you should rob God of his praise? What! Would you have all nature's beauties hidden? Why, then, hide the beauties of grace? Jesus Christ deserves to be confessed before men. He is not ashamed to acknowledge himself as our friend amid the splendors of his Father's court. Nor was he ashamed amid the mockery and spitting of Pilate's hall. Why, then, should you find it a hardship or a difficulty to acknowledge *him*? Acknowledge him! I ought to feel proud of the honor to be allowed to acknowledge him! I, who am black with sin, ashamed to call him husband who is the fairest of the children of men! I, who am poor as poverty, blush to acknowledge that the King of Kings calls himself my brother! I, who deserve the deepest hell, be ashamed to acknowledge that Christ has washed me in his precious blood, and set my feet upon a rock, and put a new song into my mouth! My Master, I cannot be ashamed of you! How can it be?

> **Jesus Christ deserves to be confessed before men**.

> No, when I blush, be this my shame,
> That I no more revere his name!

My brother, my sister, you who keep yourself in seclusion and hide your candles under a bushel, you should not do so; for the sake of his dear name, who loved you with an everlasting love, and has graven you upon the palms of his hands, come forth and declare your faith.

Secondly, doubtless Christ would have her confession be *for the good of Jairus*. Did that strike you? Jairus needed much faith. He was just informed that his child was dead. Some faith was needed to believe that Christ could heal the sick, but that he could restore the dead? What faith was needed here? Therefore, this woman's confession is put in to nourish the faith of the trembling ruler of the synagogue. You do not know, dear friends, of how much service your open confession of Christ might be to some trembling soul. One reason why we have churches, and are joined in fellowship, is that we may help the weak; that by our daring to say "Christ has saved me," others may take heart, and may come to him and find the same mercy. "Oh," but you say, "the church does not want me." Then I might say the same, and all Christians might say the same. Where would there be a visible church on earth at all? What is right for one Christian to do is right for all to do; and if it is right for you to neglect professing Christ, then it is right for all believers to do so. And then, where is the church? Where is the ministry? Where is Christ's truth? How are sinners to be saved at all? Suppose, my brother, that John Calvin and Martin Luther had said, "Well, now we know the truth, but we had better be quiet, for we can go to heaven much more comfortably. If we begin preaching we shall set all the world by the ears, and there will be a deal of mischief done; hundreds of persons will have to be martyrs for their faith, and we shall be subject to many hardships." They had quite as much right to hide their religion as you have. They had quite as much reason for the concealment of their godliness as you have. But, alas! for the world, where would have been the Reformation if these had been as cowardly as you are, and like you had snuck to the rear in the day of battle?

I ask again, What would be the wretched lot of England, what calamities would happen to our island, if all who know Christ as you know him were to act as you do? There would be no ministers to preach the gospel! Why, I might today be sitting in my own house reading my Bible, or enjoying private prayer with much comfort; I certainly would not be pleading with sinners if I imitated your example. Where would the deacons of our churches and other useful church officers be? Where? Echo only answers, "Where?" if all were like you. How would the heathen be converted? Who would be the missionary – who would venture among the heathen if they were like you? The Christian would be dumb and have no testimony; in fact, I must add there could be no Christians. Even if there could be a number of secret Christians everywhere, then the world would say, "The religion of Christ is the most despicable religion under the sun, for those who believe in it will not join together; they will not even profess it. They are so ashamed of their Master that they will not come forward any of them to acknowledge what he has done for their souls." You are acting inconsistently if you will not come forward and acknowledge your Lord. My dear brethren, do not shirk it! I mean this for some of you who have been attending here for years, and ought to have been members of this church years ago; and I mean it for others of you who have come in here today, who have known the Lord some little time, and ought to be united with other Christians. I say, how much real good you might do after you have once broken through the shell and have told others what Jesus has done. You would find that after having once made a profession, you would be obliged to speak for your Lord, and who can tell what a career of usefulness might be opened up before you if you would but dare to do this for his sake?

Moreover, I have no doubt that the main reason why Jesus Christ would have this woman declare what was done in her was for her own good. Suppose he had let her go home quietly – there she goes. When she reached home she would have said, "Ah, I stole that cure; I am so glad I have it." But there would come a dark thought: "One of these days it will die away; I shall be as bad as ever, for I never asked him." Conscience would say to her, "Ah, it was a theft"; and though she might excuse herself, still she would not feel at ease. Now Christ calls her up, and conscience cannot disturb her, for he gave her the cure before them all. She will not be afraid of the return of her disease, for Jesus said, *"Your faith has made you well."*

What a blessing it would be to some of you if you would come out and confess your Lord and Master. "Well," says one, "I do not like baptism." There are a great many naughty children in the world who do not like to do what their father tells them; but those children often get whipped, and this will probably be your lot. Our good brother who spoke here last Sunday evening astounded me by leaving out part of the text which he most frequently quoted. If he quoted a text, he should quote it all. "He that believes shall be saved," said he. I know no such text in Scripture. There are texts very much like it, and the doctrine is true; but the text is, *"He who has believed and has been baptized shall be saved."* So the text stands. Those of us who are Baptists are supposed to lay too much stress on baptism. I think the danger is in not laying stress *enough* upon it. I know this, that if my Master tells me to preach the gospel to every creature, and puts it thus, *"He who has believed and has been baptized shall be saved,"* I dare not take the responsibility of leaving out part of my Master's message. I know that he who believes is saved; but, mark you, I would not run the risk of willfully refusing to attend to the second part of my Master's command. If there be anything in Scripture that is as plain as noonday, it is the baptism of believers. The deity of Christ is a point which might quite as readily be disputed as the baptism of believers in Jesus. Let any simpleminded man take the Bible without prejudice, and I conceive that it would be impossible for him to read it without discovering that the believer in Jesus is to be buried with Christ in baptism.

Little do our friends know how much mischief they do by teaching infant sprinkling. It is an invention of man, against which Christians ought to protest every day, because infant sprinkling is a practical denial of the need for personal godliness. It is not so intended by those who use it, but it is so read and interpreted by the world. It puts into the church those who are not in the church. It gives religious rites to the unconverted. It teaches men that because their mothers and fathers were good people, therefore they are Christians. But they are not; they are heathens, and as much heathens as if they were born amid the Hottentot's village community. They are in the gall of bitterness and in the bonds of iniquity, notwithstanding all their parents' excellence. To give Christian ordinances to unconverted persons is to pervert the testimony of God's church. The baptism of the believer in the name of Christ is and must be a significant emblem of death to the world. It is the crossing of the Rubicon, the throwing away of the dagger, and the drawing of the sword against the world forever. It is an ordinance whose sign can never be erased. An ordinance which disgraces and shames a man in the world's eye more than anything else, the dishonor of Christianity, the scoff and scorn of his religion, is believer's baptism; and blessed is that man who can so look at it, and then for Jesus' sake take up his cross and follow him.

"Well," says one, "I do not see it." My dear brother, if you cannot see it, I cannot help that. Your conscience is not the rule of your duty, but God's Word is; and if God's Word commands it, whatever your conscience may say about it, you are sinning if you refuse to obey. Oh! I would press this point upon you of making an open declaration, and of doing so in Christ's way, for you have no right to do it in a way of your own. It is idolatry to worship the true God by a wrong method. Acceptable service can only be rendered to God in his own way. To the law and to the testimony; if we speak not according to that word, it is because there is no light in us. I believe that after you have once thus professed your faith before men your courage will grow; your separation from the world will be more complete. You will be a marked man, often a despised man. People will point you out and say, "There is one of your Methodists." Your profession will distinguish you from the world, and will be a bond to keep you right, a heavenly chain of gold to bind you fast to the principles of your Lord and Master's truth. Do, with this poor woman, tell the whole truth, and tell it in your Master's way.

Now I send you away, dear friends, reminding repentant ones of that with which we began – the necessity of telling Jesus all. I am still wishing, however, that you who have found the Savior would tell the world all, and bear your witness that, let others do as they will, as for you and your house, you will serve the Lord.

And unto the name of God be glory forever. Amen.

Chapter 15

Cured at Last

And a woman who had a hemorrhage for twelve years, and could not be healed by anyone, came up behind Him and touched the fringe of His cloak, and immediately her hemorrhage stopped. (Luke 8:43-44)

Though I take Luke's statement as a text, I shall constantly refer to the version of the same story which we find in Mark 5:25-29.

Here we have one of the Lord's hidden ones: a case not to be publicly described because of its secret sorrow. We have here a woman of few words and much shamefacedness. Her malady subjected her to grievous penalties according to the ceremonial law. There is a terrible chapter in the book of Leviticus concerning such a case as hers. She was unclean; everything that she sat upon, and all who touched it shared in the defilement. So that, in addition to her continual weakness, she was made to feel herself an outcast, under the ban of the law. This created, no doubt, great loneliness of spirit, and made her wish to hide herself out of sight. In the narrative before us she said not a word until the Savior drew it out of her, for her own lasting good. She acted very practically and promptly, but she was a silent seeker; she would have preferred to have remained in obscurity, if it could have been so. Some here may belong to the great company of the timid and trembling ones. If courage before others is needed to secure salvation, matters will go hard with them, for they shrink from notice, and are ready to die of shame because of their secret grief. Cowper's hymn describes their inward feelings, when it says of the woman:

> Concealed amid the gathering throng
>   She would have shunned thy view,
> And if her faith was firm and strong,
>   Had strong misgivings too.

Such plants grow in the shade and shrink from the light of the sun. The nature of their sorrows forces them into solitary self-communion. Oh, that the Lord may heal such at this hour!

The immediate cure of this woman is the more remarkable because it was a wayside miracle. The Savior was on the road to restore the daughter of Jairus; this woman's healing was an extra display of grace, a sort of over-splash of the great fountain of mercy. The cup of our Lord's power was full – full to the brim – and he was bearing it to the house of the ruler of the synagogue; this poor creature did but receive a drop which he spilled on the way. We do well if, when going upon some errand of love, we concentrate all our energy upon it, and do it well in the end. But the Savior could not only perform one great marvel, but he could also work another as a sort of byplay incidentally – I would almost say, accidentally – on the road. The episodes of the Lord Jesus are as beautiful as the main run of his life's poem. Oh, that this day, while my sermon may seem meant for one, and distinctly directed to his salvation, it may also, by the power of Jesus, save another not so clearly pointed at! While the word is aimed at one particular character, may the Lord cause the very wind of the gospel shot to overcome another. Or, to change the figure for a better one, while we spread the table for some bidden guest, may another hungry soul have grace given him to take his place at the banquet of grace! May those who hide away, and whom, therefore, we are not likely to discover, come forth to Jesus, and touch him, and live!

Let us at once speak of this much-afflicted woman, for she is a typical character. While we describe her conduct and her cure, I trust she may serve as a looking glass in which many trembling ones may see themselves. We shall carefully note *what she had done,* and then *what came of it.* This will lead us on to see *what she did at last,* and *what we also should do.* May the Holy Spirit make this a very practical discourse by causing you to follow her till you gain the blessing as she did! The preacher is very weak; and may the Lord, for this very reason, work by him for your salvation.

Consider, therefore, concerning this woman, what she had done. She had been literally dying for twelve years. What had she been doing? Had she resigned herself to her fate, or treated her malady as a small matter? Far from it. Her conduct is highly instructive.

First, *she had resolved not to die if a cure could be had.* She was evidently a woman of great determination and hopefulness. She knew that this disease of hers would cause her life to ebb away and bring her to the grave; but she said within herself, "I will have a struggle for it. If there is a possibility of removing this plague, it shall be removed, let it cost me what it may of pain or payment." Oh, what a blessing it would be if unsaved ones here would say each one for himself, "I am a lost soul; but if a lost soul can be saved, I will be saved. I am guilty; but if guilt can be washed away, mine shall be washed away. I have a hard heart, and I know it; but if a heart of stone can be turned into a heart of flesh, I long to have it so, and I will never rest until this gracious work is done in me!" Alas, it is not so with many! Indifference is the rule, indifference about their immortal souls! Many are sick with dire spiritual disease, but they make no resolve to have it cured; they trifle with sin, and death, and heaven, and hell.

Insensibility has seized upon many, along with a proud conceit; they are full of sin, and yet they talk of self-righteousness. They are weak, and can do nothing, yet they boast of their ability. They are not conscious of their true condition, and therefore they have no mind to seek a cure. How should they desire healing when they do not believe that they are diseased? How sad that beneath the ruddy cheek of morality there should lurk the fatal consumption of enmity to God! How horrible to be fair without and leprous within! Are there not many who can talk freely about religion, and seem as if they were right with God, and yet in the secret place of their hearts they are the victims of an insincerity and a lack of truth which fatally undermine the life of their profession? They are not what they seem to be; a secret sin drains away the lifeblood of their religion. May the Holy Spirit show every unregenerate person the fatal nature of his soul's disease; for this, I trust, would lead to the making of a firm resolve to find salvation, if salvation is to be had.

No doubt some are held back from such action by the freezing power of despair. They have reached the conclusion that there is no hope for them. The promises of the gospel they regard as the voice of God to others, but as having no cheering word for them. One might suppose that they had searched the Book of Life, and had made sure that their names were not written there; they act as if their death warrant had been signed. They cannot believe in the possibility of their becoming partakers of everlasting life. They are under a destroying delusion, which leads them to abandon hope. None are more presumptuous than the despairing. When men have no hope, they soon have no fear. Is not this a dreadful thing? May the Lord save you from such a condition! Despair of God's mercy is an unreasonable thing. If you think you have grounds for it, the lying spirit must have suggested them to you. Holy Scripture contains no justification for hopelessness. No mortal has a just pretense to perish in despair. Neither the nature of God, nor the gospel of God, nor the Christ of God, warrant despair. Multitudes of texts encourage hope, but no one Scripture, rightly understood, permits a doubt of the mercy of God. *"Any sin and blasphemy shall be forgiven people."* Jesus, the great Healer, is never baffled by any disease of human nature; he can cast out a legion of devils, and raise the dead. Oh, that I could whisper hope into the dull ear of yonder mourner! Oh, that I could drop a rousing thought into the sullen heart of the self-condemned! How glad should I be! My poor desponding friend, I would rather see your chains snapped, your fetters broken off! Oh, that the Spirit of God would cause you, like this woman, to resolve that if there be healing for your soul you will have it!

Alas! many have never come to this gracious resolution because they cherish a vain hope and are misled by an idle dream. They imagine that salvation will come to them without their seeking it. Certainly, they have no right to expect such a thing. It is true that our Lord is found by them that did not seek him; but that is an act of his own sovereignty, and is not a rule for our procedure. The plain directions of the gospel are: *Seek the Lord while He may be found; call upon Him while He is near.* How dare they set these gracious words aside! They imagine that they may wake up, one of these fine days, and find themselves saved. Alas! it may more likely happen to them as what happened to the rich man in the parable: *In Hades he lifted up his eyes, being in torment.* God grant that none of you may trifle your souls into such misery! Some imagine that in the article of death, they may cry, *"God, be merciful to me, the sinner!"* and so may leap into salvation. It seems to them a very slight business to be reconciled to God. They imagine that they can be converted just when they will, and so they put it off from day to day, as if it were of no more consequence than going to shop to buy a coat or a gown. Believe me, the Word of God does not set forth the matter in this way. It tells us that even the righteous scarcely are saved, and it rouses us to strive to enter in at the narrow gate. God save you from every false confidence which would prevent your being in earnest about the healing of your souls. Spiritually, your case is as desperate as that of the poor woman now before us. May the Lord sweetly constrain you to feel that you must be healed, and that you cannot afford to put off the blessed day! If beneath the firmament of heaven there is healing for a sin-sick soul, seek it till you find it. When the Lord brings you to this resolve by his good Spirit, you will not be far from the kingdom of heaven.

> God save you from every false confidence which would prevent your being in earnest about the healing of your souls.

Let us next note that *this woman having made her resolve, adopted the likeliest means she could think of.* Physicians are men set apart on purpose to deal with human maladies; therefore, she went to the physicians. What better could she do? Though she failed, yet she did what seemed most likely to succeed. Now, when a soul is resolved to find salvation, it is most suitable and proper that it should use every likely means to find it. Oh, that they were wise enough to hear the gospel, and to come at once to Jesus; but often they make grave mistakes. This woman went to gentlemen who were supposed to understand the science of medicine. Was it not natural that she should look for help to their superior wisdom? She cannot be blamed for looking to the men of light and leading. Many, in these days, do the same thing. They hear of the new discoveries of professedly cultured men, and hear their talk about the littleness of sin, and the larger hope, and the non-necessity of the new birth. Poor deceived creatures! They find in the long run that nothing comes of it, for the wisdom of man is nothing but pretentious folly. The world by wisdom knows neither God nor his salvation. Many there are who know all the less of saving truth because they know so much of what human imagination has devised, and human search discovered. We cannot blame the woman that, being a simple soul, and anxious for healing, she went to those first who were thought to know most. Let us not, with Christ so near, go roundabout as she did, but let us touch our Lord at once.

No doubt the sufferer also tried men who had diplomas, or were otherwise authorized to act as physicians. How can you blame her for going to those who were in the succession and had the official stamp? Many sin-sick souls nowadays are, at first, very hopeful that the ordained clergy can benefit them by their duly performed services and duly administered sacraments. At least good men, who are eminent in the church, may be looked to for aid; surely these know how to deal with souls! Alas! it is vain to look to men at all, and foolish to depend on official dignity or special repute. Some teachers do not know much about their own souls, and therefore know less about the souls of others. Vain is the help of man, be the man who he may. Whatever his popularity, learning, or eloquence, if you seek him for his prayers or his teachings as able to save you, you will certainly seek in vain, as this poor woman did. She is not to be blamed, but to be commended, that she did what seemed best to her according to her light; but you are warned: go not, therefore, to men.

No doubt she met with some who boasted that they could heal her complaint at once. They began by saying, "You have tried So-and-so, but he is a mere quack; mine is a scientific remedy. You have used a medicine which I could have told you would be worthless, but I have the secret. Put yourself absolutely into my hands, and the thing is done. I have healed many that have been given up by all the faculty. Follow my orders, and you will be restored." Sick persons are so eager to recover that they readily take the bait which is offered them by brazen brashness. An oily tongue and a bland manner, backed with unblushing assurance, are sure to win their way with one who is anxious to gain that which is offered. Ah, me! "All is not gold that glitters," and all the professions which are made of helping sin-sick souls are not true professions. Many pretenders to new revelations are abroad, but they are physicians of no value. There is no balm in Gilead, there is no physician there; if there had been, the hurt of the daughter of my people would have long ago been healed. There is no medicine beneath the sky that can stop the palpitations of a heart which dreads the judgment to come. No earthly surgery can take away the load of sin from the conscience. No hand of priest or presbyter, prophet or philosopher, can cleanse the leprosy of guilt. The finger of God is needed here. There is one Heal-all, one divine Cure-all, and only one. Happy is he that has received this infallible balm from Jehovah-Rophi – the Lord that heals. Yet we marvel not that when souls are afflicted with a sense of guilt, they try anything and everything which offers even a faint hope of relief. I could wish that all my hearers had an intense zeal to find salvation; for even if it led them into passing mistakes, yet, under God's blessing, they would find their way out of them and end by glorifying the grace of our Lord Jesus Christ, which never fails.

This woman, in the next place, having resolved not to die if a cure could be had, and having adopted the likeliest means, *persevered in the use of those means*. No doubt she tried many, and even opposite, remedies. One doctor said, "You had better go to the warm baths of the lake of Tiberias; such bathing will be comforting and helpful." She grew worse at the warm bath, and went to another physician who said, "You were wrongly treated; you need bracing up in the cold baths of the Jordan." Thus she went from vanity to vanity, to find both of them useless. An eminent practitioner assured her that she needed an internal remedy, and he alone could give her an infallible receipt. This, however, was of no use to her, and she went to another who said that an external application should be tried, such as Isaiah's cake of figs. What perseverance that woman must have had! I am not going to say anything about our doctors nowadays, for no doubt they are the most learned and skillful that can be; but in earlier times, surgery was murderous, and medicines were poisonous. Many of the prescriptions of those days are sickening and yet ridiculous. I read yesterday of a prescription, in our Savior's time, warranted to cure many diseases, which consisted of grasshoppers' eggs. These were supposed to exercise a marvelous influence, but they are no longer in the list of medicines. The tooth of a fox was said to possess special powers; but I noticed that one of the chief drugs of all, the most expensive, but the surest in its action, was a nail from the finger of a man who had been hanged. It was important that he should have been hanged; another fingernail might have had no effect. Poor creatures were made to suffer most painfully by cruel medicines which were far worse than the disease. As for surgical operations, if they had been designed to kill, they were certainly admirably arranged for their purpose. The wonder is that for twelve years poor human nature could stand out, not against the disease, but against the doctors. Brethren, the case is much the same spiritually. How many under their burden of sin go first to one, and then to another, practice this, and agonize after that, and pine for the other, perseveringly, and still to no avail! Travel as fast as you may in a wrong direction, and you will not reach the place you seek. Vain are all things except Jesus our Lord.

Have you been to Doctor Ceremony? He is, at this time, the fashionable doctor. Has he told you that you must attend to forms and rules? Has he prescribed you so many prayers and so many services? Ah! many go to him, and they persevere in a round of religious observances, but these yield no lasting ease to the conscience. Have you tried Doctor Morality? He has a large practice and is a fine old Jewish physician. "Be good in outward character," says he, "and it will work inwardly and cleanse the heart." A great many persons are supposed to have been cured by him and by his assistant, Doctor Civility, who is nearly as clever as his master. But I have it on good evidence that neither of them separately, nor even the two together, could ever deal with an inward disease. Do what you may, your own doings will not stop the wounds of a bleeding heart. Doctor Shame has also a select practice, but men are not saved by denying themselves until they first deny their self-righteousness. Doctor Excitement has many patients, but his cures seldom outlive the setting of the sun. Doctor Feeling is much sought after by tender spirits; these try to feel sorrow and remorse, but, indeed, the way of cure does not lie in that quarter. Let everything be done that can be done apart from our blessed Lord Jesus Christ, and the sick soul will be nothing bettered. You may try human remedies for the space of a lifetime, but sin will remain in power, guilt will cling to the conscience, and the heart will abide as hard as ever.

But this woman not only thus tried the most likely means and persevered in the use of them, but *she also spent all her substance on them.* That was perhaps the chief thing in ancient surgery – this golden ointment which did good to the physician, no matter what became of the patient. The most important point was to pay the doctor. This woman's living was wasting away as well as her life. She continued to pay, and to pay, and to pay, but she received no benefit from it all. Say, rather, that she suffered more than she would have done had she kept her gold. Thus do men waste their thought, their care, their prayer, their agony over that which is as nothing; they spend their money for that which is not bread. At last she came to her last shekel. In the end there was an end to her means, but so long as the silver lasted, she lavished it out of the bag. What would a man not give to be saved? I never wonder that dying men give their estates to priests in the hope that they can save their souls. If gold could purchase pardon, who would withhold it? Health of body, if it could be purchased with gold, would be cheap at any price; but health of soul, holiness of character, acceptance with God, assurance of heaven – these would be cheap if we counted out worlds as poor men pay down their pence for bread. There are men so mean that they would not part with a pound for a place in paradise; but if these once knew their true condition, they would alter their minds. The price of wisdom is above rubies. If we had mines of gold, we might profitably barter them for the salvation of our souls.

Beloved, you see where this woman was. She was in downright, desperate earnest to have her mortal malady healed, and so she spared neither her labor nor her living. In this we may wisely imitate her.

We have seen what the woman had done; now let us think of what had come of it. We are told that she had suffered many things from many physicians. That was her sole reward for trusting and spending; she had not been relieved, much less healed, but rather *she had suffered*. She had endured much additional suffering through seeking a cure. That is the case with you who have not come to Christ, but, being under a sense of sin, have sought relief apart from him. All that you do apart from Jesus, in order to win salvation, will only cause you increased suffering. You have tried to save yourself by prayers; your prayers have turned your thoughts upon your sin and its punishment, and thus you have become more wretched than before. You have attended ceremonies, and if you have used them sincerely, they have worked in you a solemn sense of the holiness of God, and of your own distance from him; and this, though very proper, has only increased your sorrow. You have been trying to feel good, and to do good, that so you may be good; but the very effort has made you feel how far off you are from the goodness you so much desire. Your self-denial has excited cravings after evil, and your humiliations have given new life to your pride. Efforts after salvation made in your own strength act like the struggles of a drowning man, which sink the more surely. As the fruit of your desperate efforts, you have suffered all the more. In the end, I trust this may work for your good, but up till now it has served no healing purpose. You are now at death's door, and all your praying, weeping, churchgoing, chapel-going, and sacrament-taking do not help you one bit.

There has been this peculiarly poignant pang about it all, that you are *nothing bettered*. Cheerily did you hope, but cruelly are you disappointed. You cried, "I have it this time," but the bubble vanished as you grasped it. The evil of your nature, when repressed in one place, broke out in another. You dealt with the symptoms of your disease, but you did not cut off the root of the mischief; it only showed itself in another form, but it never went away. You gave up one sin only to fall into another; you watched at the front entrance, and the thief stole in at the back door. Up till now, O soul, you have not come to Jesus, and after all your goings elsewhere, you are nothing bettered!

And now, perhaps, you are saying, "What can I do? What shall I do?" I will tell you. You can do nothing except what this woman ultimately did, of which I will speak by and by. You are now brought to this extremity – that you are without strength, without merit, without power, and you must look outside of yourself to another who has strength and merit and can save you. God grant that you may look to that glorious One before this service is over!

We read of this woman that although she suffered much, she was nothing better, *but rather had grown worse.* No better after twelve years of medicine? She went to the Egyptian doctor, and he promised her health in three months. She was worse. She tried the Syrian doctor; he was a man who had great knowledge of the occult sciences, and was not ashamed to practice enchantments. She was bitterly disappointed to find herself decidedly weaker. Then she heard of a Greek practitioner who would cure her in an instant. She paid her remaining money, but she still went backward. She bought disappointment very dearly. Friend, is this your condition? You are anxious to be right, and, therefore, you are earnest in every effort to save yourself; but still you are nothing bettered. You climb a treadmill, and are no higher after all your climbing. You drift down the river with one tide, and you float up again when it turns. Night after night you pull up in the same old creek that you started from. Oh, pitiful condition! Getting gray, too: becoming quite the old gentleman, and yet no nearer eternal life than when, as a lad, you used to attend the house of God, and wished to become a child of God. Nothing bettered? No, she grew worse. Fresh mischief had developed; other diseases fed upon her weakness, and she was more emaciated, more lifeless than ever. Sad result of so much perseverance! And is not that the case with some of you who are in earnest, but are not enlightened? You are working, and growing poorer as you work. There is not about you so much as there used to be of good feeling, or sincere desire, or prayerfulness, or love for the Bible, or care to hear the gospel. You are becoming more careless, more dubious than you once were. You have lost much of your former sensitiveness. You are doing certain things now that would have startled you years ago, and you are leaving certain matters undone which once you would have thought essential. Evidently you are caught in the current, and are nearing the waterfall. The Lord deliver you!

This is a sad, sad case! As a climax to it all, the heroine of our story had now *spent all that she had.* She could not go now to the Egyptian doctor, or to the Syrian doctor, or to the Hebrew doctor, or to the Roman doctor, or to the Greek doctor. No; now she must do without their flattering unction in the future. As for those famous medicines which raised her hopes, she can buy no more of such costly inventions. This was, perhaps, her bitterest grief; but let me whisper it in your ear – this was the best thing that had yet happened to her, and I am praying that it may happen to some of you. At the bottom of your purse I trust you will find wisdom. When we come to the end of self we come to the beginning of Christ. That last shekel binds us to the pretenders, but absolute bankruptcy sets us free to go to him who heals diseases without money and without price. Glad enough am I when I meet with a man who is starved out of self-sufficiency. Welcome, brother! Now you are ready for Jesus. When all your own virtue has gone out of you, then shall you seek and find that virtue which goes out of him.

This brings to our notice, in the third place, what this woman did at last. Weaker and weaker had she become, and her purse had become lighter and lighter. She hears of Jesus of Nazareth, a man sent of God who is healing sick folks of all sorts. She hears attentively; she puts the stories together that she hears; she believes them; they have the likeness of truth about them. "Oh," says she, "there is yet another opportunity for me. I will get in the crowd, and if I can only touch the bit of blue which he wears as the border of his garment, I shall be made whole." Splendid faith! It was thought much of in her own day, and we may still more highly prize it now that faith has grown so rare.

Note well *she resolved to trust in Jesus in sheer despair of doing anything else.* My dear friend, I do not know where you are sitting today – I almost wish I did, that I might come up to you and say to you personally, "Try Jesus Christ, trust him, and see whether he will not save you. Every other door is evidently shut; why not enter by Christ the door? There is no other life buoy; lay hold on this! Say with our songwriter:

> I can but perish if I go;
>   I am resolved to try;
> For if I stay away, I know
>   I must forever die.

Exercise the courage which is born of desperation. May God the Holy Spirit help you now to thrust forth your finger and get in touch with

Jesus! Say, "Yes, I freely accept Christ. By God's grace, I will have him to be my only hope. I will have him now." Be driven to Jesus by force of circumstances. Since there is no other port, O weather-beaten ship, make for this one! Wanderer, here is a refuge! Turn in to this place, for there is no other shelter.

After all, *this was the simplest and easiest thing that she could do.* Touch Jesus. Put out your finger, and touch the hem of his garment. The prescriptions she had purchased were long; but this was short enough. The operations performed upon her had been intricate; but this was simplicity itself. The suffering she had endured had complicated her case; but this was as plain as a spear. "Touch with your finger the hem of his garment; that is all." O my hearer, you have tried many things, great things, and hard things, and painful things; why not try this simple matter of faith? Believe in the Lord Jesus Christ, and you shall be saved. Trust Jesus to cleanse you, and he will do it. Put yourself into your Savior's hands once for all, and he will save you.

Not only was this the simplest and easiest thing for the poor afflicted one, but certainly *it was the freest and most gracious.* There was not a penny to pay. Nobody stood at the door of the consulting room to take her money; and the good physician did not even give a hint that he expected a reward. The gifts of Jesus are as free as the air. He healed this believing woman in the open street, in the midst of the crowd. She had felt that if she could but get into the throng, she would, by hook or by crook, get near enough to reach the hem of his garment, and then she would be healed. It is so today, dear hearer. Come, and receive grace freely. Bring no good works, no good words, no good feelings, no good resolves, as the price of pardon; come with an empty hand, and touch the Lord by faith. The good things which you desire, Jesus will give you as the result of his cure; but they cannot be the cause or the price of it. Accept his mercy as the gift of his love! Come empty-handed, and receive! Come undeserving, and be favored! Only come into contact with Jesus, who is the fountain of life and health, and you shall be saved.

> Bring no good works, as the price of pardon; come with an empty hand, and touch the Lord by faith.

This was the quietest thing for her to do. She said nothing. She did not cry aloud like the blind men. She did not ask friends to look on and see her make her venture. She kept her own counsel, and pushed into the press. In absolute silence, she took a stolen touch of the Lord's robe. O my hearer, you can be saved in silence. You have no need to speak to any person of your acquaintance, not even to your mother or father. At this moment, while in the pew, believe and live. Nobody will know that you now are touching the Lord. In later days you will own your faith, but in the act itself you will be alone and unseen. Believe on Jesus. Trust yourself with him. Be done with all other confidences, and say, "He is all my salvation." Take Jesus at once, if not with a hand's grasp, then at least with a finger's touch. O you poor, timid, bashful creature, touch the Lord! Trust in his power to save. Do not let me tell you to do it in vain, but do it at once. May God's Spirit cause you to accept Jesus now!

This is *the only effectual thing*. Touch Jesus, and salvation is yours at once. Simple as faith is, it is never-failing. A touch of the fringe of the Savior's garment sufficed; in a moment she felt in her body that she was healed of that plague. "It is twelve years ago," she said to herself, "since I felt like a living woman. I have been sinking in a constant death all this while, but now I feel my strength come back to me." Blessed be the name of the great Healer! She was exceedingly glad. Tremble she did, lest it should turn out to be too good to be true; but she was most surely healed. O my dear hearer, do trust my Lord, for he will surely do for you that which none other can achieve. Leave feeling and working, and try faith in Jesus. May the Holy Spirit lead you to do so at once!

And now, poor convicted sinner, here comes the driving home of the nail. Do as this woman did. Ask nobody about it, but do it. She did not go to Peter, James, and John, and say, "Good sirs, advise me." She did not beg from them an introduction to Jesus, but she went of her own accord, and tried for herself the virtue of a touch. You have had advising enough; now come to real work. There is too much tendency to console ourselves by conversations with godly men; let us get away from them, and speak to their Master. Talks in the inquiry room, and chats with Christian neighbors are all very well; but one touch of Jesus will be infinitely better. I do not blame you for seeking religious advice; this may be a halfway house to call at, but do not make it the terminal. Press on till, by personal faith, you have laid hold of Jesus. Do not tell anybody what you are about to do; wait till it is done. Another day you will be happy to tell the minister and God's people of what the Lord has done for you, but for the present, quietly believe in the Lamb of God who takes away the sin of the world.

Do not even ask yourself about it. If this poor woman had consulted with herself, she might never have ventured so near the Holy One of God. So clearly shut out from society by the law of her people and her God, if she had given the matter a second thought, she might have abandoned the idea. Blessed was the impetuosity which thrust her into the crowd and kept her head above the throng, and her face towards the Lord in the center of the press. She did not so much reason as dare. Do not ask yourself anything about it, but do it. Believe, and be done with it. Stop not to confer with your own unbelief, nor answer your rising doubts and fears; but at once, in an instant, put out your finger, touch the hem of his garment, and see what will come of it. God help you to do so while I am speaking!

> Put out your finger, touch the hem of his garment, and see what will come of it.

Yield to the sacred impulse which is just now operating upon you. Do not say, "Tomorrow may be more convenient." In this woman's case, there was the Lord before her; she longed to be healed at once, and so, come what may, into the crowd she plunged. She was so enfeebled that one wonders how she managed to get near him; but possibly the crowd took her off her feet and carried her onward, as often happens in a rush. However, there was her chance, and she seized it. There was the fringe of the Lord's garment; out went her finger, it was all done. O my friend, you have an opportunity now, by God's great grace, for you are in his house of prayer. Jesus of Nazareth passes by at this moment. He who speaks to you is not trying to say pretty things, but he is pining to win your soul for Jesus. Oh, how I wish I could lead you to that saving touch! The Spirit of God can do it. May he now move you to cry, "I will believe in the appointed sacrifice, and trust my soul with Jesus!" Have you done so? You are saved. *He who believes in the Son has eternal life.*

"Oh, but I tremble so!" So did she whom Jesus healed. Her hand shook, but she touched him all the same for that. I think I see her quivering finger. Poor emaciated woman, with pale and bloodless cheeks!

What a tapered finger was that which she held out, and how it quivered! However much the finger of your faith may tremble, if it does but touch the hem of the Lord's garment, virtue will flow from him to you. The power is not in the finger which touches, but in the divine Savior who is touched. So long as there is a contact established between you and the almighty power of Jesus, his power will travel along your trembling finger and bring healing to your heart. A telegraph wire may shake with the wind and yet convey the electric current, and so may a trembling faith convey salvation from Jesus. A strong faith, which rests anywhere but in Jesus, is a delusion; but a weak faith, which rests alone on Jesus, brings sure salvation. Out with your finger! Dear soul, out with your finger! Do not go away till you have touched the Lord by a believing prayer or hope. Holy Spirit, do not permit any to leave the tabernacle until, by a believing desire, or trust, or confidence of some sort, they have established a contact between themselves and Jesus, and have felt the virtue enter them for their instant healing. O Lord, save this people! Why do you come, Sunday after Sunday, in such crowds? and why must I stand here and bleed my heart away in love for your souls? Is the sole result to be that I help you to spend an hour and a half in a sort of religious amusement? What a waste it is of my labor, and of your time, unless some gracious work is done! O sirs, if you are not brought to Christ, my preaching will prove a curse to you! It appalls me to think that the preaching of the gospel will be a savor of death unto you unless it brings you life. Put not the day of grace from you. By the living God, I do implore you, trust the living Redeemer. As I shall meet you all, face to face, before the judgment seat of Christ, I do implore and beg you, put out the finger of faith, and trust the Lord Jesus, who is so fully worthy to be trusted. The simple trust of your heart will stop the death which now works in you. Lord, give that trust, for Jesus' sake! Amen.

Chapter 16

She Had Not Escaped Notice

When the woman saw that she had not escaped notice, she came trembling and fell down before Him, and declared in the presence of all the people the reason why she had touched Him, and how she had been immediately healed. (Luke 8:47)

Last Sabbath morning we spoke upon the woman who was healed of her issue of blood. After having spent all her living on physicians, and being disappointed in them all, she touched the Savior's garment and was healed immediately. She came behind him, for she did not wish to be seen. She said not a word; she had not the courage to ask for the blessing in an open manner. When cured, she slunk away into the crowd; she was anxious about being unobserved. Now, if the story had ended here, you would not have been surprised. It was a case of extreme delicacy that might seem to require a specially secret ending by the woman's being permitted to go her way home, happy and whole.

But now, suppose that, in the tenderness of our Savior's sympathy with this trembling woman, he had permitted her to depart without making an open confession; what would have been the consequence? The Savior willed that the miracle should be recorded in three of the four Gospels, and if it had ended where we left it last Sabbath morning, then such is our human nature that we should have drawn from it the inference that saving faith need not be confessed. Our natural love of ease, and our desire to avoid the cross, would have made us follow this woman's example, and we would have tried to touch the Lord for healing, and then run away from him without making any profession of discipleship. Many would have quoted her case as a reason why they might be allowed to escape the responsibilities, duties, and sufferings which discipleship might involve. If the Savior had permitted this woman to retreat in silence, many cowardly believers would have said that the Savior's silence gave consent to her retreating without a word, and that they might safely imitate her. I know the men and their style of reasoning. This would have been fine nonsense for them. Think how this story would have been used in times of martyrdom. The cowardly would have argued, "We may have to go to prison or to the stake if we confess Christ; why should we be so needlessly daring? We can receive grace from Jesus quite unknown to anybody, and having gained salvation we can mingle with the crowd and avoid exposing ourselves to danger." The Savior would not allow us to find in this case an apology for an evil course, and so he called out the woman whom he had cured. The spirit of hiding, thank God, was not found in the church in martyr times; for holy men and women came forward and confessed their faith with more than common eagerness.

If the narrative had ended where we left it last Sunday, what a release it would have afforded to those good, peace-loving people who, in these days of blasphemy and rebuke, will take no sides at all! "Anything for a quiet life." They are very comfortable, and they mean to remain so. What does it matter to them though the whole church should be rotten with error? They hope to go quietly to heaven – indeed, they feel they are going there; and, if they are not soldiers of the cross, still they trust they are followers of the Lamb; if they do not contend earnestly for the faith once delivered to the saints, still they eat the fat, and drink the sweet, and enjoy the privileges of a comfortable religion. That is the present policy of many, and gladly enough would they have sheltered themselves behind this woman. She, however, *had not escaped notice,* nor may they. We have enough apologies for selfishness and ease and compromise, without the Savior's supplying us with one; and so he took special care in this instance that nothing so evil should be made out of it. What might have been a defense for guilty silence he turns into a grand argument for open confession. He will not allow concealment in this case, because he will not tolerate it in any case, but will have us take up our cross and follow him.

That is the subject for today. May I be helped by the Holy Spirit so to handle it that any here who are sincere in their love for Christ but yet have never declared it, may be forced to come out at once, and before the Lord Jesus Christ and his people declare that they have touched him, and that they have been healed immediately.

Let me say to you first, *her hiding seemed very excusable;* but secondly, *her hiding was not permitted;* and thirdly, *your hiding should not be excused nor permitted, but should come to an end at once.*

First, then, we say concerning this woman, that her hiding seemed very excusable. I have already said that if, in any instance, a cure might have been concealed, this was one; and it was so for many reasons. First, because of *this woman's natural timidity, and because of the nature of her malady.* It would appear that if in any case the thing might have been done in a corner, or if done in a crowd might have been passed over without remark, this was an evident case in point. Yet the Savior, tenderly considerate as he is, will not have it so. And you, dear friend, may say, "I am naturally so very timid and shy; pray excuse me." This woman was not only bashful, but her sickness also made her rightly wish to remain in obscurity. "I would not like my story to be known," says one. She might have justly said the same. It must have been hard indeed for her to confess what the Lord had done. Yet she had to acknowledge his grace openly, and so must you. She is a woman sick and faint, who for twelve years has been growing weaker and weaker, yet when she is healed she must come forward and confess the cure. Does this seem hard to you? Surely it is the least she can do, and she ought to do it of her own accord. Yet if silence might have been allowed in any case, hers was so delicate a matter that she might have had the doubtful privilege of receiving mercy without acknowledging it.

In addition to this, remember that *the Savior did not invite publicity.* He laid no injunction upon those whom he healed that they should tell everyone of the marvel. He did not seek fame or observation; he did not strive nor cry, nor cause his voice to be heard in the streets. In several cases he commanded the healed ones to tell no man what was done; and in this case he had given the cure without any open request for it. Might she not from this conclude that her secret act of faith was approved, and that it might continue to be secret, since it had gained the benefit? You may reason in that way about yourself, and say that Jesus does not need that you should testify for him. Indeed, it is true that he does not need anything from any of us; but is this a proper way of treating your Lord? You may say that quietude on your part would be excusable; but as the Savior did not think so in this woman's case, I believe that he will not think so in your case. I trust that in his mercy he will deal with you as with her, and compel you to come out and acknowledge the wonders of his grace.

There was another reason why she might have thought she need not make a public confession, and that was that *the Savior was at that time exceedingly occupied*. The multitude thronged him, and he was on the way to the house of the ruler of the synagogue to attend to his child; she would only be stopping him in his career of love. Should the Savior be detained for her? Already Jairus did not look upon her very cheerfully when he saw that Jesus stopped for her; what would he do if she caused a still longer delay? Besides, she might naturally argue, "Why should such an insignificant person as I am detain the prophet? What am I that I should take up even a second of his time? Jairus is before me; let him take his turn. I have the blessing, and there is no need to detain the Lord." You know how ready we are to make excuses when a duty is not pleasant; I suppose you are very handy at it yourself. But now since this excuse, if it ever occurred to the woman, was soon disposed of, I would advise you also to cast away all subterfuges, and remember that it is written, *If you confess with your mouth Jesus as Lord, and believe in your heart that God raised Him from the dead, you will be saved,* or quoting an equally plain Scripture, "He who has believed and has been baptized shall be saved." The faith and the confession are put together by the Holy Spirit: "*What therefore God has joined together, let no man separate.*"

> **The faith and the confession are put together by the Holy Spirit.**

Excuse might also have been found for the healed woman in the fact that *her cure would make itself known by its results*. When she returned home everybody would see that she was quite another person; and when they asked how it came to pass, she could tell them all about it. They would see in her life the best evidence of the work of our Lord upon her. Is it not better to speak by your life than by your lips? Exactly so, and herein lies the apparent force of this excuse for disobedience. It needs some truth to keep a falsehood on its legs. Note well that this woman was not permitted to withhold the open declaration of her indebtedness to Christ, even though it was certain that her health and her conduct would witness to his power. I know what you say: "I need not join a church, I can be a Christian at home. Better live a Christian life than wear a Christian name." My friend, we never proposed to you that you should put the wearing of a Christian name in the place of a Christian life – we have solemnly spoken the reverse of such a notion. We would earnestly remind you of our Savior's words: *"These are the things you should have done without neglecting the others."* Attention to one duty is no justification for the neglect of another. I charge you, disobey not in any point. Confess your Lord, acknowledge what he has done for you, and be sure that the outcome of your life supports your confession. Have the shaft of godly living by all means, but crown it with the heart of a brave confession.

Another pretext might have served this woman, if she desired an excuse. She might truthfully have said, "It is evident that *an open confession is not essential to my cure, for I am cured.*" She was healed immediately, and it is added that she felt in her body that she was healed of that plague, so that she knew that she was healed, and it was clear that a declaration of her faith was not necessary to her receiving that great help from the Lord. Therefore, many argue, "To confess Christ and join with his people is not necessary to my salvation." Who said it was? Open confession is not necessary – no, is not permitted – till you are saved. How could this woman have made any confession of a cure till she was cured? But being cured, it then became necessary that she should confess it: not necessary to the cure, that is clear, but necessary because of the cure. It is always necessary for a disciple to do what his Lord bids him. It is essential for a soldier of the cross to follow his Captain's orders. Jesus bids us to let our light shine; dare we hide it away? If we have received grace at his hands, he would have us confess that we have received it, and surely our sense of justice makes it needful for us to acknowledge our obligation.

Thus I have shown you that in her case many excuses might have been made; and yet after all, it would not have been a fitting thing if she had stolen away in the crowd and gone home cured without praising and blessing her Lord. It would have been to her everlasting dishonor. I think she felt this when the Savior fixed those dear eyes of his upon her and said, *"Someone did touch Me."* What a vision of loving-kindness and peace it was to her! In a moment she must have thought, "How foolish I was to go behind him! The very look of his face is comfort, the glance of his eye is joy. He would have granted my request with a smile." When she saw what he was like, and perceived the right royal bearing of the Bountiful One, she blushed that she had thought to steal a cure from one so ready to give it. The sight of him was rebuke enough for her clandestine snatching at the blessing. As to going away then without thanking him, why, I think the moment she saw his majestic mercy, the divine royalty of his goodness, she could not do otherwise than fall at his feet and worship such a glorious Lord. Within herself she felt that it was a marvelous cure which had come to her by a touch of him, and she could not praise him enough. The stones would have cried out against her if she had not confessed his miracle of gracious power, and the earth would have refused to bear up such a monster of ingratitude. Instantly she fell down before him and told him the whole truth. The thoughts of her heart were revealed by her Lord, and never was Jesus more truly adored than by this poor creature, whose silence stood rebuked by her Lord's love, and condemned by his immeasurable goodness.

Secondly, her hiding was not permitted by the Savior. I told you, in the opening of the discourse, that to have let her story finish without bringing her out would have been an encouragement to that practical denial of Christ which consists of concealing our faith in him. The unearthing of this woman from her hiding place was brought about by the Savior himself, and therefore, with all its apparent roughness, we may be sure that it was the kindest thing that could have been done. Her being brought out had the best of consequences.

For, first, an open confession on her part was needful *in reference to the Lord's glory.* Beloved, the miracles of Christ were the seals which God gave to his mission. He was the Man sent from God, and the wondrous things that he did proved that God was with him. If the wonders which he worked were not made known, the seals of his mission would have been concealed, and so would have lost much of their effect. How would men know that he was the very Christ if they never heard that the sick were healed? If this woman concealed her cure, others might do the same; and if they all did it, then Christ's commission would have no visible endorsement from the Lord God. I should like to impress this idea upon those of you who do not confess your Lord: whatever is right for you to do is right for other people to do. If it is right for one Christian not to confess Christ, and join a church, it must be allowable for other Christians to do the same. Where would be churches, where would be the continuance of gospel ordinances, and for the matter of that, who would be bound to be a preacher if no one is even bound to make an open profession? If *you* may go to heaven by the back stairs, then so may I, and God's grand entrance to the kingdom may be deserted. Who will care to go to heaven by the open way, with all its responsibility and opposition, if you can just as easily take the snug road behind the hedges, and slink into glory without observation? It will not do, brethren, if we consider what the Lord Jesus Christ deserves from us, and how our open confession tends to certify his mission. The change worked in the spiritual and moral condition of the saved is God's attestation of the gospel; and if this is not to be spoken of, how is the world to know that God has sent the gospel at all?

Further, remember that *our Lord's miracles were illustrative of his teaching.* Properly viewed, the miracles of Christ are the pictures of a volume of which his sermons are the text. You take *The Illustrated London News,* and you get the description of a public building, or the account of a grand ceremony. You are glad of the printed account, but you are much helped to form an idea of the whole business by the pictures. You would not like to lose the pictures, which are the chief feature of value in the paper. Now, in our Savior's ministry his words were the text, and his miracles were the pictures. If the picture is to be torn away, or pasted over, a great injury is done to the paper; and even so our Lord's teaching would be greatly marred if its miracles were concealed. I showed you, last Lord's Day morning, that the healing of this woman was a wonderfully instructive incident; how could it remain unknown? Must it be passed over to gratify her fear? Must Jesus work this wonder and nobody ever hear about it? As God is seen in his works of creation, Jesus is seen in his miracles of grace. Shall we rob him of his glory? God forbid that we should do him this serious dishonor. When first I knew the Lord, if anybody had said to me, "You will be ashamed to confess Christ although he has saved you. The day will come when you will blush to acknowledge his name," I would have felt indignant at the suggestion. Why, I wanted to tell everybody of the Savior's love. If there had been nobody else to hear me, I should have had to tell the cat. I felt like Bunyan did when he said he wanted to tell the crows on the plowed land all about it. I cannot understand how it is that you who know the Savior, or think you do, can imagine it to be right to hide away and cover up the glory of Christ. Oh, tell it! Tell it all the world over that he has healed us, forgiven us, and saved us.

But the confession had to be made *for the sake of others*. Do any of you wish to live unto yourselves? If you do, you need saving from selfishness. I have seen it brought as a charge against evangelical religion that we teach men to look to their own salvation first, and that this is a kind of spiritual selfishness. Ah, but if that salvation means salvation from selfishness, where is the selfishness of it? It is a very material point in salvation to be saved from hardness of heart and carelessness about others. Do you want to go to heaven alone? I fear you will never go there. Have you no wish for others to be saved? Then you are not saved yourself. Be sure of that. What is the most natural plan to use for the salvation of others but to bear your own personal testimony? Our Lord healed this woman for the good of the whole crowd. They must have all been astonished when they heard her story. He did it especially for the good of Jairus. Jairus's little daughter had been living twelve years, and this poor woman had been dying twelve years – note the exact time in each case. Surely there was a loud call to Jairus in this cure to exercise faith in Jesus, and it must have greatly helped his faith, which was not quite so strong as it seemed.

Do you not think that her public declaration was required *for the good of our Lord's disciples*? When they heard her story, did they not treasure it up, and speak of it to one another in later days, and thereby strengthen each other's faith? The remembrance of these remarkable miracles, which they saw their Master work, would serve them in good stead in times of persecution. Beloved, had not the Lord an eye even to you and to me, who were to be borne by his grace centuries later on? Do you not think that he fetched the healed one out on purpose so that this being put into the Gospel might bring out hidden ones throughout all generations? Did not our Lord foresee that many would be encouraged to touch the hem of his garment by faith through hearing of her cure? Thus, you see, the trembling woman must acknowledge her Lord, so that her Lord's household may be blessed thereby.

But especially she had to do this *for her own good*. The Savior had designs of love in bringing this poor trembling one forward before all the people. By this he saved her from a host of fears which would have haunted her. Suppose she had gone home healed and had never confessed it; surely she would have felt uneasy. A sense of having stolen the benefit without leave or license would have caused her uneasy dreams and sad dread. She would worry herself with the fear that the disease would soon return again, or that she would die from a fearful judgment. Besides, she would have said to herself, "I was little better than a thief. I did not come in by the door, but climbed over the wall. I am afraid it will go hard with me at the day of judgment. Will a man rob God? Have not I robbed the Savior himself?" All such fears were rendered impossible by her open confession and that which followed upon it. Jesus assured her that he had taken no offense; he wished her to have no fears, for, said he, *"Your faith has made you well; go in peace."*

She had been a very timid and trembling woman, but now she would shake off all improper timidity. I have known many persons cured of timidity by coming forward to confess Christ. I could mention cases of persons who have been very reserved, and scarcely able to say a word upon any subject, but when they joined the church and were baptized, their open confession broke the ice, and the waters of their life were set in motion. Our Lord removes this infirmity by our obedience: *In keeping [My commandments] there is great reward.*

Our Lord also gave her an increased blessing after her confession. Perhaps the Lord is reserving some great favor for some of you when you profess his name. You hide indoors, and he allows you milk enough to live upon; but if you would come out and confess him, he would feed you with the strong meat of the kingdom. You would become a braver and more useful person if you would take up your cross. You are now like Saul, the son of Kish, hiding among the stuff; come out and be a king. Confess what Christ has done for you. For what did the Savior give her?

He gave her clearly to know her relationship to him. He said, *"Daughter."* I do not know that the Savior ever called any other woman "daughter," for he was guarded in his speech to women; but to this one woman he said, *"Daughter."* Oh, may the Lord give trembling ones to see and feel the near and dear relationship which exists between Christ and their souls! May your sonship come up before your minds most vividly, as a reward of obedience. May Jesus say to some of you, "Son, be of good comfort"; or to another, "Daughter, be of good cheer, your faith has saved you." "What I would give," says one, "if Jesus would call me *daughter*!" Give him your whole self by believing in him, and confessing him, and see if he does not reveal to you his love. What choice revelations you lose through sinful silence I cannot tell you, but assuredly you miss many a cheering word from your Lord's own lips. If you will not acknowledge him, how can you expect him to give you the spirit of adoption? If you receive instead the spirit of bondage, you cannot wonder why.

Next note that our Lord gave her joyousness. He said, *"Daughter, take courage."* Smooth those wrinkles from your brow, my daughter.

> Why should the children of a king
> Go mourning all their days?

"Take courage." Ah, friends! you hang your heads. Perhaps if you had grace enough to acknowledge Jesus more fully, you would hold your heads up, and the sun would shine into your faces, and you would march joyfully all the rest of your lives. I advise you to try it. One of the best medicines for low spirits will be found in a courageous obedience to

Jesus. Keep close to the Crucified One, and your own cross will grow light in fellowship with him.

Next notice that he gave a commendation to her faith: *"Your faith has made you well."* Why, it was not her faith which made her whole, was it? No, but Jesus puts his own crown upon the head of faith. It is always safe for Jesus to crown faith, because faith always crowns Jesus. Her faith would answer, "Lord, I did nothing, you did it all," and, therefore, Jesus ascribes her healing to her faith. How much I desire that you, who are now afraid of your own faith, would win your Lord's praise by coming out and bearing witness to what he has done for you! Then will you not only believe, but you will also know that you have believed, and end forever your present state of miserable doubt.

Then the Lord gave her a word of precious quieting. He said, *"Go in peace."* This is as much as to say, "Do not stop in this crowd, to be pushed about or stared at, but go home in quietness. Go home to your house, and to your friends, with a light heart. All is well. You enjoy my favor. I have called you 'daughter,' and I will never disown you. I have blessed you, and you shall be blessed. I give you peace on earth and peace in heaven." O you that do love the Lord, and trust him, but yet have never declared your faith according to his command, you say, "We do not know how it is, but while we hear of God's people having great peace, we do not enjoy it." You cannot expect to have peace and still be disobedient. If you do not side with Jesus, do you expect him to be at your side? You shall have bread and water so that your soul shall be kept alive; but you cannot taste the wines on the dregs, nor the fat things full of marrow, so long as you do not confess your Lord. The dainties of the cupboard are not for disobedient children. Are you ashamed of Jesus? How, then, can you expect him to give you the kisses of his mouth? That he should save you will be more than his promise; but as he loves you, he must and will discipline you unless you confess his name and his work. Why do you lose present comfort by neglect? All in the train of faith will go to heaven, but why do so many ride third-class, or even get into cattle trucks? Why not ride first-class? To be out-and-out for Christ is to ride first-class. Confess your Lord. Determine never to hide your colors. Be heart and soul a Christian. Live for Jesus, and be ready to die for him; this is to go to heaven first-class, and why should you not?

Why will you be fretting and fuming, moaning and mourning, when you might as well be singing and dancing and feasting in the presence of your Lord and his household? Do you hesitate to acknowledge your Lord and Master? Ah, me! how shall I sufficiently grieve over you? Let not another day pass over your head till you have left Cowards' Castle and come into the ranks of the army of the Lord of Hosts.

Thus I have already reached my last point: your hiding ought to be ended. "Whom are you speaking to, sir?" Well, not to you, dear friends, who are always to the front, lifting the banner of the cross. "Whom are you speaking to, sir?" To you, my friend, if you are really a disciple, but secretly, for fear of the Jews. If you keep yourself to yourself, it is to you that I am speaking, and I desire to press upon you your obligations. *What do you owe to my Lord?* You are washed from your uncleanness. You are clothed with the robe of righteousness. You are accepted in the beloved. You know that you have passed from death to life. Unless fearfully mistaken, you know that you are the Lord's. Well then, own it. Do not be ashamed to take your place in the cross-bearing procession, and follow the Lamb wherever he goes. By your love for Jesus, do not turn to the right, seeking your own ease, nor to the left, aiming at the peace of others, but go straight on where duty and Jesus lead you. This is still the way to honor and immortality.

> **Those who are sowers of the seed know what a joy it is to see it spring up.**

Do you not think *you owe something to the church of God,* which kept the gospel alive in the world for you to hear? Did not a band of godly men and women meet together, and see that the gospel was preached? Was it not so that you were saved? Should you not help to keep that church going by whose means you were brought to Jesus?

May I be permitted also to say, I think *you owe something to the minister who led you to Jesus.* What a cheer it is to us when we get a letter from one who has found the Lord through our teaching; and better still, when face-to-face we meet one who has trusted the Savior through our poor instrumentality! Those who are sowers of the seed know what a joy it is to see it spring up. Who are the people who cause us needless depression? Who are those who withhold needful encouragement? Why, those who do not come out and tell what grace has done for them. For the sake of those who labor among you in word and doctrine, I implore you to come forward. Common gratitude should lead you to let us know that our labor is not in vain in the Lord.

Besides, *you owe it to yourselves.* Are you going to be mere bats, fluttering out when none will observe you, and hiding from the light? Are you going to be like mice, which only come out at night to nibble in the pantry? Conduct yourselves like men! O you that are hidden in the clefts of the rocks, let the Savior hear your voices and see your countenances!

You owe it to your family. You should tell your household what grace has done for you. Many a person wonders that his sons and daughters do not turn out well, when he himself has never been openly on the Lord's side. "Oh?" says one, "but then I am right in my heart." But is the light within to be shut up in a dark lantern? Who is to read a closed book? We want to see in the shopwindow of your life some of the goods which are stored in the warehouse of your heart, or how can you trade for your Lord? When a man boldly says, "I believe in Jesus," and proves it by his actions, it has a holy influence upon his children, his servants, and his companions; do you not desire to influence them correctly?

Do you not think *you owe it to your neighbors to show your colors*? Why, there are whole streets in this city where scarcely a single person goes to a place of public worship. Should he slink there as if half ashamed of it? What is to become of us if the little salt loses its savor? There are regions in this city in which dwell hundreds of thousands of inhabitants in which attendance at public worship is so scanty that the churches and chapels have only a sprinkling of people. Should not you that love the Lord be very earnest to let it be known that there is still a God to be worshiped, a Savior to be trusted? In these evil days above all others –

> Ye that are men now serve him,
>   Against unnumbered foes;
> Your courage rise with danger,
>   And strength to strength oppose.

Many crowd around him when Christ is on the winning hand. What is the worth of their hosannas? The style of man that a crucified Christ delights in is he who follows his Lord in the day of blasphemy and reproach. A true soldier of Jesus can stand up for his Lord alone. He is as true to Jesus when he is the only one as he would be if all the millions went after him. Blessed is he who is not offended with Jesus, nor ashamed of his cross. O you saved ones, run up your colors; fly them at the masthead and nail them there, and never let the enemy take them down. Oh, that God would move everyone here that has been a little shy or backward to go outside the camp and bear the Lord's reproach!

Now let me hear some of your objections, and answer them. I hope I have been answering them all through my sermon. Here is one: "Well, you know, Mr. Spurgeon, I am such an insignificant person. It cannot make any difference what I do." Yes, and this woman was a very insignificant person – only a woman! When I speak thus in English, it is a very ungallant speech, but if a rabbi had said it in Christ's day, it would not have seemed at all out of place, for they taught that no holy person ought, in the streets, to allow a woman's dress to touch him, lest he should be defiled thereby. They thought that if a scribe tried to teach a woman the law, he dishonored the law by doing so. Religious men lightly esteemed women in the Savior's day. Our divine Lord never gave the slightest sanction to such an abominable spirit, and I am not going to lend any sanction to your saying "I am only a poor feeble woman." God thinks much of the lowly; you must not talk so. Besides, many of you do not think so meanly of yourselves as you pretend to do when you want to avoid your duty. Do not excuse yourselves through pretended humility. If the Lord bought you with his blood, you are not so insignificant that you can be allowed to deny him your service.

"But coming out and joining a church, and all that, is such an ordeal." So it may be. In this woman's case, it was a far greater ordeal than it can be to you. Picture her, with her delicacy of feeling, called into the midst of all that crowd to confess her cure! Ready to sink into the earth! An unclean person who had broken the ceremonial law! How she longed to hide herself away! Yet the tender Lord, for her own sake, would have her stand forth, and what seemed an ordeal became a joy. Jesus does not excuse one of his healed ones from acknowledging the work of his grace.

A dear lady, who has long since gone to glory, was once an honored member of this church. It was Lady Burgoyne, and when she wished to unite with us she said to me, "Dear sir, I cannot go before the church. It is more than I can manage to make a confession of Christ before the members." I told her that we could make no exception for anybody, and especially not for her, who was so well established in the faith that she could surely answer a few questions before those who were brethren and sisters in the Lord. She came bravely, and spoke most sweetly for her Lord. Some of you may remember her, with her sweet countenance and revered demeanor. When she had acknowledged her Lord, she put both her hands on mine, and said emphatically, "With all my heart I thank you for this; I shall never be ashamed of Christ now. When aristocratic friends call upon me I will speak to them of my Lord." She did so constantly. You never found her slow to introduce the gospel, whoever might be with her. She frequently said to me, "Oh, what a training that was for me! I might have been a timid one all my days if I had not made that confession before the church." Now I say to you, if it be an ordeal, undergo it for Christ's sake. But indeed, it should be a pleasure to acknowledge your Lord among his own disciples.

"Alas!" says one, "I could not tell of what the Lord has done for me, because mine is such a sorrowful story. You know what I used to be, sir; sovereign grace has made me different, but my former life silences me!" Was it not so with this woman? How could she tell her story? But then it was to the glory of God, and so *she told Him the whole truth*. Whatever you were before you were converted, never boast of it; but at the same time do not deny it, but honor your Savior. Remember how often Paul tells us what he was before conversion. If any rake up your old sin, answer that it is sadly true, but you have been washed, and much has been forgiven you. Acknowledge that you were the chief of sinners, and that even now you are less than the least of all saints, but the Lord has brought you from death to life to the glory of his name.

> Whatever you were before you were converted, never boast of it; but at the same time do not deny it, but honor your Savior.

"I have so little to tell," says one. That is a good reason why you should tell it, for it will be all the easier for you to do so. He that has little to tell should tell it straightaway. I will give you no other answer than that. But still, if you can tell that the Lord Jesus has washed you in his precious blood, I do not think it is a little thing to tell. If you can say, *"Though I was blind, now I see,"* say it, and do not think it a little thing. Once you thought it the greatest fact you could possibly know: think so still. Don't garnish the story, but state it just as it happened.

"But perhaps people may not believe me." Did I tell you that you were to make them believe you? Is that your business? You are to do right, whatever the consequences may be. But they will believe you if you deserve to be believed. When we meet together as believers, and hear the story of a sinner saved by grace, we are none of us suspicious, although sometimes we are a little too quick to believe, and are apt to be deceived. Do not fear that you will be distrusted. Confess your faith at any rate, and God will bless your testimony.

"Ah!" says one, "but suppose after I had confessed Christ I should become as bad as ever." Suppose that this woman had supposed such a sad thing, and had said, "O Lord, I cannot confess that you have healed me, for I do not know how I may be in six months' time." She was not so mistrustful. "But suppose the Lord should leave me, and permit me to leave him." Yes, and suppose you were to leave off supposing anything of the sort, and just take his promise as it stands: *"He who believes has eternal life." "He who has believed and has been baptized shall be saved."* Do you believe his Word? Then lay aside such suspicions. Jesus does not give us a nonsensical, temporary salvation; he does not save us for a quarter of a year and then leave us. If saved by him, you will be forever saved! He is the Author of eternal salvation. If he gives you a new heart, it is a new heart, and it will never become an old one. If he puts the water of life within you, he does not put it there as you sprinkle the pavement in front of your shop in the morning, which is soon dried up; but he says, *"The water that I will give him will become in him a well of water springing up to eternal life."* When I trusted Christ, I did not trust him to save me for a year or two, but forever. When you go the heavenly journey, take a ticket all the way through. Some of our friends take a ticket to the next station, and then rush out to get another. Take your ticket for the New Jerusalem, and not for a halfway house. The train

> **Jesus does not give us a nonsensical, temporary salvation.**

will never break down, and the track will never be torn up. If you can trust Jesus Christ to carry you through to glory, he will do it. Let not that fear disturb you.

"Ah!" says one more, "it seems too good to be true. I cannot think that such a one as I may dare to link myself with the Lord Jesus Christ who is so great and so glorious." Yet this is your only hope. You are only saved through being in Christ. This may be too great, too good for us to imagine, but then we need not imagine it; it is clearly revealed in the infallible Word of God. He that believes in Jesus is one with him. Come, then, and acknowledge that blessed oneness.

Be one with Christ today in his humiliation, and you shall be one with him by and by in his glory. Be despised and ridiculed for his sake, and you shall be honored and glorified with him in the day when he appears. God bless you for Christ's sake! Amen.

Charles H. Spurgeon – A Brief Biography

Charles Haddon Spurgeon was born on June 19, 1834, in Kelvedon, Essex, England. He was one of seventeen children in his family (nine of whom died in infancy). His father and grandfather were Nonconformist ministers in England. Due to economic difficulties, eighteen-month-old Charles was sent to live with his grandfather, who helped teach Charles the ways of God. Later in life, Charles remembered looking at the pictures in *Pilgrim's Progress* and in *Foxe's Book of Martyrs* as a young boy.

Charles did not have much of a formal education and never went to college. He read much throughout his life though, especially books by Puritan authors.

Even with godly parents and grandparents, young Charles resisted giving in to God. It was not until he was fifteen years old that he was born again. He was on his way to his usual church, but when a heavy snowstorm prevented him from getting there, he turned in at a little Primitive Methodist chapel. Though there were only about fifteen people in attendance, the preacher spoke from Isaiah 45:22: *Look unto me, and be ye saved, all the ends of the earth.* Charles Spurgeon's eyes were opened and the Lord converted his soul.

He began attending a Baptist church and teaching Sunday school. He soon preached his first sermon, and then when he was sixteen years old, he became the pastor of a small Baptist church in Cambridge. The church soon grew to over four hundred people, and Charles Spurgeon, at the age of nineteen, moved on to become the pastor of the New Park Street Church in London. The church grew from a few hundred attenders to a few thousand. They built an addition to the church, but still needed more room to accommodate the congregation. The Metropolitan Tabernacle was built in London in 1861, seating more than 5,000 people. Pastor Spurgeon preached the simple message of the cross, and thereby attracted many people who wanted to hear God's Word preached in the power of the Holy Spirit.

On January 9, 1856, Charles married Susannah Thompson. They had twin boys, Charles and Thomas. Charles and Susannah loved each other deeply, even amidst the difficulties and troubles that they faced in life, including health problems. They helped each other spiritually, and often together read the writings of Jonathan Edwards, Richard Baxter, and other Puritan writers.

Charles Spurgeon was a friend of all Christians, but he stood firmly on the Scriptures, and it didn't please all who heard him. Spurgeon believed in and preached on the sovereignty of God, heaven and hell, repentance, revival, holiness, salvation through Jesus Christ alone, and the infallibility and necessity of the Word of God. He spoke against worldliness and hypocrisy among Christians, and against Roman Catholicism, ritualism, and modernism.

One of the biggest controversies in his life was known as the "Down-Grade Controversy." Charles Spurgeon believed that some pastors of his time were "down-grading" the faith by compromising with the world or the new ideas of the age. He said that some pastors were denying the inspiration of the Bible, salvation by faith alone, and the truth of the Bible in other areas, such as creation. Many pastors who believed what Spurgeon condemned were not happy about this, and Spurgeon eventually resigned from the Baptist Union.

Despite some difficulties, Spurgeon became known as the "Prince of Preachers." He opposed slavery, started a pastors' college, opened an orphanage, led in helping feed and clothe the poor, had a book fund for pastors who could not afford books, and more.

Charles Spurgeon remains one of the most published preachers in history. His sermons were printed each week (even in the newspapers), and then the sermons for the year were re-issued as a book at the end of the year. The first six volumes, from 1855-1860, are known as *The Park Street Pulpit*, while the next fifty-seven volumes, from 1861-1917 (his sermons continued to be published long after his death), are known as *The Metropolitan Tabernacle Pulpit*. He also oversaw a monthly magazine-type publication called *The Sword and the Trowel,* and Spurgeon wrote many books, including *Lectures to My Students, All of Grace, Around the Wicket Gate, Advice for Seekers, John Ploughman's Talks, The Soul Winner, Words of Counsel for Christian Workers, Cheque Book of the Bank of Faith, Morning and Evening,* his autobiography, and more, including some commentaries, such as his twenty-year study on the Psalms – *The Treasury of David.*

Charles Spurgeon often preached ten times a week, preaching to an estimated ten million people during his lifetime. He usually preached from only one page of notes, and often from just an outline. He read about six books each week. During his lifetime, he had read *The Pilgrim's Progress* through more than one hundred times. When he died, his personal library consisted of more than 12,000 books. However, the Bible always remained the most important book to him.

Spurgeon was able to do what he did in the power of God's Holy Spirit because he followed his own advice – he met with God every morning before meeting with others, and he continued in communion with God throughout the day.

Charles Spurgeon suffered from gout, rheumatism, and some depression, among other health problems. He often went to Menton, France, to recuperate and rest. He preached his final sermon at the Metropolitan Tabernacle on June 7, 1891, and died in France on January 31, 1892, at the age of fifty-seven. He was buried in Norwood Cemetery in London.

Charles Haddon Spurgeon lived a life devoted to God. His sermons and writings continue to influence Christians all over the world.

Other Similar Titles

***Life in Christ (Vol. 1, 2 & 3),*
by Charles H. Spurgeon

Men who were led by the hand or groped their way along the wall to reach Jesus were touched by his finger and went home without a guide, rejoicing that Jesus Christ had opened their eyes. Jesus is still able to perform such miracles. And, with the power of the Holy Spirit, his Word will be expounded and we'll watch for the signs to follow, expecting to see them at once. Why shouldn't those who read this be blessed with the light of heaven? This is my heart's inmost desire.

– Charles H. Spurgeon

Available where books are sold.

Jesus Came to Save Sinners, **by Charles H. Spurgeon**

This is a heart-level conversation with you, the reader. Every excuse, reason, and roadblock for not coming to Christ is examined and duly dealt with. If you think you may be too bad, or if perhaps you really are bad and you sin either openly or behind closed doors, you will discover that life in Christ is for you too. You can reject the message of salvation by faith, or you can choose to live a life of sin after professing faith in Christ, but you cannot change the truth as it is, either for yourself or for others. As such, it behooves you and your family to embrace truth, claim it for your own, and be genuinely set free for now and eternity. Come and embrace this free gift of God, and live a victorious life for Him.

Available where books are sold.

**Words of Warning,
by Charles H. Spurgeon**

This book, *Words of Warning,* is an analysis of people and the gospel of Christ. Under inspiration of the Holy Spirit, Charles H. Spurgeon sheds light on the many ways people may refuse to come to Christ, but he also shines a brilliant light on how we can be saved. Unsaved or wavering individuals will be convicted, and if they allow it, they will be led to Christ. Sincere Christians will be happy and blessed as they consider the great salvation with which they have been saved.

Available where books are sold.

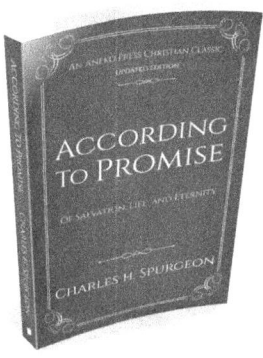

According to Promise,
by Charles H. Spurgeon

The first part of this book is meant to be a sieve to separate the chaff from the wheat. Use it on your own soul. It may be the most profitable and beneficial work you have ever done. He who looked into his accounts and found that his business was losing money was saved from bankruptcy.

The second part of this book examines God's promises to His children. The promises of God not only exceed all precedent, but they also exceed all imitation. No one has been able to compete with God in the language of liberality. The promises of God are as much above all other promises as the heavens are above the earth.

Available where books are sold.

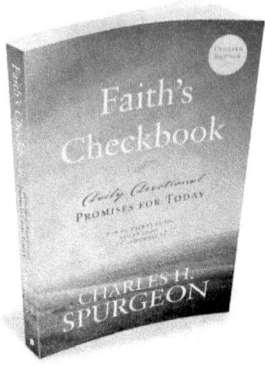

***Faith's Checkbook*, by Charles H. Spurgeon**

Faith's Checkbook is a one-year devotional meant to encourage you to take God at His Word – to take hold of God's promises by faith. Each day you will be presented with a specific promise from the Bible, along with accompanying exhortation by Charles Spurgeon.

This is your "spiritual checkbook," if you will. God's bank account of provision is ample, and it cannot be overdrawn. Every situation you might face is equally met with a promise that, if accepted, will sufficiently see you through.

"God has given no promise that He will not redeem. He does not offer hope that He will not fulfill. To help my brethren believe this, I have prepared this little volume." – Charles H. Spurgeon

Available where books are sold.

***Morning by Morning*, by Charles H. Spurgeon**

Charles H. Spurgeon's devotionals *Morning by Morning* and *Evening by Evening* have inspired, encouraged, and challenged Christians for generations. Spurgeon, with his masterful hand, carefully selected his text from throughout the Bible and covered a broad range of topics, in order to present a well-balanced and fruitful daily devotional for readers both young and old.

Now updated into more-modern English for today's readers, and again separated into two volumes as originally published, with morning devotionals in one volume and evening devotionals in the second. We chose a 11-point font for the sake of legibility, and formatted the devotionals so each fits on a single page.

Available where books are sold.

Faithful to Christ, by Charles H. Spurgeon

I believe that many Christians get into a lot of trouble by not being honest in their convictions. For instance, if a person goes into a workshop, or a soldier into a barracks, and if he does not fly his flag from the beginning, it will be very difficult for him to run it up afterwards. But if he immediately and boldly lets them know, "I am a Christian, and there are certain things that I cannot do to please you, and certain other things that I cannot help doing even though they might displease you" – when that is clearly understood, after a while the peculiarity of the thing will be gone, and the person will be let alone.

However, if he is a little dishonest and thinks that he is going to please the world and please Christ too, he can depend on it that he is in for a rough time. If he tries the way of compromise, his life will be like that of a toad under a harrow or a fox in a dog kennel. That will never do. Come out. Show your colors. Let it be known who you are and what you are. Although your course will not be smooth, it will certainly not be half as rough as if you tried to run with the hare and hunt with the hounds, which is a very difficult piece of business.

Available where books are sold.

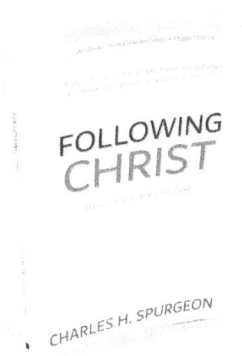

Following Christ, **by Charles H. Spurgeon**

You cannot have Christ if you will not serve Him. If you take Christ, you must take Him in all His qualities. You must not simply take Him as a Friend, but you must also take Him as your Master. If you are to become His disciple, you must also become His servant. God-forbid that anyone fights against that truth. It is certainly one of our greatest delights on earth to serve our Lord, and this is to be our joyful vocation even in heaven itself: *His servants shall serve Him: and they shall see His face* (Revelation 22:3-4).

Available where books are sold.

www.ingramcontent.com/pod-product-compliance
Lightning Source LLC
Chambersburg PA
CBHW070130080526
44586CB00015B/1635